AF379133

Transforming Japanese Workplaces

Transforming Japanese Workplaces

Takashi Sakikawa

Professor of Organizational Behavior, Niigata University, Japan

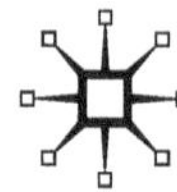

First published 2012 by
PALGRAVE MACMILLAN

Palgrave Macmillan in the UK is an imprint of Macmillan Publishers Limited, registered in England, company number 785998, of Houndmills, Basingstoke, Hampshire RG21 6XS.

Palgrave Macmillan in the US is a division of St Martin's Press LLC, 175 Fifth Avenue, New York, NY 10010.

Palgrave Macmillan is the global academic imprint of the above companies and has companies and representatives throughout the world.

Palgrave® and Macmillan® are registered trademarks in the United States, the United Kingdom, Europe and other countries.

ISBN 978–0–230–29991–7

This book is printed on paper suitable for recycling and made from fully managed and sustained forest sources. Logging, pulping and manufacturing processes are expected to conform to the environmental regulations of the country of origin.

A catalogue record for this book is available from the British Library.

A catalog record for this book is available from the Library of Congress.

To Kaoko and Souko

Contents

List of Figures and Tables

Figures

Tables

Foreword

The days are long gone when Westerners sang praises of the Japanese economy, as did Ezra Vogel 30 years ago in his book *Japan as No. 1*. For a while, Japan was overrun by academics, journalists, and business people seeking to learn the secrets of Japanese economic success. As the period of slow growth took hold in the 1990s, however, Japan became a cautionary tale of how *not* to organize a modern economy and its corporations. The West shifted from student to teacher as it prescribed various remedies to revive the Japanese economy. Foreign investors, most from North America, urged the Japanese to shed old ways of corporate governance in order to revive profitability. At the macro level, Western experts urged Japan to reduce the power of government to guide the economy. For corporations—the meso level—the prescription was to put far more emphasis on shareholders than ever had been done, which, it was said, would force firms to become more efficient in their use of labor and capital. Now, after the financial crisis, it has come full circle with the yen once more a powerful currency, with the yen once more a powerful currency, Japanese banks in better shape than those in the West, and Japan still a very prosperous, if slow growing and shrinking, nation.

But today Westerners say—and know—much less about the micro level: production methods and work organization at the establishment level. In the pre-1995 period things were different. There was close analysis of Japanese factories and their work groups. The micro level was put, pun unintended, under a microscope—it is not a joke. A slew of articles described the technological practices of Japanese factories, such things as just-in-time inventory systems, continuous improvement, quality control, and waste elimination.

Other studies dug into the factory's human resource management (HRM) practices: self-managing teams, quality circles, multi-skilled frontline workers, job enlargement, and more. This included organization-wide HRM practices such as strong corporate cultures, relatively low status barriers between blue- and white-collar workers, enterprise unions, and employment security. Often the two sides of the coin—technology and HRM—were analyzed jointly to show how they interacted and supported each other. The touchstone for all of this was Toyota and its Toyota Production System (TPS). In Western universities, the HRM side of the Toyota system came to be known as high-performance work practices (HPWP). During the early years of the Clinton administration, American companies were offered incentives to adopt a greater number of these high-performance practices.

During Japan's heyday in the West there also was close study of the business strategy of Japan's corporations. The Japanese approach gave rise to what is known as the resource-based view (RBV) of business. Companies were said to compete not only on price but also on the development of inimitable organizational practices—including corporate culture and human resource (HR) systems—that sustained technological and manufacturing prowess.

Not only academics but also representatives of US companies studied their Japanese competitors and began putting into practice some of the lessons they had learned. But it was often slow going. The status of HR executives in the US was low compared to their Japanese counterparts, meaning that it was more difficult for them to push their companies to adopt relatively costly changes such as employment security and high levels of training expenditures. Employees, at least those at the front line, remained more of a commodity than an asset. There also was a reluctance to give employees the responsibility and autonomy necessary for *kaizen*—the continuous improvement of quality and efficiency.

The RBV view of strategy also ran into barriers. Companies gave lip service to the claim that "employees are our most important asset," but less often practiced it. None of this is to deny the fact that high-performance practices found their way into US manufacturing plants. But there was lots of picking and choosing. While the impact of HPWP on productivity was high, the perception and reality that they were important to overall business strategy remained low. At this point, somewhere in the late 1990s, Japanese factories fell off Western radar screens.

Because of that inattention, many Western observers do not understand the extent to which Japanese factories have restructured since the late 1990s in response to cost competition from China and Korea (and now India and Brazil), the strengthening yen, and other factors. First, there have been very large increases in the use of nonregular employees who are paid less and have less job security than regular staff. Nonregular employees now constitute a whopping 35 percent of the labor force, up from 25 percent in 1999 and 20 percent in 1990. Second, there has been extensive outsourcing to Southeast Asia of supply chains and assembly of less sophisticated products. Third—and least well understood—industries other than automotive manufacturing have turned to cell production methods. While Westerners understand cell production in the automotive industry, with Toyota being the paradigmatic example of lean production, far less is known about its recent use in other industries.

Sakikawa makes an important contribution with his detailed analysis of cell production in the electronics industry. The industry generally has not paid its production workers as well as those in automotive; its workforce always has been *relatively* more dependent on contingent workers, including women. Sakikawa studied production teams in 20 factories producing items such as copying machines, game consoles, air conditioners, and machine tools. It is an area and an industry about which very few studies have appeared in English in recent years (or before). Cell production is a batch alternative to mass production. It entails more intensive use of space, faster responses to customer needs, and build-to-order methods. Cell production has been adopted in the production of many high value-added products still produced in Japan. Major electronics companies such as Canon, NEC, Sharp, and Sony have pursued it in order to sustain the competitiveness of their Japanese factories.

What Sakikawa shows is that cell production comes hand in hand with the kind of HPWP for which companies like Toyota are well known: extensive training, self-managing teams, total quality management (TQM), employment security, multiskilling, team-based pay, and so forth. That is, Japanese electronics companies are restructuring in the face of competition not only through the "low road" of irregular employment but also along the "high road" of investments in human capital. Training includes nonregular employees – that is, cell production rests on people as a key asset. Frontline workers and their supervisors are given responsibility for many aspects of production, with the cells treated as profit centers having their own profit/loss accounting.

Sakikawa uses a variety of methods to explore these issues: structured interviews, surveys, and statistical analysis. He finds that HPWP improves performance under cell production. His variables include production volume, inventory minimization, product quality, error signaling (*pokayoke*), efficient parts supply (*mizusumashi*), and HPWP. His performance measures include inventory levels, lead time, and quality. The message is that HPWP remains critical to cell production, even in the electronics industry. He also shows how cell production interacts with technology and with business strategy. What remains unclear, however, is the extent to which competitiveness also rests on the use of irregular employees, whose pay is relatively low, and whose hours and employment can be moved flexibly up and down.

The second part of Sakikawa's book examines another area that was of interest to Western observers in the 1980s and 1990s: strong, encompassing organizational cultures. In those decades, corporate culture brought white-collar managers and professionals together with blue-collar workers with a high commitment to the company's success. Most regular employees at the time were men. Today, however, there is more diversity in Japanese firms with respect to the age of employees (irregular employees are more likely to be young) and with respect to career paths (irregular employees are more likely to hop from job to job). The number of female employees is also more, though less often at the company's highest levels. Of course, the amount of diversity is less than that found in US companies, especially as regards gender, race, and ethnicity. Nevertheless, it's interesting to study whether encompassing organizational cultures can be sustained as Japanese firms become more fragmented in terms of employment status, age, and gender. What Sakikawa finds is that the old type of culture is eroding somewhat and giving way to a greater number of subcultures and to greater variation in pay and career paths.

The third part of Sakikawa's study is a fascinating comparison of Japan and China based on a study of 16 companies and 129 production teams in the Dalian area. He finds that not all Chinese factories are following the "low road" of relatively unskilled mass-production assembly. Rather, the factories he studied are using advanced HR practices such as HPWP, as well as some cell production. In other words, the ground is fertile for more rapid introduction of cell methods. As this occurs, what will happen to advanced manufacturing methods in Japan? Will Japan be able to maintain a competitive edge in manufacturing production? In the US—with Apple Inc. being the best-known example—production is done almost entirely outside the country. What's left are high-end engineering and design jobs. The problem is that producing a dollar of revenue now requires far fewer US jobs. Manufacturing jobs are good jobs as compared to those in the service sector, where pay levels are lower. For high school graduates, these good jobs are becoming increasingly scarce. Will this be Japan's future, or at least the future of its electronics industry? Will cell production and advanced HR methods be enough to secure relatively high-paying blue-collar jobs in Japan?

Thus far, there has been some mixed success in restructuring Japanese manufacturing, certainly more so than in the United States. Ironically, however, Japan's restructuring methods—especially the high level of irregular employment—may undermine the ability of Japanese manufacturers to keep production in Japan. Although training for irregulars may be similar to regular employees, this is not always the case. And irregulars lack the attachment and dedication to the company that are the hallmarks of the regular worker, the *kaisha-in*. Will a more transitory labor force be able to sustain the practice of *kaizen*, which requires a willingness to put not only one's body but also one's brain on the line?

These questions are important not only for Japan. Currently the United States is engaged in a debate over the future of manufacturing. Some argue that manufacturing can never again be a major employer or a major industry in the United States. At best, US firms will be like Apple, relying on overseas workers to assemble products "designed in California." Their US workforce will consist of people doing research and development (R&D) and similar high-end jobs. But blue-collar jobs will disappear. The fact that Chinese companies are ready to do not only mass production but also advanced batch production using cell methods suggests that the United States will not be able to sustain blue-collar manufacturing jobs.

On the other hand there are those who argue that manufacturing still has a future in the United States, especially if a greater number of industries imitate Japanese electronics and adopt the kind of advanced HR and production methods that Sakikawa describes. Those methods can be used not only in high-wage industries like automobile manufacture and assembly, but the US must do other things as well. Because employers do less training than in Japan, there has to be better funding for high schools and community colleges, which are key to creating a skilled workforce. There has to be better education for high school students and greater emphasis on vocational skills. Companies have to do more than give lip service to the idea that workers are assets and not only costs. In other words, it's not enough to simply take production methods from Japan and plunk them down on American soil. The institutional underpinning is different.

It's a pleasure to write this foreword to an excellent and much-needed study. It should be helpful to a wide range of readers interested in the Japanese economy as well as those interested in the future of manufacturing in Western Europe and North America.

Sanford M. Jacoby
UCLA

Preface and Acknowledgments

Over the past decades, Japanese companies have drawn the attention of business leaders, scholars, and even the general public from around the world for both good and bad reasons. The nation rose from the ashes of World War II and, in the 1960s, became the world's second largest economy after the United States. Japan's stunning postwar economic growth was driven largely by Japanese companies, particularly those in the manufacturing sector, rather than public and government institutes. These manufacturing companies captured a large portion of worldwide markets for automobiles, electronic appliances, electronic precision equipment, steel, and other products from their US and European counterparts. Japan seemed likely to surpass the US and become the world's largest economy in terms of the amount of products and services it created. Business leaders, scholars, and journalists outside the nation attributed the spectacular postwar success of Japanese companies to their unique management styles, which they praised. Some US scholars attempted to theorize the Japanese styles of management, and US business leaders, particularly those in the manufacturing sector, also tried hard to learn various management practices from Japanese companies and introduce them into their factories.

In the early 1990s, the Japanese economy overheated, and shortly thereafter, the bubble economy suddenly collapsed, plunging Japan into a decade-long economic downturn. Showing no sign of recovery from the prolonged slump, even after the dawn of the new millennium, the Japanese economy has continued to decline. It has experienced the so-called two lost decades. Japanese companies have been bogged down by two decades of economic stagnation, and their earnings have been substandard by international standards. The economic woes facing Japanese companies have been compounded by fierce competition from foreign companies, including not only old competitors—American and European companies—but also new global business players, for instance, South Korean, Taiwanese, and Chinese companies. Japanese companies have struggled and are continuing to struggle to survive economic woes and global competition.

Nevertheless, business leaders and scholars from around the world were interested in Japanese companies through the 1990s and made those companies the target of their criticism. They criticized Japanese companies for sticking to outdated management styles, which they considered no longer effective in the days of global competition. After the turn of the new century, however, they did not even criticize and seemed to have lost all interest in Japanese companies. Instead, they turned their attention to companies in emerging economies such as China and India. Articles about Chinese and Indian companies appeared in almost every issue of global management periodicals such as the *Academy of Management Journal* during the decade after the new millennium. It is quite clear that management practitioners and scholars outside Japan had less interest in Japanese companies or their management practices than they had in the 1980s, when Japanese companies and their competitiveness were noticeable in the international business arena.

However, ever since Japan was hit hard by a massive earthquake and the subsequent tsunami and nuclear accident on March 11, 2011, business leaders, journalists, politicians, commentators, and scholars from around the world have become interested once again in Japanese companies. They have learned that even small and unknown Japanese companies play a vital role in global supply chains, and business activities of these companies can largely affect those in the rest of the world and, ultimately, the global economy. They were also surprised to watch the behavior and attitudes of Japanese people affected by the triple disasters that were televised worldwide, such as their orderliness, discipline, politeness, teamwork, and calm response in the face of adversity. These Japanese people are the ones who are working on the front lines of communities, companies, and other areas damaged by the earthquake, tsunami, and nuclear accident. Some are working at front lines inside the damaged nuclear reactors, being exposed to a lethal level of radiation. The March 11 disasters reminded people around the world of the resilience, stoicism, perseverance, well-coordinated actions, altruistic behavior, and other traditional Japanese qualities that are also crucial parts of the strength possessed by frontline organizations in Japanese companies.

When Japanese companies were over-represented in the international business settings in the 1980s and early 1990s, numerous books and articles were published about them and their management styles. These books included *In search of excellence* by Peters and Waterman (1982), one of the best-selling business books of all time, and *Theory Z* by Ouchi (1981), a seminal book in the field of Japanese management. Books on Japanese companies published at that time are not just about personnel management and organizational structures unique to the country but also about production systems prevalent among Japanese manufacturers.

One of the most popular books concerning Japan's manufacturing is *The machine that changed the world,* written by Womack, Jones, and Roos (1990), who coined the term "Lean Production System." Even after the collapse of the Japanese bubble economy, some business authors continued to be inspired by Japanese companies. Among their books is *Competing for the future* by Hamel and Prahalad (1994). At around the same time, *The knowledge-creating company,* co-authored by Japanese scholars Nonaka and Takeuchi (1995), discussed Japanese companies and has since been read worldwide. In this book, the authors attempted to theorize the process of knowledge creation in organizations on the basis of the information obtained from Japanese companies.

Numerous books on Japanese companies were also published outside Japan. However, the number of these foreign books has reduced, particularly since the turn of the twenty-first century. It was around this time that business leaders and scholars started losing interest in Japanese companies and instead became interested in companies in emerging economies. However, it is not that Japanese companies have done nothing. Rather, they have transformed and continue to transform in the wake of the shifting economic and competitive environments and the challenges and difficulties they face, even if the scale and scope of these transformations are not equal across these Japanese companies. Although Japanese companies may not have been in the spotlight in recent years, it would be difficult or even impossible to gain an understanding of Japanese companies and their management practices and organizational structures without noting the transformations that Japanese companies have undergone more than a decade since the beginning of the twenty-first century, a period during which Japanese companies have faded into oblivion, but have been struggling to survive and transform. It is imperative to bridge the gulf between what is known about Japanese companies in their heyday and what is unknown about them struggling to survive and transform in the past decade or more.

Scholars have explored whether and how Japanese companies have undergone a transformation over the past decade or longer from several perspectives, including those of business strategies, organizational structures, corporate governance practices, and research and development activities. In this book, I first explore the transformations of Japanese companies in terms of human resource management (HRM) practices. Studies on this aspect have already been conducted, one of the most prominent of which is the research conducted by Jacoby (2005). Around the turn of the century, according to the author, Japanese companies followed the

US lead in introducing market-oriented work practices such as pay-for-performance policies and personnel outsourcing. Japanese companies, however, continued to utilize conventional and organization-oriented work practices, such as seniority-based evaluation and job security, more widely and intensively than did their US counterparts.

Although Jacoby investigated how Japanese companies transformed their HRM, his research focused on HRM policies, which are formulated by HRM staff at corporate headquarters and whose effect is company-wide yet general. In his study, Jacoby took a "macro" perspective and approached HRM issues involving US and Japanese companies. By contrast, in this book, I take a "micro" perspective by focusing more on operational practices, the so-called HRM practices, which are actually performed by rank-and-file or first-line workers. In Part I, I shed light on these practices at Japanese workplaces and empirically assess their effectiveness.

Next, I explore macro-level transformations surrounding Japanese companies by studying their organizational culture. No prior work has utilized theories from the organizational culture literature to examine the transformation of traditional Japanese workplaces. In addition to their unique management practices, Japanese companies are well known for their strong and homogeneous culture resulting from these practices. In Part II, I examine the traditional and transforming cultural situations in Japanese companies.

In Part III, by considering the impact of different national environments, I explore and assess the effect of new HRM practices introduced by Japanese manufacturers by using evidence from production teams at Japan- and China-based manufacturers. The China-based manufacturing companies that participated in my survey were affiliated with Japanese companies. This made it possible to examine the transforming landscape of overseas Japanese workplaces.

Thus, in this book, I examine and present the transforming landscape of Japanese workplaces. I also empirically assess the effectiveness of Japanese companies' new approaches regarding management practices and organizational culture. One reason I use the term "workplaces" in the book's title is that my interest lies in places where people actually work. Indeed, in field sites, I observed and examined what occurred inside the companies and at their workplaces. This book is based on the research I have conducted over the past decade and the conference papers I have presented in Japan and abroad. This book is based largely on a collection of my studies, published by my university, titled *The new Japanese workplaces* (Sakikawa, 2010). I have extensively refined and rewritten the information presented in those papers and have also presented new ideas. I hope that this book will help management practitioners and scholars around the world to better understand Japanese companies and their management practices and organization. I also hope that it will add to and advance the knowledge in the fields of human resource and organizational behavior.

I am grateful to many people for their generous advice and encouragement in the process of conducting my work and publishing this book. I am grateful to Yasuo Okamoto, management professor emeritus at the University of Tokyo, for providing many opportunities for me to conduct surveys with him and his research team at field sites in Japan and abroad. My participation in his international survey on overseas Japanese companies' management practices from the late 1990s through the early 2000s made me interested in frontline organizations and management practices and was my first step toward publishing this book. I am also thankful to Sandy Jacoby, HRM professor at the Anderson Business School, University of California, Los Angeles, for arousing my interest in HRM issues in the US, Japan, and elsewhere. His Ph.D. class gave me many opportunities to learn that several aspects of Japanese management practices were shared by high-performing US companies though termed differently as "high-performance work practices." Many other people have helped and encouraged me to conduct my work and publish this book, some of whom are practitioners at home and abroad and others are academics, particularly members of the Japan Academic Society of Organizational Science. Additionally, I would like to thank Zeng Ying, then a doctoral student at Japan's Niigata University, and Jian Chun Hua, then a lecturer at China's Dalian University, for their support of my Chinese survey. Despite the immense support and encouragement I received from those people, if any mistakes remain in this book, they are my own.

Finally, I thank The Japan Ministry of Education, Culture, Sports, Science and Technology for funding the series of my work that led to publishing this book through the Grant-in-Aid for Scientific Research (C: 21530353).

Part I
Transforming Management Practices in Japanese Workplaces

1
Japanese Workplaces in Transition

The rise and fall of Japanese companies

Japanese companies and Japanese styles of management attracted attention from business leaders and scholars and even the general public around the world when, after Japan achieved an "economic miracle," the then Harvard University sociology professor Ezra F. Vogel (1979) extoled the nation in the late 1970s by using the expression: "Japan as number one." The Japanese economy rose from the ashes after World War II and enjoyed high growth throughout the 1960s, achieving an average annual growth in gross domestic product (GDP)—the value of all goods and services a nation generates—of about 10 percent. During the same period, Japanese companies gained a large share of the global market for products such as automobiles, motorcycles, electrical appliances, precision instruments, textiles, steel, and shipbuilding. The nation expanded sufficiently to become the world's second largest economy after the United States in 1968. During the 1970s, the US's trade imbalance with Japan approached 10 billion dollars a year. The term "Japanese economic miracle" was coined in reference to the nation's spectacular postwar economic growth.

The nation's high economic growth ended at the start of the 1970s. The economy experienced a stable growth period from the mid 1970s through to the early 1990s and expanded about 4 percent annually during this period. Nevertheless, Japanese companies still stood out, and played a leading role, in the international business arena. In its survey on the competitiveness of nations, the World Competitiveness Yearbook, the Switzerland-based International Institute for Management Development (IMD) ranked Japan in first position in the early 1990s. Due to the success of Japanese firms, company executives, management scholars, business consultants, and other professionals (e.g., business journalists) around the world took a strong interest in Japanese styles of management and many books on the subject were published. These people asserted that Japanese styles of management lay behind the success of Japanese companies and even the nation's economy.

In the late 1980s, the Japanese economy witnessed stock and real estate prices continuing to increase in what was called the "bubble economy." These prices more than doubled during the period 1988 to 1990 when Japan's share of world exports was at its peak. Japan appeared to be on the brink of surpassing the United States to become the world's largest economy. However, the bubble economy abruptly burst in the early 1990s. Thereafter, Japan's economic growth rate plunged to 1 percent, a rate which persisted throughout the 1990s. During this period, the Japanese economy never bounced back from its economic stagnation, and thus it experienced a "lost decade." As the Japanese economy weakened, many Japanese companies' balance sheets deteriorated. The Japanese firms that had made an excessive investment in various business areas, including unprofitable ones, at the time of the bubble economy were shackled by the "three excesses" of overcapacity, overemployment, and overinvestment after the collapse of the bubble. Such companies had to dispose of these negative legacies of the bubble economy age in order to move forward. Although Japanese companies were known for their employment security, some of them had no choice but to streamline their business structure and even cut jobs due to the increased pressures on them from Japanese and non-Japanese shareholders to improve their earnings, which were substandard in comparison to those of foreign (e.g., US) companies.

Meanwhile, Japanese companies' overseas competitors, especially those from the United States, regained their competitiveness against Japanese companies by taking several measures; for example, they delivered innovative and state-of-the-art products in the areas of microprocessors, personal computers (PCs), operating systems, and other information technology (IT)-based products. Japanese companies faced competition not only from these innovative American companies but also from South Korean and Taiwanese companies and other new global players that had not been prominent in international business settings in the 1980s. In the face of fierce challenges from these overseas competitors, Japanese companies gradually began to lose their global market shares to these new challengers as well. For example, Japanese semiconductor makers such as NEC Corp. and Toshiba Corp. dominated the global market from the mid 1980s through to the early 1990s.

However, in the early 1990s, Intel Corp., a US semiconductor maker, recaptured the number one position in the worldwide market share for semiconductor products that it had lost to those Japanese semiconductor manufacturers in the mid 1980s by delivering innovative and high value-added microprocessors. Taiwanese and South Korean semiconductor makers caught up with Japanese manufacturers and obtained a large portion of the global market for dynamic random-access memory (DRAM)—a commodity type of semiconductor products for speeding up processing in such products as PCs by temporarily storing data—in the 1990s even though this market had been dominated in the 1980s by Japanese semiconductor makers. They quickly developed the latest DRAM models and delivered a large volume of these products, the unit cost of which was considerably lower than that of the same products made by their Japanese counterparts, to the market. As Japanese companies lost momentum and showed a lack of competitiveness during the 1990s, business journalists and management scholars abroad and even at home started criticizing them and their management styles.

Even after the dawn of the new millennium, Japan's economic growth still remained weak, with an average GDP growth of 2.1 percent per annum from 2003 to 2007. Among overseas markets, the North American market was lucrative for export-dependent Japanese companies such as automobile and electronics manufacturers. However, the US economy was hit hard by the collapse in September 2008 of Lehman Brothers Holdings Inc., then the fourth largest US investment bank. Consequently, Japanese companies lost opportunities to sell their products in the US market and posted poor quality of earnings in the last quarter of 2008 and throughout the following year. The Japanese economy lost steam, although it appeared to be finally getting out of its prolonged stagnation. The yen's high surge against the US dollar in recent years has also reduced the competitiveness of Japanese companies. The Japanese currency hit a postwar high of 75.32 yen to the US dollar in Oceanian trading on October 31, 2011. The strength of the yen adversely affects the overseas earnings of Japanese exporters when these earnings are repatriated. They have to raise the prices of exported products to compensate for the loss caused by the yen's appreciation, and this makes their products less cost-advantageous in overseas markets. In the meantime, among Japanese companies' foreign competitors, South Korean automobile and electronics manufacturers are taking advantage of the depreciation of their nation's currency, the won, against the US dollar and acquiring large portions of the global share for automobiles and electronic appliances that had previously been held by Japanese companies.

Japan's GDP growth rate was –0.7 percent in 2009 and –5.2 percent in 2010. The Japanese economy has continued to shrink over the two decades since the collapse of the bubble economy, experiencing the "two lost decades." Meanwhile, China has rapidly expanded its economy, gaining the position of the world's second largest economy from Japan in 2010. Japan was ranked 26th out of 59 countries in the IMD's 2011 World Competitiveness Yearbook, while other parts of Asia (namely, Singapore, Hong Kong, and Taiwan) were ranked in the top 10. Against the backdrop of the current situation regarding Japanese companies, business leaders, management scholars, and journalists from around the world have given much attention to companies in emerging economies such as China and India over the past decade. Meanwhile, they have shown little interest in Japanese companies and their management practices (Makino and Roehl, 2010).

The Japanese economy suffered its first trade deficit in over three decades in 2011 due to the disruption of supply chains caused by the earthquake and tsunami of March 11, a historic rise in the yen, and a sharp drop-off in global demand stemming from the euro financial crisis. Meanwhile, the nation has had to rely heavily on imported energy due to the nuclear crisis that followed the natural disasters.

Shifting environments that awoke Japanese companies

Over the past two decades, Japanese companies have been mired in prolonged stagnation at home and have faced fierce challenges from overseas competitors. However, in facing these woes, they have not merely weathered them and done nothing. In the wake of shifting environments, they have taken several measures and have attempted to regain their competitiveness, although the majority of Japanese companies are still struggling to survive.

As I suggested earlier, Japanese companies had been expanding their business areas into ones unrelated to their core operations and carrying unprofitable business areas when the bubble economy collapsed. Consequently, they had no choice but to realign, simplify, and streamline their business structure and even cut jobs in order to turn themselves around and survive their financial problems. Facing greater pressures from shareholders at that time, compared to earlier days when shareholders were acquiescent in Japanese business society, Japanese companies had to lay off part of their workforce. Many Japanese companies appeared to abandon the idea of job security which they had long espoused. However, the majority secured jobs for their core members (i.e., permanent and regular employees) but did not guarantee jobs for nonpermanent and nonregular employees (e.g., part-time workers, contract workers, and temporary workers dispatched from personnel staffing agencies or subcontracted companies).

In recent times, Japanese companies have employed nonpermanent or casual employees for various reasons; for example, as their earnings have shrunk due to the prolonged economic slump, they cannot afford to employ a large number of regular workers who are assigned to peripheral jobs but receive generous wages and benefits. For these companies, carrying superfluous employees after seasonal demands have reached their peak is a financial burden; thus, they now hire casual and contingent workers as "seasonal workers" who are employed for a limited period (Fu, 2012). Hence, for more than a decade, the number of nonpermanent employees in Japanese workplaces has risen while the number of permanent employees has fallen (Fu, 2012).

With job security intact, at least for regular and core workers, Japanese companies have totally or partially changed the seniority system, one of the management policies which, along with job security, has long been espoused by Japanese companies since the end of World War II. Some Japanese companies have replaced the traditional Japanese seniority system with the American pay-for-performance style. One reason for this is their belief that the US Internet-based dot-com companies and other innovative companies located in Silicon Valley generate dynamism inside their organizations by means of meritocracy, thereby building up their competitiveness against their competitors, including Japanese companies. Other Japanese companies have not completely abandoned the seniority system; instead, they have added a flavor of meritocracy to their traditional seniority system. These Japanese companies learned indirectly by word of mouth or directly from their experiences that pay-for-performance policies do not necessarily work in Japan's egalitarian society where harmony among people is highly valued. They have eclectically combined seniority- and merit-based principles in such a way that nonmanagerial employees are evaluated based on their seniority while managerial employees are assessed according to their performance outcomes. They have also added a flavor of meritocracy to the seniority system in such a way that they place the same weight on meritocracy as on seniority when evaluating employees.

Japanese companies, particularly those in the manufacturing sector, have made progress toward globalization over the past decade. Japanese manufacturers have transferred production facilities to overseas countries that provide abundant, cheap labor forces so that they can cut costs and be more competitive against their rivals both at home and abroad. Their overseas production has accelerated in recent years as the yen has highly appreciated against the US dollar. Roughly 18 percent of all of the products made by Japanese companies in 2010 came from their overseas factories (*Nikkei Newspaper*, November 4, 2011). This figure is projected to reach over 20 percent in 2015, and this has raised the concern that the hollowing out of the Japanese manufacturing industry will accelerate. Japanese plants abroad, for instance in China, Southern Asian countries such as Thailand and Malaysia, and elsewhere, are typically responsible for mass-producing a large volume of goods for shipment to Japan and other marketplaces worldwide. A large number of the operators working in these plants work on long assembly lines. Meanwhile, homeland factories make a small number of high value-added products for shipment to the domestic market. Operators working in these factories are required to perform multiskilling tasks, in other words, to handle multiple work tasks in order to assemble various models of products in small-lot sizes.

The examples provided previously represent only some of the measures taken by Japanese companies in the wake of changes in their environments. They have taken numerous other measures, some radical enough to involve business restructuring and others benign enough to almost keep the status quo. These measures, both radical and benign, include reforming corporate governance, building partnerships with rivals both at home and abroad, concentrating resources on future promising business areas such as social infrastructures and solar panels, digitizing business transactions, halting new graduate recruitment, and cutting back on the cost of entertaining customers. These efforts demonstrate that in the face of several adversities, Japanese companies have transformed, and these transformations will not stop: Japanese companies and their workplaces are still transforming.

Prior studies (e.g., Haghirian, 2010; Miyoshi and Nakata, 2011; Numagami, Kawabe, and Kato, 2010) have attempted to examine whether and how Japanese companies have changed over past years in terms of business strategies, organizational structure, corporate governance, and the like. Unlike these previous studies in this area, in this book, I present the transformations of Japanese companies and workplaces that have taken place since the turn of the twenty-first century in terms of management practices and organizational culture. Some scholars (e.g., Jacoby, 2005) have examined the same issues that I address in this book, including human resource management (HRM) issues for Japanese companies, but they focused on the so-called HRM policies formulated by HRM staff employees in company headquarters or by people in high-ranking positions within an organization. However, I focus more on operational HRM practices that are actually performed by people in their workplaces. Before describing the transforming landscape of Japanese workplaces, in the following sections I discuss traditional Japanese management and the traditional organizational culture of Japanese companies.

Traditional Japanese management

Traditional Japanese management is exemplified by the three pillars of Japanese management: lifetime employment, the seniority system, and enterprise unionism. These elements of traditional Japanese management correspond to parts of the organization-oriented employment system (Jacoby, 2005). Once new college or high school graduates have landed a job with Japanese companies, their employment is guaranteed until they reach retirement age, usually around the age of 60. Japanese employees whose jobs are secure can develop skills specific to their companies. These skills can be more broadly categorized as tacit knowledge as opposed to articulate knowledge (Nonaka, Toyama, and Hirata, 2008). Thus, such skills are difficult for competitors to emulate because they are tacit or hardly communicable and can only be shared between those who have spent years working together at the same workplace. Lifetime employment has been deemed to be superior because it can help to develop firm-specific skills (an aspect of tacit knowledge), thereby building and sustaining a company's competitiveness. Not only can Japanese companies committed to job security promote the development of firm-specific skills, but they can also gain the loyalty of their employees in exchange for job security.

The seniority system is not used in isolation but rather together with lifetime employment. Given that people are employed until they reach retirement age, the seniority system is utilized. Alternatively, provided that employees are evaluated on the basis of their tenure or seniority, lifetime employment can be viable and effective. Employees are promoted to a higher position or paid a higher wage according to the length of their service to their companies, that is, how long they have worked for their current employers. Companies using the seniority system are unlikely to hire people from outside the company when a position is vacant; instead, they fill the vacancy by promoting an employee within the company. Thus, labor markets have been established inside Japanese firms, and this so-called internal labor market is a phenomenon unique to Japanese companies. Meanwhile, labor markets have not developed as much outside Japanese companies. Internal labor markets have helped to develop firm-specific skills or tacit knowledge inside Japanese firms.

The last of the three pillars of Japanese management is enterprise unionism. Japanese companies have unions within the firm. In Japanese business society, employers bargain with representatives from company unions. Even if employees are members of an enterprise union, they can be promoted to a managerial position in the future. Thus, both Japanese general employees—whether union members or not—and managerial employees are concerned about the future of their company. Japanese unionized employees are not as hostile toward their company as their counterparts in the rest of world, where industrial unions are the norm and powerful (e.g., in the United States). Both nonmanagerial and managerial employees cooperate well with each other in Japanese companies, and this cooperation has forged a family-like or paternalistic atmosphere in Japanese workplaces.

These three pillars are all about the personnel policies that are formulated by those in charge of HRM at company headquarters, but they are not exactly the management practices that are actually implemented by people in the workplace. Numerous and various management practices are in place in Japanese workplaces. Some of these practices are employed behind the scenes and are not as well known as the three pillars, but they have had a significant effect on the success of Japanese companies. Among these management practices, team-based practices have been widely used among Japanese companies and can be regarded as crucial elements of traditional Japanese management in addition to the three pillars of Japanese management.

As can be seen in an automobile factory where workers assemble parts components, Japanese workers exercise their multiskilling ability and handle a wide range of work tasks. Their ability to perform multiskilling tasks allows for team-based or interdependent jobs and teamwork is a source of the high level of productivity and competitiveness demonstrated by Japanese companies. Jobs in these work environments are not demarcated as much as those in Western workplaces and are designed to be carried out by a team of workers. Helping colleagues with a problem on the same production line or in the same workplace and other team activities can facilitate team-based jobs; thus, teamwork, a practice popular in Japanese workplaces, is required to achieve team-based jobs. One reason why team-based jobs and practices are common among Japanese companies is that Japan is a collectivist society. Japanese workers are inclined to work together and are skilled at teamwork.

Table 1.1   The traditional styles of Japanese management

Among management policies, the three pillars of Japanese management:
lifetime employment
seniority system
enterprise unionism

Among management practices, the following team-based practices:
multiskilling tasks
interdependent jobs
teamwork
autonomous team structures
decisions made in the interest of the team
improvement activities
QC circles

Japan is also an egalitarian society, and the difference between managerial and general employees in terms of authority and remuneration is small. Accordingly, Japanese team structures are not that hierarchical and all employees are allowed to make decisions. The nature of Japanese teams involves a large amount of discretion or autonomy in decision-making. Decisions are occasionally group oriented in that each employee makes a decision in the interests of her or his team, not in his or her own interests.

Improvement activities are among the team-based management practices deemed to be common across Japanese companies. These activities are quite often performed off the line by a team of employees rather than by individual ones. Quality control (QC) activities represent one type of improvement activities and are prevalent in Japanese companies in both the manufacturing and nonmanufacturing sectors. These improvement activities are sometimes assessed on the basis of team performance, and members of a QC circle are thus rewarded according to the team's outcomes.

Team-based management practices have contributed to improved efficiency, as demonstrated particularly by Japanese companies in the manufacturing sector, and, eventually, to greater competitiveness. Table 1.1 summarizes the traditional styles of Japanese management.

Traditional organizational culture of Japanese companies

Japanese companies hold collectivist values because they are embedded in the regional context where Confucianism is traditionally espoused.

Japanese society is considered to share the same values as other Asian and Confucian countries and regions, such as China, South Korea, and Taiwan (House et al., 2004). Japanese employees are thus apt to act in the best interests of their group or organization rather than in their own best interests. Although it is regarded as being the same type of Confucian country as China, South Korea, and other Asian countries, Japan is also an egalitarian society and stresses harmony and equality among people to a greater extent than other Asian and Confucian countries. Thus, Japanese people working for Japanese companies dislike large differences in terms of wages, authority, and hierarchy. It is noted that Japanese companies care about equality among employees not only in terms of wages and authority but also in terms of company clothing, cafeterias, parking lots, and other symbols that have a profound effect on employees' perceptions of the similarities or disparities in their workplaces. Thus, even Japanese rank-and-file workers are allowed to participate in decision-making. Compared to people and organizations in high power distance societies (e.g., China), both individual employees and work organizations in Japan can be characterized as discretional and autonomous. Egalitarian values bolster the seniority system that is widely used in Japanese companies, but they could also cause performance-based promotion and remuneration to malfunction in the Japanese business context.

As Hofstede (1980) identified in his famous cross-culture studies, Japan is also characterized as a masculine society in the sense that, generally, males and their values are more likely to be favored than their female counterparts and female values. Masculinity prevails over femininity inside Japanese companies, and male employees traditionally dominate Japanese workplaces, in particular managerial or higher ranking positions. Japanese companies' organizational culture means that it is more likely that male employees rather than female employees will occupy managerial positions and finally end up in the highest ranks of the organization.

The nature of an organizational culture can be characterized in terms of the extent to which it is homogenous or heterogeneous. The organizational culture of Japanese companies is traditionally homogenous and strong. Japanese society is known for its homogenization of cultural values. This stems from the fact that Japan's geographic position, surrounded as it is by sea, insulates the nation from the rest of the world and that Japanese governments have traditionally prevented a massive influx of foreigners into the country. Consequently, the majority of the workforce in Japanese companies is composed of Japanese citizens.

Table 1.2   The traditional organizational culture of Japanese companies

---

The types of organizational culture:
collectivist culture
egalitarian culture
masculine culture

The nature of organizational culture:
homogeneous and strong culture

This demographic composite has facilitated cultural homogenization in Japanese companies. Japanese employees share the nation's cultural values and consequently their organization has become culturally homogeneous. This situation has helped to develop a strong culture in Japanese companies, through which people are well integrated.

In addition to the nation's geographic position, Japanese management practices also seemingly aim to homogenize organizational culture, and these practices have further enhanced cultural homogeneity and strength in Japanese companies. Job security policies, one of the three pillars of Japanese management, prevent employees from being laid off. It is argued that as Japanese employees whose employment is secure are emotionally attached and committed to the goals and values of their organizations in return for their job security, a strong organizational culture is likely to develop within Japan's organizations. The seniority system can also facilitate the development of strong organizational culture by promoting internal labor markets. Additionally, enterprise unionism can build a strong culture within a company by forging a family-like atmosphere in the workplace. Against the backdrop of these situations within Japanese firms, a homogeneous, strong culture is more likely to develop in these organizations. What is more, this strong culture has been considered to be a competitive edge for Japanese companies. Strong culture can motivate people to work harder or allow them to work without a bureaucratic control mechanism. A summary of the traditional organizational culture of Japanese companies is provided in Table 1.2.

The purpose of this book

As I have argued so far, Japanese companies have transformed and are transforming. In this book, I present the transformations that have taken place since the dawn of the new millennium and are currently taking place in Japanese workplaces in terms of management practices, particularly in the area of HRM, and organizational culture. I also empirically assess the effectiveness of the new approaches introduced by Japanese companies with regard to management practices and organizational culture based on my hypotheses and evidence collected from Japanese companies. Thus, I aim not only to explore every aspect of Japanese companies and their workplaces but also to generalize and theorize management issues by observing these companies.

Some readers may wonder why I am publishing a book on Japanese companies and their management and organization when they seem to be ailing and their presence is not remarkable in the global business arena. I have written and published this book for several reasons. First, management studies should not be faddish. Management scholars are attracted to success stories about companies or to in-vogue management techniques as they jumped on the Japanese management bandwagon in the 1980s and early 1990s. However, management scholars should be responsible for studying not only successful companies and popular management ideas but also what is going on in actual or seemingly unsuccessful companies. They may discover "something new" by studying successful companies and fashionable management ideas; but even in actual or seemingly unsuccessful companies and outdated management ideas, they may also capture "something important" which they might not figure out through studying successful companies or management ideas that are in vogue. Japanese companies have tried to transform in the face of woes that companies in the rest of the world have not yet experienced. Thus, it is highly likely that management scholars would capture something important or significant to an understanding of both management theories and practices by studying what Japanese companies have done (and how) over the past decade or longer.

Second, and related to the previous point, management scholars are required to study companies, regardless of their success or failure, not just in the short term but also over a long period so that they can enhance our understanding of these firms' management and organization. In Japanese companies' glory days, Japanese styles of management influenced business leaders and scholars. These Japanese companies undeniably shaped, and left their deep footprints on, the history of management theories and practices. Thus, it is pointless to stop studying or documenting Japanese companies and their management and organization.

Third, business leaders and even public policymakers outside Japan can draw and learn lessons from the experiences of Japanese companies over the last decade or more. Thus, an important task for management scholars is to document these experiences. Companies in emerging economies such as China and India have enhanced their presence in global business settings in recent years as they have enjoyed these economies' rapid and continued high growth. However, these economies will not continue to develop forever; their growth will stop sometime in the future. Then, companies in these emerging economies may face the same problems that Japanese companies have experienced over the past decade or so. If so, they might be able to learn how to address these problems from Japanese companies' experiences and efforts. I hope that by reading this book, readers, including business leaders, scholars, students, and even the general public around the world, will be able to gain an understanding of the transforming landscape of Japanese workplaces. I hope that they will also be able to draw and learn lessons from Japanese firms' experiences and to understand what they should do (and how) in the future in the face of challenges such as those that Japanese companies have faced.

2
Management Practices in Japanese Workplaces: Myth and Reality

Introduction

In the past, the management styles and organization of Japanese companies were frequently and earnestly compared to those of their US counterparts by people from the two countries and beyond for one reason or another. First, in the late 1970s and the 1980s, when the competitiveness of American companies decreased compared to that of Japanese companies, American corporate leaders and business scholars started taking a special interest in Japanese management and, subsequently, in comparing both countries' management styles. Second, differences in management styles and business practices between America and Japan became so pronounced as a result of business conflicts between the two countries that academics, policymakers, and bureaucrats from both countries made comparative studies of American and Japanese management. Third, as Japanese management and organization—some of which seem to be in sharp contrast to those of the United States—are unique and indigenous to Japanese society, it was intellectually interesting, especially for management scholars not just from the two countries involved but also from other parts of the world, to compare and study both countries' management and organizational styles. Fourth, in order to catch up with and then surpass American companies, both Japanese bureaucrats and corporate leaders, who deemed these companies to be world business forerunners, needed to learn a lot from these US firms by comparing different management styles in the two countries.

The traditional view held by management scholars and practitioners of Japanese companies was clearly different to their view of American companies: Japan's management and organizational practices are flexible while those of the United States are bureaucratic. In this chapter, I verify the conventional view based on my case studies of Japanese companies in the automobile and electronics industries in order to explore the existing landscape of Japanese workplaces around the turn of the twenty-first century. I attempt to do so by drawing on the notion of what scholars call high-performance work practices (HPWPs) and exploring their prevalence in Japanese workplaces. I begin by clarifying the conventional view of the management practices in Japanese workplaces in more detail in the next section.

Conventional view of Japan's management practices

One of the most well-known studies that have ever attempted to compare and characterize the management and organization of both US and Japanese companies is Ouchi and Jaeger's work (1978). In their classic work in this area, they called the typical type of American organizations and Japanese organizations "Type A" and "Type J" organizations, respectively. Type A organizations are characterized by their use of standards, explicit rules, hierarchy, highly classified jobs, and other elements of a mechanical system; Type J organizations are characterized by their use of job security, horizontal coordination, group-oriented decisions, implicit rules, and strong culture and other elements of an organic system. Thus, Ouchi and Jaeger regarded the nature of Type J organizations as being organic or flexible, as opposed to the mechanical and bureaucratic nature of Type A organizations.

Aoki (1990), a Japanese economics professor, also expressed his views of the management practices and organization of US and Japanese firms; these views stressed the contrast between companies in the two countries. In his model, American organizations were characterized by their use of vertical coordination to achieve both the efficiency of hierarchical coordination and economies of specialization. He designated these American organizational and management practices as the H-mode ("H" standing for hierarchy). Meanwhile, Japanese organizations were characterized by their use of horizontal coordination and information sharing across departments or subunits. Aoki called these Japanese management and organizational practices the J-mode ("J" standing for Japanese). He supposed that Japanese companies that are driven by J-mode principles (e.g., horizontal coordination) are more adaptive to changes in environments than their US counterparts that operate based on H-mode principles (e.g., hierarchical coordination).

Scholars such as Womack, Jones, and Roos (1990) have considered Toyota Motor Corp. to exemplify Japan's nimble and efficient organizational methods. This Japanese automaker uses a production system called Toyota Production System (TPS), which has often been compared to the mass production or Fordism invented by Ford Motor Co. in the early part of the twentieth century. TPS is also known as Lean Production System in the United States and other parts of the world (Womack, Jones, and Roos, 1990). A crucial part of TPS is the just-in-time (JIT) delivery principle, by means of which it is expected that a suitable, not excessive, amount of product parts can be supplied to a production line in time for the time point they are required. Consequently, inventories, which are regarded as piling up waste rather than adding value by Toyota workers, can be kept at as low a level as possible and not only inventory costs but also lead time and even return on investment (ROI) can be improved.

In sum, legend had it that the management practices of Japanese workplaces are more flexible and innovative, as opposed to their American counterparts' bureaucratic and outdated ones. In order to verify this view, I explore the management practices of Japanese workplaces around the turn of the century by drawing on the notion of HPWPs. I do this because this notion will offer a clue to the extent to which these innovative and flexible management practices were common across Japanese workplaces at that time.

HPWPs and their prevalence among American workplaces

In the past, managing people was considered not to be greatly associated with companies' bottom lines. It was believed that the people in charge of human resource management (HRM) generated profits only by cutting back on the workforce or their paychecks. Behind such a view of HRM was the assumption that personnel are a cost or expense to be minimized. However, scholars began to offer a different view of HRM in the early 1990s. These scholars, for instance Arthur (1994), Cutcher-Gershenfeld (1991), Ichniowski et al. (1996), Huselid (1995), and US Department of Labor (1993), posited that personnel are not a cost or expense but rather capital to be invested in. They argued that management practices can develop highly committed employees who can be a source of a firm's competitiveness and that the use of these practices can enhance company performance. They called these practices HPWPs because they expected them to generate high performance. The term "HPWPs" was used interchangeably with other terms, such as high commitment, innovative, flexible, and alternative management practices. These management practices stand in contrast to traditional practices, which correspond to parts of the compliance human resource (HR) system identified by Mossholder, Richardson, and Settoon (2011).

Baron and Kreps (1999) argued that the term "high commitment management practices" is a general catchphrase used for an ensemble of HRM practices that aims at getting more from workers by giving them more work. They went on to argue that there is no single one-size-fits-all array of practices; instead, people in charge of HRM must select management practices that are relevant to their particular company. The following management practices are among those proposed by Baron and Kreps:

- Employment guarantees: workers will not be dismissed except, perhaps, for grave errors of omission or commission.
- Egalitarianism in word and deed: distinctions among workers at different levels of the hierarchy are aggressively de-emphasized. Everyone is part of one big team. Symbolic distinctions—for instance, separate bathrooms or dining facilities and reserved parking spots for executives—are eliminated or downplayed, and real distinctions (most significantly, in compensation levels) are also de-emphasized.
- Emphasis on self-managing teams and team production.
- Job enlargement (job includes more tasks than is typical) and enrichment (variety and challenge of tasks is greater than usual).
- Extensive socialization and training of employees, including cross-training.
- Extensive job rotations.
- Open channels of communication: employees at all levels are allowed and expected to contribute ideas. Associated with this—and with the downplaying of hierarchical distinctions—are flattened hierarchies.
- Extensive screening of prospective employees, emphasizing cultural fit.

Becker and Gerhart (1996) argued that what some scholars considered as constituting a set of HPWPs or a high-performance work system was sometimes different from what others expected. For example, Arthur (1994) downplayed the role of variable pay as a high-performance work practice, while Huselid (1995) and MacDuffie (1995) stressed this practice as being part of a high-performance work system. Huselid (1995) and Pfeffer (1994) designated internal promotion and employee grievance procedures as HPWPs, while Arthur (1994) and Ichniowski and colleagues (1996) regarded these practices as parts of the rigid HRM system that sometimes results in less productive work environments. Becker and

Huselid (1998) thought of these two practices as bureaucratic HRM practices and found them to have economically and statistically significant negative effects on company profitability. Thus, scholars seemed not to agree on what constituted HPWPs and the like. However, as Baron and Kreps (1999) argued, Western scholars (e.g., US Department of Labor, 1993) seemed to agree that the numerous management practices they designated as high-commitment HRM practices had a certain character, namely, management styles seen in traditional top-tier Japanese firms (e.g., employment security), and that these HPWPs might come from Japanese companies.

Several studies have examined the extent to which HPWPs and the like were prevalent among US companies around the turn of the twenty-first century; these studies include a national cross-industry study (Osterman, 2000), a California-based establishment study (Erickson and Jacoby, 2003), and an HRM-performance relation study (Huselid, 1995). Osterman's study (2000) found that high-performance work organizations (HPWOs) took root in American workplaces in the early 1990s. He defined HPWOs as being constituted by self-managed teams, total quality management (TQM), quality circles, and job rotation. American establishments with at least 50 employees in the private for-profit sector participated in his surveys. In his 1992 survey, Osterman found that 40.5 percent of establishments had self-managed teams, 24.5 percent had TQM, 27.4 percent had quality circles, and 26.6 percent had job rotation. The use of HPWO practices grew considerably in the five-year period following his first-round survey in 1992 with one exception: self-managed teams, which was at almost the same level as in 1992. He also revealed that establishments that had had HPWO practices in place in 1992 were able, by and large, to sustain them over the subsequent five years while a large number of establishments that had not had them struggled to introduce these innovative practices into their workplaces.

These new American workplaces characterized by their use of HPWPs were epitomized by SAS Institute Inc. and Xilinx Inc. I had a chance to visit these companies and to interview managerial employees and observe their workplaces. With regard to SAS Institute, I only visited SAS Institute Japan. As for Xilinx, I visited both its headquarters in Silicon Valley and its Japanese office. SAS Institute makes software packages for use in statistics (SAS originally stood for "statistical analysis system") and also provides business solutions to corporate customers worldwide. At the time of my visit, it was known for carrying out practices that were hardly ever seen in typical American workplaces, let alone the software industry, where cutthroat competition is the norm both outside and within companies (O'Reilly and Pfeffer, 2000). It provided staff benefits including a daycare center at work, profit sharing systems, a job security policy, an extensive education system, team practices, free health insurance, and an on-site medical clinic. SAS Institute carried out these practices because it enjoyed one of the lowest staff turnover rates in the software industry, no more than 5 percent a year, because of the use of such practices. In 1999, the company had a professional turnover of less than 4 percent, losing 131 out of 3292 employees, while the industry average was five times that at slightly over 20 percent (Fishman, 2000).

Xilinx, a Silicon Valley-based semiconductor company, also employed and implemented so-called HPWPs. Like other semiconductor and high-technology companies, it experienced an extremely difficult time when it faced a significant downturn in the industry in 2001 following the September 11 terrorist attacks. While other companies decided to cut jobs, Xilinx avoided firing its employees because the then chief executive officer (CEO) Wim Roelandts had repeatedly told his employees that layoffs were a last resort and he believed that he would lose employees' trust if he did what he had promised not to do, that is, lay off people (Delong and Darwall, 2003a, 2003b). Indeed, the company did not dismiss anyone during these difficult times, and Xilinx's employees responded positively to a pay-cut plan because they were loyal to and trusted the CEO and the company. After weathering and getting out of the severe economic conditions, Xilinx finally generated high levels of financial performance, possibly because of their use of HPWPs.

In sum, it seems that a comprehensive set of HPWPs was not prevalent among American firms around the turn of the century. However, the majority of US companies had adopted some aspects of a high-performance work system even if they did not have a full set of such practices in place. American companies responded to the current difficulties facing them by adopting these management practices (O'Toole and Lawler, 2007).

Prevalence of HPWPs among Japanese workplaces

Legend had it that Japan's management practices are innovative and flexible. In this section, I examine whether such innovative and flexible management practices as HPWPs were indeed common across Japanese workplaces around the turn of the century based on my case studies of Japanese automotive and electronics manufacturers. I provide the case of Toyota as one example of the Japanese companies that were expected to utilize HPWPs because Japanese automobile makers were well known for using these practices and outperforming their foreign competitors (MacDuffie, 1995). I then provide cases of some Japanese electronics manufacturers and further explore the prevalence of HPWPs among Japanese workplaces. I provide these cases because the Japanese electronics industry was—and still is—as important as the automotive industry for the Japanese economy since, along with the automobile industry, it was the driving force behind the growth of the Japanese economy in the post-World War II period. By examining Japanese electronics manufacturers as well, I can compare the management practices of both Japanese automotive and electronics manufacturers and enhance our understanding of the prevalence of HPWPs among Japanese workplaces. The cases in this section were written largely based on my joint research with colleagues (Okamoto, 2002). It should be noted that I examine operational management practices at the front-line level, not more general and abstract management policies at the company level (Arthur and Boyles, 2007).

The Japanese automotive industry: Toyota Motor Corp.

Toyota Motor Corp. (TMC), best known globally as Toyota, is headquartered in the city of Toyota, Aichi Prefecture, in the center of Japan and home to the nation's automobile industry. When I surveyed Toyota in 2000, a total of 12 domestic plants operated by the company were located in the Aichi district. In addition to these plants close to company headquarters, Toyota also had factories in the other areas: Kyushu, Hokkaido, and Tohoku. I visited Toyota Motor Kyushu Inc. (TMK) with my colleagues in February 2000. Located on the southern Japanese island of Kyushu, TMK was and is a manufacturing company wholly owned by TMC. It started operations in 1992. A subsidiary affiliated to TMC not as a budget center but as a profit center, TMK is responsible for its profits and losses and thus is treated as an independent firm from the parent company. When I visited TMK in 2000, the Harrier, Windom, Chaser, and Mark II models were manufactured in its plants. TMK is currently designated as one of the Toyota group's companies that primarily manufactures Toyota's top luxury vehicle, the Lexus, for shipment to both the domestic market and to overseas markets such as North America and China.

When I studied Toyota, there were many automotive parts suppliers around the Toyota plants in the Aichi district. By taking advantage of their proximity to those suppliers, the plants were able to procure the appropriate amount of parts components they needed no later than the designated arrival time. This became a competitive edge for the Aichi district Toyota plants. Compared to these plants, the number of suppliers around TMK was considerably smaller. It was difficult for TMK to depend on automotive suppliers in the Aichi district to deliver parts components because its site was far from the Aichi district and it took a long time to transport components to TMK. Thus, TMK had no option but to rely on local nascent suppliers to supply parts, which was considerably disadvantageous to the manufacturing company in terms of parts procurement. Nevertheless, the unparalleled efficiency and quality achieved by TMK's workers compensated for this disadvantageous procurement position.

TMK redesigned their conventional long manufacturing lines and introduced autonomous complete assembly lines. Each of the traditional long lines was broken down into several mini-lines. Production teams were organized along these mini-lines and a team of operators was engaged in production activities on the line they were in charge of. A typical front-line production team was composed of one supervisor and around 15 operators. This production team was also a front-line work organization. The supervisor had around three team leaders who reported to him or her. Each leader was in charge of around five general operators. The production team was "self-sufficient" or autonomous in that the operators, as a team, were responsible for the whole production process on the divided and mini production line.

Upon the introduction of these autonomous complete assembly lines, the roles and responsibilities of supervisors were strengthened (Fujimoto, 1999). Each supervisor, now in charge of a mini-line, was allowed a larger amount of discretion with regard to daily operations. In addition, several supportive tools and facilities, ranging from switches for planned line stops (to control lines), monitoring displays (to share on-site information), training centers (to upgrade skills), and rest areas (to motivate workers), were offered to each mini-line.

Workers took part in total quality control (TQC) activities and tried hard to find and solve problems in order to improve quality. Each quality control (QC) circle always had about four themes to address and was expected to complete each one in three to four months; thereafter, the QC circle team was supposed to figure out new themes and tackle the new targeted themes. Workers were not only engaged in improvement activities through QC circles but also had several opportunities to take part in such activities. TMK's operators routinely tried to address and improve problems concerning product quality, costs, worker safety, and their work environment; for example, an increase in the number of female workers at TMK made employees feel that they needed work environments and workplaces that were comfortable not only for male workers but also for female workers. In response to this demand, TMK operators modified an 18 kg (approximately 40 lb) hammer to 3.3 kg (around 7 lb) so that female workers could easily work with this tool. This effort was part of the company's proud record of continuous improvement activities. Operators were rewarded for their suggestions if they were found to benefit TMK and translate into future profits.

In line with TMK's personnel policy of gradually expanding workers' skills, workers were required to be multiskilled and to deal with a wide range of work processes. Assembly workers were not just asked to assemble parts but also to maintain or repair equipment and tools. This was because TMK had little new equipment and, consequently, workers had to maintain outdated equipment as part of their work; for instance, two-thirds of the press machinery installed at TMK was secondhand from their parent company (TMC). Some TMK workers made jigs themselves so that they could enhance their understanding of the tool. Operators were also asked to broaden their range of skills so that their work tasks would not become boring.

In this fashion, TMK adopted and implemented such HPWPs as problem-solving and continuous improvement activities, TQC, QC circles, intensive and systematic training for multiskilled workers, job enlargement, pay for good suggestions (translating into improvements), and intrinsic rewards such as comfortable work environments. It adopted these practices not only to humanize the work environment but also to be more efficient and competitive. The TMK plant manager whom my colleagues and I interviewed asserted that the workforce itself was a source of competitiveness for the company. Indeed, TMK operators were more motivated in this work environment characterized by autonomous complete assembly lines than they had been in their previous environment, which was characterized by traditional long lines (Fujimoto, 1999). In addition, they were a source of a high standard of productivity and quality for TMK.

The Japanese electronics industry: Canon Inc.

Along with the automobile industry, the Japanese electronics industry bolstered the Japanese economy and drove growth after World War II. Japanese electronics companies demonstrated their strength on the international business scene by challenging US dominance in the global market in the 1970s and 1980s. However, Japanese electronics companies were mired in the nation's prolonged economic stagnation triggered by the collapse of the asset-inflated bubble economy in the early 1990s. Consequently, they fell into dire financial straits and their financial performance indices, such as profitability and ROI, declined. During this time, they also faced increasingly fierce competition from foreign companies in their business area. They lost portions of the market share that they had acquired to their foreign competitors, and this led to a further deterioration in their financial situation, which had already been affected by the economic slump after the bubble economy burst. These new business environments posed serious threats to Japanese electronics manufacturers.

Despite these relentless threats facing the Japanese electronics industry, Canon Inc. demonstrated relatively favorable financial performance throughout the 1990s and the early 2000s compared to other Japanese electronics companies. For example, in 2001, Canon posted a net profit of 167,561 million yen (US$1378 million) compared to 121,227 million yen (US$997 million) for Sony Corp., 56,603 million yen (US$466 million) for NEC Corp., and 41,500 million yen (US$341 million) for Matsushita Electric Industrial Co. Ltd. (whose company name was later changed to Panasonic Corp.) in the same Japanese fiscal year ending March 31. Canon improved its bottom lines, especially after Fujio Mitarai's appointment as CEO of the company in 1995. I examine the case of Canon with a focus on its efforts to turn itself around, which were primarily led by Mitarai, around the turn of the century.

Canon was founded in 1933. The original name of the company was Precision Optical Instruments Laboratory. Canon was originally a camera manufacturer, but it has diversified into several business areas, such as business machines, copying machines, printers, and semiconductor production equipment. Canon is a research-oriented company and has invented and developed several types of new technology, as the company's philosophy, represented by the company's *San-Ji* spirit jargon, indicates. *San* means "three" in Japanese, and the Japanese word *Ji* suggests "oneself" or "by oneself." By *San-ji*, the company means three types of do-it-yourself mind-sets: spontaneity, independence, and self-awareness. The prefix for all three Japanese terms is *Ji: Ji-hatsu* (spontaneity), *Ji-ritsu* (independence), and *Ji-kaku* (self-awareness). Thus, *San-ji* signifies the ensemble of these three do-it-yourself mind-sets. Canon employees are required to work hard and tackle their work with a *San-ji* spirit.

Like other Japanese electronics manufacturers, Canon strived to improve its cash flows and other financial performance indices when it launched its Excellent Global Corporation Plan in January 1996. In line with this plan, Canon decided to allow its shares to be traded on US soil and to go public there. After it improved its bottom lines, Canon was listed on the New York Stock Exchange (NYSE) in September 2000. Behind this improvement in performance were the efforts made by Canon, spearheaded by CEO Mitarai, to turn the company around.

Canon had been an electronics conglomerate, but since 1998, the company has divested itself of its unprofitable business segments, such as PCs, typewriters, FLC (ferroelectric liquid crystal) displays, and optical cards. Meanwhile, it has concentrated resources on the business areas involving its core technology (i.e., optoelectronics), such as digital cameras, printers, and steppers. In the face of financial adversities caused by the drop in demand in Japanese markets following the collapse of the bubble economy, Japanese companies were under pressure to restructure their business structure. They trimmed unprofitable business areas and instead focused their resources on lucrative and prospective business segments. Before the bubble economy burst, it seemed as though Japanese firms, both in the manufacturing and nonmanufacturing sectors, wanted to be involved in a wide range of business areas, even ones unrelated to their core operations, and becoming a conglomerate company seemed to have become a status symbol for Japanese companies. However, after the bubble economy burst, companies divested themselves of unprofitable business areas under their restructuring plans. Unlike other Japanese companies, Canon still strived to achieve a synergy among several business domains while axing a bunch of unprofitable business areas, namely, PCs, typewriters, and so forth.

After taking over as CEO, Mitarai exerted strong leadership to reorient Canon's entire business activities. Parts of the company's research and development (R&D) functions were transferred to factories in order to enhance the effectiveness of research activities. For example, Canon's engineers had been engaged in R&D for office imaging products, such as copying machines, fax machines, and image scanners, at the company's headquarters in the Japanese capital of Tokyo. Upon taking the helm at Canon, Mitarai attempted to redeploy R&D teams to the company's Toride plant located in a suburb of Tokyo in 1997. As the Toride plant included both manufacturing and R&D functions, product development lead time—the length of time required to complete all research activities—was reduced by around 25 percent compared to the same benchmark before reorganization.

Canon started implementing supply chain management (SCM) around 1999. A supply chain is a network where upstream suppliers, manufacturing facilities, and downstream retailers are all integrated. SCM is an integrated approach for dealing with the planning and control of the flow of materials from suppliers to end users (Kanji and

Wong, 1999). To put it simply, it is a technique for managing these supply chains with the aim of matching demand with supply and keeping a lower volume of inventory. Canon Hi-Tech (Thailand), located in Ayutthaya, 60 km (around 38 miles) north of Bangkok, was the first Canon plant in the world to introduce SCM. It manufactured items such as bubble jet printers, personal-use copying machines, and multi-function facsimile machines, and when I studied Canon in 2001, 4703 people worked for this manufacturing company. Other Canon group factories at home and abroad learned how to introduce and implement SCM from Canon Hi-Tech (Thailand). CEO Mitarai took the initiative in introducing SCM and asked managers at Canon's affiliated companies and plants worldwide to renew product codes so as to synchronize the product codes of the Canon group and to install the new procurement system. The process of introducing SCM demanded meticulous work and a considerable amount of time, but Canon eventually succeeded in introducing SCM globally among its group companies.

In line with the introduction of SCM, Canon attempted to replace its production system with a new method. Like many other Japanese manufacturers, Canon had employed a traditional large-scale automation and conveyor belt production system. Mitarai witnessed the team-based production method when he visited Mitsumi Electric Co. Ltd., a medium-sized Japanese electronics manufacturer, in March 1997 and Sony Kisarazu, Sony's affiliated manufacturing company, in July of the same year. He was interested in a new production method that Sony called "cell production." This led to Canon departing from traditional conveyor production systems and introducing a cell production system. In a cell production work environment, workers perform multiple production tasks in a manufacturing cell arranged in either a U-shape or another form such as a straight line.

A committee for management turnaround, led by CEO Mitarai as its chairman, was set up at Canon's headquarters in April 1998. This committee had eight subcommittees. The production and logistics subcommittee spearheaded the introduction of the new production system into Canon group companies worldwide. Canon Nagahama, the company's affiliated manufacturing company that made laser beam printers, bubble jet cartridges, and so forth, was designated as the pilot factory to adopt and implement cell production systems when Canon kicked off its management turnaround initiatives. Canon's Japan-based plants competed with one another to become the second factory after Canon Nagahama to adopt and implement the cell production method. This competition was what members of the committee for management turnaround had expected to witness because they believed that it would promote the adoption and spread of cell production among Canon group companies worldwide. As a result of this competition, the cell production method was employed first by the Toride plant and then by Oita Canon, whose products included digital cameras. Canon Chemicals, which manufactured toner cartridges, chemical products, and so forth, followed these forerunners, as did Canon's Fukushima plant, which manufactured bubble jet printers. Manufacturing facilities overseas, such as in the United States and Mexico (Tijuana, a city straddling the border between the United States and Mexico), also started cell production.

Canon expected that the use of the cell production method would allow the company to achieve a range of goals: (1) humanization of work environment, (2) improvement in productivity, (3) reduction in inventory, (4) effective use of work space, (4) quick response to changes in customers' needs and demands, (5) high-variety and small-lot production, and (6) success of build-to-order (BTO) manufacturing strategies. More importantly for Canon, the method was also instrumental in implementing SCM and ultimately improving its bottom lines or net profits. The plants that introduced and operated cell production played a vital role in meeting demands from sales sites so that supply chains could be linked between production and sales sites. Innovations such as multitasking workers, job rotations to develop multiple skills, and products, jigs, and equipment designed to match the cell production work environment, were vital to the implementation and success of this production method.

Indeed, Canon improved several performance measures and enjoyed good performance by using the cell production method. For example, at Canon's Ami plant, one of the plants well known for its introduction of cell production, 27 conveyor belts, equivalent to a total length of 2700 meters (around 2468 yards), were removed as a result of the use of the new production method. People at the plant also scrapped the large-size equipment used on the traditional manufacturing lines. Individual workers manufactured 1.3 times as many products in the cell production work environment as they had done in the traditional manufacturing work environment. Compared to line workers, cell operators found their work more challenging and fulfilling. Osterman (2000) argued that the adoption of HPWPs produced redundant workers and was significantly related to reductions in the number of workers or layoffs. Indeed, after Canon adopted management practices entailing the use of cell production, the number of workers required was reduced: the number of people who were deployed to the manufacturing cells was smaller than the number of operators who had worked on the traditional mass production lines. However, Canon moved these saved or "surplus" workers to other workplaces or manufacturing cells where production work on new business or products was about to begin.

Canon started production and workplace innovation activities six to eight years later than other Japanese electronics manufacturers. CEO Mitarai was inspired to introduce cell production into the company when he went on a plant tour at Mitsumi Electric and Sony Kisarazu. Despite Canon's late introduction of cell production, the company reaped benefits from such innovation activities much earlier than other Japanese companies that had introduced these activities long before it had done so because all of its employees were engaged in these activities, or, to put it more simply, because of the efforts of the entire company.

The Japanese electronics industry: NEC Corp.

NEC Corp. was once a leading electronics corporation in the areas of computers, communications equipment, and semiconductors in Japan and the world. Its current name came from an abbreviation of its previous name, Nippon Electric Company, Limited. NEC occupied a large share of the domestic market for PCs in the early days of Japan's PC industry. It also held lead position in global semiconductor sales rankings from the late 1980s through to the early 1990s. NEC's semiconductor business unit was dubbed "a department store for semiconductor products." As the epithet suggests, NEC delivered a broad range of semiconductor products from dynamic random-access memory (DRAM) commodity-type chips to more customized application-specific integrated circuit (ASIC) chips for shipment to certain producers (e.g., a game console maker). In this fashion, not only did NEC diversify into various business areas, it also expanded product models in specific business areas, and this was the company's strength.

However, NEC started losing its competitiveness against overseas competitors in the early 1990s. In the semiconductor business, NEC lost the top position in the world semiconductor sales rankings to Intel Corp., an American semiconductor manufacturer that delivered innovative and high value-added microprocessors. It also lost the large share of the global DRAM market it had held to new chip makers from South Korea and Taiwan that had been obscure in the global marketplace in the 1980s. Likewise, although NEC dominated the PC market at home from the 1980s through to the mid 1990s, it lost the large share of this market to foreign PC makers such as Dell Inc. and Hewlett-Packard (HP)

Co. Fierce competition from overseas manufacturers weakened NEC's sales and profits, which had already been damaged by the collapse of the Japanese bubble economy. NEC steadily increased its sales after the early 1990s, but its profitability lagged far behind its US rivals such as Intel, Micron Technology, HP, and IBM. NEC's profitability (operating income/net sales) for the year 1998 was 2.2 percent while Intel's was 43.2 percent, Micron's was 14 percent, HP's was 12.2 percent, and IBM's was 16.7 percent.

In response to declining profits and profitability, NEC introduced what it called production innovation initiatives and attempted to disseminate these activities to NEC group companies nationwide in the early 1990s. As the first step in these initiatives, NEC set up a production innovation team composed of 15 people, ten from the production department and five from the design department. The new team was responsible for studying the principles of the TPS and then disseminating these across NEC's manufacturing plants nationwide. Even though, at first, people employed at NEC plants showed resistance to the production innovation initiatives, they eventually started to replace their outdated production system with the new one, that is, TPS or cell production.

One of the plants that was remarkably successful in introducing the new production system was NEC Yonezawa. Located in the rural city of Yonezawa around 240 km (150 miles) north of Tokyo, NEC Yonezawa was a manufacturing company that was 100 percent owned by NEC, and its main products were PCs when I studied this company in 2001. It is currently operated by NEC Personal Products Ltd., a 51 percent stake in which China's Lenovo Group Ltd holds, with the remaining 49 percent stake owned by NEC. NEC Yonezawa started its production innovation initiatives in 1995. Then, in 1998, it began to implement the company's original management innovation program—Big Challenge 21. The program's goal was to turn NEC Yonezawa around so that it could become strong enough to compete with its domestic and overseas rivals even though it was small in comparison to them. Thus, although it was a manufacturing company, NEC Yonezawa sought to improve not just operating outcomes, such as productivity and total cost, but also financial ones, such as profitability and capital turnover.

In line with the Big Challenge 21 program, in 1998, NEC Yonezawa employed the BTO manufacturing strategy to produce and deliver laptop PCs to its corporate customers. If manufacturers carry out this strategy appropriately, it allows them to assemble parts components immediately after receiving orders from their customers and to deliver the completed products to them within the required time frame. In

1999, NEC Yonezawa started utilizing the BTO strategy to manufacture and deliver laptop PCs to its non-corporate and individual customers. With this new strategy, it hoped to improve customer satisfaction by providing them with the desired products at the desired time. Indeed, it obtained large gains by implementing its BTO strategy correctly. The strategy allowed NEC Yonezawa to reduce its total lead time—the total time it takes a manufacturer to create a product and then deliver it to customers after receiving orders from them. In 1997, before its utilization of the BTO strategy, NEC Yonezawa's manufacturing lead time, a part of total lead time, was 8.2 hours; in 2000, after the introduction of the BTO strategy, this figure was reduced to 5.5 hours.

The cell production method allowed for flexible output and played a vital role in NEC Yonezawa's implementation of its BTO manufacturing strategy. When NEC Yonezawa employed a conventional mass production system, about 30 workers used to assemble PC components on a PC production line; however, after it adopted the cell production system in 1998, the PC assembly line was composed of a sub-assembly line where about four workers operated and a final assembly line where three workers were deployed. TPS consultants advised NEC Yonezawa's engineers to adopt linear manufacturing cells instead of the popular U-shaped cells as they believed that cell workers were able to detect problems more easily on a linear cell than on a U-shaped cell or other forms of manufacturing cells. Sub-assembly lines were finally combined with final assembly lines. The combined lines were used when products were manufactured in small-lot sizes. A small number of cell workers (e.g., three operators) worked on these integrated manufacturing cells.

With regard to the production lines for dot printers, NEC Yonezawa used U-shaped cells where one worker performed all of the work tasks required to manufacture a dot printer. The one-person, U-shaped manufacturing cells were introduced because the volume of dot printers manufactured by NEC Yonezawa was relatively small compared to its other products (e.g., PCs).

Other NEC domestic plants and manufacturing companies also made considerable efforts to replace their old production systems and associated workplace practices with new ones. For example, NEC Kagoshima, a display manufacturing company under the control of NEC, introduced its production innovation initiatives in 1995 and attempted to transform its outdated production system. The attempts made by NEC Kagoshima finally paid off: production lead time was halved, labor productivity doubled, and all expenses were reduced by more than 30 percent. These plant-level production innovation initiatives, as seen in

NEC Yonezawa and Kagoshima, developed into a company-wide SCM innovation initiative in 2000 in order to involve all NEC employees, not just those from production sites but also those involved in procurement, logistics, sales, and other functions, in innovation activities. By integrating and synergizing different functions, NEC sought to survive intense global competition.

The Japanese electronics industry: Sony Corp.

Sony Corp. was founded in 1946 by Masaru Ibuka and Akio Morita. Ibuka created the company's founding prospectus, which stated the company's purpose as being to establish an ideal factory that enjoys a spirit of freedom and open-mindedness and where dedicated engineers can exercise their technical skills to the highest level. Sony is known for its invention and production of state-of-the art products, such as Walkman portable music stereos and digital video recorders, and for tapping the expertise of the capable engineers working in its "ideal factory." Sony is involved in a wide range of business fields, ranging from electronics, music, movies, and games to financial services. Around the turn of the twenty-first century, more than half of Sony's total revenues still came from the electronics business area. Despite the smaller scale, in term of sales and workforce, of its games, movies, and financial services compared to its electronics business, these fields made a much greater contribution to the increase in Sony's operating incomes. Sony was no longer merely an electronics manufacturer. At that time, people outside and inside Sony sometimes said that the electronics maker was no longer interested in manufacturing and was far from having the "ideal factory" described in its founding prospectus. This tendency has become more apparent in recent years as Sony has outsourced its production activities to electronics manufacturing services (EMS) manufacturers overseas (e.g., Taiwan) and sold its manufacturing facilities at home and overseas to these contracted manufacturing companies.

Since the Plaza Accord of September 1985, which was followed by the sharp appreciation of the Japanese yen against the US dollar, Sony has expanded its sales and the number of its employees overseas. When I examined Sony around the turn of the century, it was transferring much of the production function to China and concentrating its manufacturing facilities there, as were other Japanese manufacturers, because China-based factories were more advantageous in terms of labor costs than Japan-based ones. At that time, labor costs in China were very low compared to those in Japan, although they have increased considerably in recent years due to continued growth of the Chinese economy and the ensuing strong demand for labor. In addition to the labor-cost advantage, China, with over 300 million households, was the largest growing market in the world. The emerging market was attractive to Sony and other electronics manufacturers worldwide. In order to tap China's cheap labor and the emerging huge market, Sony decided to mass produce low-end products in China for shipment not only to Japan and other international markets but also to Chinese markets.

Meanwhile, Sony's 13 domestic manufacturing facilities that were in charge of the final assembly of electronic products were reorganized and finally brought under the control of Sony EMCS (Engineering, Manufacturing, and Customer Services) Corporation, which was set up in 2001. The new company was an independent manufacturing company wholly owned by Sony. Sony EMCS was established because it was expected that Sony's manufacturing plants would be more efficient and profitable under the control of Sony EMCS than they had been before. Sony's manufacturing functions had not contributed to profits as strongly as other functions had done, such as design, R&D, logistics, sales, and services; other Japanese manufacturers also experienced a similar situation. Sony EMCS was responsible not only for final assembly but also for production-process design, materials procurement, production planning, inventory control, logistics, customer services, and so on. Sony EMCS was designated as a service company, rather than a manufacturing company, providing customers with a high standard of service, that is, quality and speed. The plants under the control of Sony EMCS were required not only to cut costs but also to gain and sustain profits and be self-sufficient. Sony EMCS was allowed to provide its services not only to Sony but also to other companies if it could offer a high standard of service and quality and then generate profits.

Pressed by Sony EMCS to be more efficient and profitable than before, employees working in EMCS plants made efforts to turn around operations at their plants. The plants competed to survive with other Japanese and international manufacturers and even Sony's plants overseas. It was reported that one of the plants that made very serious efforts in this direction was Minokamo TEC (MKM) (Sakatsume, 2002). MKM's major products included digital video cameras, PlayStation game devices, and mobile phones. Using cell production, MKM saved, on average, the equivalent of nine workers' salaries per cell line following its introduction of this manufacturing method in the mid 1990s. It also reduced the shop floor space needed to produce 600 units of PlayStation game consoles a day from 65.5 m^2 to 45.3 m^2 in 23 months. This progress was achieved largely through the continuous improvement activities conducted by MKM's production workers. They were willing to suggest ideas for work environment improvement while working closely with production engineers. They devised new jigs and tools to improve their work environment. They also invented mounting devices that were more suitable for their working conditions than previous ones, thus reducing physical movements and saving time wasted on the lines.

Myth and reality of management practices in Japanese workplaces

Conventional wisdom had it that management practices in Japanese workplaces are flexible and innovative, as opposed to their American counterparts' bureaucratic and outdated practices. This view was supposedly established or reinforced by such classic works in the area of Japanese management as Ouchi and Jaeger (1978). Assuming that Japan's management practices are characterized by their use of high performance or commitment work practices, I have sought to verify this notion based on the cases of major Japanese manufacturers in the automotive and electronics industries. My conclusion is that this view was a myth. Furthermore, the reality with regard to American workplaces was that some, if not all, of them used some HPWPs and that their practices were not necessarily bureaucratic and outdated. Although the cases I studied do not present the entire picture, they convey the existing landscape in some of the most representative Japanese workplaces around the turn of the century.

The case of Toyota showed that TMK, a manufacturing company wholly owned by Toyota, adopted and implemented HPWPs such as TQC, problem-solving and continuous improvement activities, QC circles, intensive and systematic training for multiskilled workers, job enlargement, and so on. TMK adopted these practices to become more efficient and to offer a humanized work environment. The workforce at TMK was an important source of the company's competitiveness. Toyota's case verifies the conventional view of Japanese companies and their management practices and organizations, namely, that they are characterized by the use of HPWPs.

The cases of Japanese electronics manufacturers offer a view of Japanese companies and their management practices and organization that is at odds with the conventional view. These companies used some of the conventional management practices, as did US firms, before the beginning of the new century. In the wake of economic and competitive woes, they tried to replace conventional production systems with innovative production systems and, at the same time, to transform conventional management practices into HPWPs. Japanese electronics companies had used large-scale automation and conveyor belt production systems and management practices relevant to those systems. In line with their undertaking to introduce production innovation initiatives and employ the cell production system, Japanese electronics manufacturers put HPWPs in place in their workplaces. Up until then, they had not utilized, or at least not made full or systematic use of, continuous improvement activities, intensive or extensive training for multiskilled workers, job enlargement or enrichment practices, opportunities for workers to make discretionary decisions, self-managing teams, provision of compensation for knowledge, and other elements of a high-performance work system.

One of the reasons why Japanese electronics companies were late in adopting HPWPs and innovative production systems was that in the late 1980s, the time when the nation reached the peak of its asset-inflation-backed bubble economy, these firms were eager to invest the abundant cash they were earning in those days into large-scale and automated production systems and computer-integrated manufacturing (CIM) (Isa and Tsuru, 2002). In contrast to the electronics companies, the Japanese automotive industry—led by Toyota—redesigned work teams in the 1970s to take full advantage of production technology innovations. These facts could lead to the claim that Japanese carmakers began workplace transformations far earlier than Japanese electronics manufacturers. Japanese carmakers seemed to have already employed and carried out so-called HPWPs at the time when Japanese electronics manufacturers were struggling to adopt and establish these practices in their workplaces around the turn of the century.

Concluding remarks

Based on my arguments so far, I conclude that contrary to the conventional view that the management practices of Japanese workplaces are flexible and innovative, the reality was that Japanese workplaces did not necessarily utilize, or at least did not make full or systematic use of, HPWPs—as opposed to traditional and bureaucratic management practices—around the turn of the twenty-first century. Nevertheless, the cases I studied highlighted Japanese workplaces in the process of transition, becoming workplaces where people were beginning to utilize new management practices.

As the cases demonstrate, the efforts made by Canon, NEC, and Sony seemed to pay off, at least for their factories. Before closing this chapter,

I shall attempt to explain why their workplace transformations paid off by drawing on the perspectives presented in the strategic human resource management (SHRM) literature, which I discuss in more detail in the following chapters.

First, I discuss the question from the universalistic perspective that posits that best practices or HPWPs matter across organizations irrespective of their strategies, structures, and other organizational conditions. Based on this perspective, the reason why Japanese electronics companies improved their performance measures is that they simply adopted the so-called HPWPs involved in the new production method being introduced (namely, the cell production system). These workplace practices contributed greatly not only to reductions in costs, workforce, space, and inventory but also to a high standard of quality, which ultimately led to improvements in company performance.

Second, I discuss the question taking into consideration the contingency perspective that assumes that the effect of management practices on company performance is dependent on an organization's strategies, technology, structures, and other parameters. I could argue that the Japanese electronics manufacturers' efforts to transform their workplaces paid off because they employed the management practices required, or relevant to, the implementation of high-variety and small-lot production or BTO manufacturing. For example, by employing management practices involved in the use of cell production, Canon's factories and NEC Yonezawa were able to implement BTO manufacturing strategies and then respond flexibly to changes in customer demands and keep a low level of inventory. Furthermore, it could be assumed that the business models or meta-strategies under which these manufacturing strategies are subsumed interacted with the management practices employed by these electronics manufacturers. The business models developed by these companies were concerned with SCM, whereby they linked upstream parts suppliers with downstream customers and built supply chains. In order to implement SCM and link suppliers with markets, Canon and NEC Yonezawa introduced and carried out management practices associated with cell production. Then, these manufacturers improved not just factory-level operating performance measurements, such as lead time and the efficient use of factory space, but also company-level performance indices, such as cash flows and net profits.

In addition to exploring emerging management practices in Japanese front-line organizations, in the next chapter, I also continue my examination of whether and how Japanese manufacturers improved performance by means of their use of relevant and effective management practices.

3
Emerging Management and Organizational Practices

Introduction

Japanese companies have lost their competitiveness since the asset-inflated bubble economy burst in the early 1990s. They were dragged down by the three excesses of overcapacity, overemployment, and overinvestment after they had made an excessive investment in various business areas at the time of the bubble economy. They had to dispose of these negative legacies of the bubble economy age, but this was a daunting task and they could not move forward. In addition to macroeconomic woes, Japanese companies faced threats from fierce competitors around the world and lost their competitiveness. From the perspective of business strategies, these competitive threats had a more significant effect on Japanese companies' lost competiveness than the collapse of the Japanese bubble economy (Numagami, Kawabe, and Kato, 2010). Overseas competitors acquired a large portion of the global markets that Japanese companies had once dominated largely because they had learned their business and management practices from their Japanese counterparts; for example, it is well known that Dell Inc., a US PC manufacturer, learned the direct-sales model from Toyota.

Japanese industry as a whole had not regained its lost competitive edge by the turn of the twenty-first century. However, Japanese companies in the manufacturing sector tried hard to turn themselves around, and they gradually regained some of their competitiveness. Some Japanese manufacturers—for example, Canon Inc. and Ricoh Co. Ltd., both of which make copying machines and other electronic products—attained higher levels of financial performance indices, such as sales, profits, and profitability, than they had done before the Japanese bubble economy burst. These companies took several measures to turn themselves around and regain their lost competitiveness: downsizing their operations; changing their traditional practices of corporate governance; building new procurement and replenishment systems; the use of IT as a competitive weapon, and so on. As the previous chapter demonstrated, among these efforts was the replacement of traditional mass production with cell production, which was significant in terms of its effect on workplace innovation. The introduction of the new production method entailed changes in management practices. This new manufacturing method was also considered to have improved both operating and financial performance measures, such as productivity, quality, lead time, cash flow, capital turnover, and net profits. However, not only the manufacturing method, but also the relevant management and organizational practices, could have affected these outcomes.

In this chapter, therefore, I examine management and organizational practices emerging on Japan's production front lines as a result of the change in manufacturing system. Based on this examination, I generalize the relations between management practices and manufacturing performance and present tentative propositions on these associations. I begin by reviewing the literature that examined the technical and human or organizational aspects of manufacturing systems in the next section.

Production systems and management practices

Organizations have something to do with technology or vice versa: this is the view that the socio-technical systems (STS) approach postulated and presented in the early 1950s (Trist and Bamforth, 1951). This approach suggests that work organizations are limited by technology or, conversely, that technology requires relevant organizations. One form of organization can be replaced by other types of organization in line with the introduction of new technology. Thus, an examination of a productive system requires detailed attention to both the technological and the social components of the system. Accordingly, it is important to identify work organizations or management practices centered on a focused manufacturing system.

MacDuffie (1991) presented four organizational or structural characteristics of mass production. The first organizational characteristic is the extensive division of labor. Mass-production organizations can seek to achieve efficiency by giving operators a specialized task that takes them less time to learn. The second is the factors that mediate the link between the market and the production system—product diversity, lot size, and organizational buffers; that is, mass production organizations are characterized by standardized product design, large-lot production, and a large buffer composed of inventory, space, and people. The third characteristic is a centralized hierarchy to integrate the many specialized tasks within the organization. The fourth is the separation of conception from execution. Mass-production organizations enhance efficiency by establishing one set of specialists to think and another set of relatively low-skilled specialists to do. This means that a team of operators in mass-production environments are not given the discretion to make decisions on their own, and thus they are characterized by a considerably low level of autonomy.

These organizational practices, such as specialization/standardization/simplification (the 3S's), large organizational buffers, centralization, and separation of conception from execution, are in contrast to elements of the so-called high-performance work system, namely, opportunities to participate in self-managing teams, extensive training to develop multiskilled and knowledgeable workers, and appropriate incentives. These practices of mass-production organizations are more similar to conventional or traditional management practices than to innovative management practices or high-performance work practices (HPWP). Traditional management practices in the United States are remnants of the industrial relations of the 1930s and are characterized by tightly defined jobs with associated rates of pay; clear lines of demarcation separating the duties and rights of workers and supervisors; decision-making powers retained by management; communications and conflicts channeled through formal chains of command; grievance procedures, and so on (Ichniowski et al., 1996). Mass production relegates production workers to the status of common labor, and workers are widely viewed as an expense to be minimized by reducing labor costs (Arthur, 1994).

MacDuffie (1995) studied management practices by focusing on automobile plants worldwide. He conducted a survey of 62 automotive assembly plants located in the United States, Japan, Europe, and other parts of the world. He found that assembly plants were driven not only by flexible production systems, such as the Lean Production System, but also by the use of a bundle of innovative management practices. These practices included self-directed work teams; problem-solving groups; employee suggestions; job rotation; decentralization; recruiting applicants with interpersonal skills and a willingness to learn new skills; contingent compensation; no status differentiation; and a higher level of training for new and experienced employees. He also found that these plants outperformed the assembly plants that operated with traditional mass-production systems and associated management practices in terms of both productivity and quality.

The high-performance work system in the manufacturing sector

MacDuffie (1995) presented effective management practices, or what he called innovative management practices, for manufacturing activities. His work was different from the STS approach in that he attempted to explore the impact of such management practices on manufacturing performance by presenting the notion of a bundle of innovative management practices, the use of which was more likely to improve productivity, quality, and other aspects of performance than using any one of the practices in isolation. MacDuffie's work has been cited by scholars in the area of strategic human resource management (SHRM) when seeking to explore the impact of management practices. In order to explore the impact of management practices, MacDuffie sought not only the "horizontal" fit between similar management practices but also the "vertical" fit between those management practices and the manufacturing system. In the SHRM literature (Becker and Huselid, 1998; Bowen and Ostroff, 2004), the horizontal fit approach is concerned with the systems or configurational perspective and the vertical fit approach is associated with the contingency perspective.

Based on their survey of US manufacturing companies in the steel, apparel, and medical electronic instruments and imaging industries, Appelbaum and colleagues (2000) presented what they called the high-performance work system. Their work was different from the STS approach in that it sought to examine whether and how management practices were associated not only with work outcomes, such as workers' organizational commitment and job satisfaction, but also with operating outcomes, including productivity and space utilization. In their work, these researchers defined so-called HPWPs more clearly than other existing works in the literature by presenting the components of a high-performance work system. They posited that a high-performance work system consists of three basic components: opportunities to participate, skills, and incentives. Providing opportunities to participate can be achieved by several operational management practices, such as substantive participation in self-directed teams or off-line problem-solving activities and empowering people. Appropriate incentives include employment security and pay-for-performance policies. Skills can be upgraded, for example, by selection policies that guarantee an appropriately skilled workforce and the provision of formal training. Based on their models of a high-performance work system, Appelbaum and colleagues examined the management practices utilized in steel, apparel, and medical electronic instruments plants. They noted that it is through the effective elicitation of discretionary effect that management practices positively influence a plant's performance. This notion suggests that discretionary effort mediates the relationship between a high-performance work system and a plant's performance. Discretionary effort is concerned with the contribution of effort from workers above and beyond what is called for in their job description (Harrell-Cook, 2001). Management practices regarding opportunities to participate, skill enhancement, and appropriate incentives are instrumental in eliciting discretionary effort from workers.

Appelbaum and colleagues discussed the reasons why several types of economic gains are potentially available to plants that operated under a high-performance work system. First, adopting such a system can reduce the total number of employees, including supervisors, service workers, and warehouse staff, that a plant requires. This increases labor productivity while reducing overhead cost and the plant's unit labor cost.

Second, the system can reduce costs and make profits in a variety of ways. Inventory buffers can be reduced by using the system. An increase in annual inventory turns is associated with small inventory carrying costs. A high-performance work system can reduce scrap and waste by improving product quality. It may also lower the amount of space required for producing output, thereby requiring less capital expenditure.

Third, since the system can reduce equipment failure or other interruptions to the production process, the actual production of plants can more closely approximate potential production. Finally, regardless of whether a high-performance work system can reduce costs or not, it can lead to economic gains for plants by increasing revenues. This can occur when a more participatory work organization allows the plant to manufacture complex products and/or to achieve reliable on-time delivery of such products.

Cell production and roles of production workers

Japanese electronics companies began to redesign their manufacturing lines and to replace mass production with cell production around the mid to late 1990s. They decided to abandon mass production or automated conveyor belt lines and introduce cell production in the hope that the new production method would enable them to regain the competitiveness lost to overseas rivals and become their competitive edge. At that time, a large number of Japanese manufacturers began to transfer their production facilities to overseas sites offering cheap labor, especially China, where they manufactured a small variety and a large volume of products for shipment to both Japan and the global market. Against this backdrop and in the hope of keeping manufacturing operations in Japan, Japanese manufacturing companies also decided to manufacture a high variety of products in small-lot sizes for delivery to the Japanese domestic market only using manufacturing cells.

It was reported by Japanese newspapers and business journals when cell production began to spread among Japanese manufacturers that leading Japanese electronics companies, such as Sony Corp., Canon Inc., and NEC Corp., were employing the new production method and that they had improved their business performance. Other Japanese manufacturing companies, small-, mid-, and large-size, in the electronics, machine tools, metal-making, and other industries followed the lead of the major Japanese electronics manufacturers in transforming their manufacturing system and employing cell production. Cell production attracted much attention from business people, in particular those working in manufacturing industries, business consultants, journalist, and scholars in Japan. It eventually became media hype.

However, cell production is not an entirely new manufacturing method. On the one hand, manufacturing cells are said to have evolved out of U-shaped production lines (Tamaki, 1996). This suggests that cell production originated from the Toyota or Lean Production System. The manufacturing method with U-shaped production lines is described as a special type of manufacturing used in just-in-time (JIT) production environments along with pull production, piece flow, and multiprocess handling (Miltenburg, 2001). Machines are arranged around a U-shaped line on which operators perform production work. Product parts are placed at the entry of the U-line. They are then processed or assembled on the U-line by operators and the completed product comes out at the end of the U-line. Production activities proceed in accordance with the product flow. On the other hand, cell production is said to have originated in cellular manufacturing, which is based on group technology. Cellular manufacturing was invented with the aim of grouping together dissimilar machines to produce a family of products (Hyer and Brown, 1999). An American producer of semicustom heavy machinery for the paper industry, the Langston Company, began cellular manufacturing in the late 1960s (Hyer and Wemmerlöv, 2002).

Although cell production has a lot in common with production on U-shaped manufacturing lines and cellular manufacturing in general, it is slightly different from them in some respects. Both the U-shaped production line and cellular manufacturing methods are typically used for parts processing, while the cell production method is used for assembling processed parts components. In addition, cellular manufacturing is a replacement for job shop production by which to manufacture dissimilar parts with work organizations engaged in specific functions, while cell production is an alternative to mass production. There are such differences between the U-shaped production line/cellular manufacturing methods and cell production, but the U-shaped line and cellular manufacturing methods are also reported to be used for assembling parts components (Miltenburg, 2001; Hyer and Brown, 1999). Furthermore, the forms of manufacturing cells seen in Japan's cell production environments, such as "divided sub-cells" and "rabbit chase," are reported to have been adopted in overseas cellular manufacturing environments as well (Nicholas, 1998).

Huber and Brown (1991) argued that cell operators are central to cell manufacturing, underscoring the fact that a cell is more than just an arrangement of equipment. Likewise, Isa and Tsuru (2002) regarded Japan's cell production as a human-centered production method. In Japanese publications and newspapers, it was said that the implementation and success of cell production was dependent on people. This is because the degree to which operators exercise skills and knowledge is higher in cell production than it is in mass production or conventional manufacturing. A team of cell operators also has the discretion of handling work tasks on a self-contained unit (Shinobu, 2003). When visiting plants that adopted cell production during my fieldwork, the plant managers quite often told me that the employees working in the plants were the best of all of the available resources they had and that their plants' policies were therefore focused, first and foremost, on educating employees to become capable and high-quality workers. Thus, workers are considered to play a key role in cell production. Although the status of rank-and-file workers is relegated to common labor or an expense to be minimized in a mass production environment, it appears that their status has been reinstated and that they are regarded as human capital in the new cell production environment. Thus, it is imperative to shed light on the human or organizational aspects of cell production and to identify the management practices that are used in cell production environments. However, most of the past descriptions of cell production are anecdotal, and little is known about these management practices.

Cell production and management practices

In order to examine the human resource (HR) aspects and related issues of cell production adopted by Japanese manufacturers, particularly in the electronics industry, I draw on the work of Appelbaum and colleagues (2000) because they present the notion of the high-performance work system that would be relevant and effective in a cell production environment as well. I explore the management practices involved in cell production in terms of the elements of a high-performance work system, namely, opportunities to participate, enhancement of skills, and the provision of appropriate incentives to motivate people. Furthermore, I examine whether and how these management practices boost performance. I also seek to understand work organizations centered on cell production.

I utilize evidence from my fieldwork and information from prior work to examine HR issues on cell production. Between 2000 and 2005, when I completed the work upon which this chapter is based, I visited around ten plants that employed cell production, including PC, copying machine, printer, air conditioner, lighting product, and electrical appliance factories, and a few of the headquarters that oversaw these plants. When visiting these facilities, I interviewed plant managers, production managers, personnel managers, and other people in charge of cell production. These people were the informants for my survey.

Opportunities to participate

In traditional manufacturing plants, conceptualizing and planning what needs to be done is separated from carrying out work tasks and executing plans. Most production workers have little autonomy or control over their work tasks and methods (Appelbaum et al., 2000). Managers coordinate information-gathering and processing activities that blue-collar workers are supposed to perform. Information is concentrated within the management ranks and only a limited number of managerial employees are allowed to make decisions based on information acquired. There are few chances for ideas to flow upward from front-line workers. On the contrary, in cell production, a group of operators is allowed to take control of its own work tasks and methods even though, according to Shinobu and Mori's work (2003), such autonomy is not unlimited. A situation in which cell operators can exercise a high degree of discretion enriches their jobs and makes them feeling intrinsically motivated.

In some of the plants I visited, supervisors or team leaders were in charge of production scheduling, follow-up control, staffing and arranging operators, evaluating these operators, and so on, tasks which had previously been the responsibility of engineers or technicians. It became difficult or no longer appropriate to distinguish the roles of operators from those of technicians or engineers. It seemed that managerial employees shared their work tasks with nonmanagerial employees.

In a few plants I visited, operators working in cells were empowered to perform administrative jobs while as a team, they bore the responsibility commensurate with this empowerment. The cells at these plants were regarded as "pseudo" mini profit centers and the supervisors were the "presidents" in charge of their cell lines. At these plants, this frame for managing cells was called the "line company system;" this was reminiscent of business unit systems. According to Tani and Mitsuya (1998), in the line company system, cells are expected to generate profits by increasing sales—which is calculated in such a way that the prices set within the plants are multiplied by the number of products manufactured by each cell—and by decreasing costs, including labor costs, inventory costs, space rents, and other expenses incurred in running the cells. However, at those plants I visited, the profits and losses that the cell lines were held accountable for were not actually linked to those of the company. Thus, the cells were not evaluated directly according to their financial outcomes. It seems that line company systems were introduced into the plants in order to enhance workers' awareness not just of cost and productivity but also of profits and losses, not to evaluate them by means of the new system.

I can also give an intriguing example of the opportunities to participate and for autonomy in cell production environments. Replenishment is instrumental in implementing cell production. Replenishment workers play a vital role by supplying various parts components on time to cells that need them. By doing so, they allow the cells to manufacture a high variety of products in small-lot sizes and to keep a low level of work-in-process inventory. Replenishment workers are called *mizusumashi*, which means "whirligig beetles" in Japanese. Just as these insects swim in streams and in water in fountains, *mizusumashi* replenishment workers move between cells quickly and smoothly and supply parts components to the cells. They also carry completed products to the shipping yard in the plant. In one PC plant I visited, *mizusumashi* workers played a vital role in that they correctly picked up and carried a variety of components to the workers on the cell assembly lines who were then expected to promptly make a large variety of PCs in small-lot sizes. Importantly, *mizusumashi* workers at the PC plant acted upon the instructions given on *kanban* cards; these cards provided details of the parts items, the volume of items, and the cells to which the parts components were to be delivered, and other pieces of information. The *mizusumashi* workers were autonomous in the sense that they largely controlled their own work according to the *kanban* cards.

By empowering cells, managers at the plants with manufacturing cells I visited hoped to build and run customer-oriented manufacturing lines that could flexibly respond to changes in customer demand. Thus, cell production was designated as the production method necessary for implementing supply chain management (SCM), through which the managers attempted to integrate the supply chain from suppliers through manufacturers to retailers and to respond quickly to customers' needs. Many of the managers I interviewed said that cell production was instrumental in implementing SCM. In addition, cell production at the plants I visited made a significant contribution to having few or no buffers of raw materials, work-in-process inventories, and finished products because it allowed high-variety and small-lot production and even one-piece flow production. As a result, the new manufacturing method improved cash flows, capital turnovers, and profits.

Furthermore, with regard to empowerment, it is important to note that operators working in cells often take part in improvement activities; in the plants I visited, they were involved in improvement activities through total quality management (TQM), quality control (QC) circles, total productive maintenance (TPM), suggestion systems, and so on. This is because cell lines are not as fixed as automated conveyor belt lines and, consequently, cells are designed to reflect the improvements made by operators and technicians. The amount of investment into manufacturing cells is very low compared to that into automated and conveyor mass production lines. This heightens the flexibility of the forms of the cells. Against this backdrop, operators in cells are encouraged to learn how to build more efficient cells through improvement activities.

Cell operators learn and improve not only by attending formal improvement activities, such as QC circles and suggestion systems, but also by taking advantage of more casual learning opportunities. At a copying machine plant I visited, teams of cell operators enhanced their production capabilities by learning more efficient operations from other cells on the same shop floor. Meanwhile, they competed with each other for better performance. A cell team learned more efficient operations from another cell team who had previously learned these operations from other cell teams. This learning process was called "horizontal development" at the plant. At one PC plant I visited, regular workers frequently exchanged know-how with nonregular workers dispatched from subcontracted manufacturers. At these plants, learning made significant contributions not only to high levels of quality and productivity but also to a reduction of work areas and the workforce. The work spaces saved were used for new cells set up to manufacture new types of products, and the operators saved were not fired but deployed to these new manufacturing cells.

Skills

In traditional manufacturing plants, blue-collar jobs are fragmented into monotonous and repetitive tasks and workers receive little training (Appelbaum et al., 2000). The emphasis is on individual efficiency. Blue-collar workers learn, from constant repetition, to do their tasks expertly, but they have little actual knowledge. This type of work organization, with its emphasis on the mastery of routine tasks and the maximization of individual productivity, is a good fit with the mass production of commodity- and single-type products. In cell production plants I visited, however, a group of operators handled multiple work tasks or processes. The number of operators deployed per cell was determined by estimating the volume of products that needed to be produced in a certain day. For example, a single operator was deployed to a cell designed to manufacture a small amount of products, but with variations. One cell operator was engaged in one-piece flow production, making single products one at a time. In a one-operator cell, the operator alone was supposed to handle all of the work tasks required in the cell and was asked to acquire the skill level commensurate with the current job. Meanwhile, a larger number of operators were deployed to a cell designed to manufacture a large amount of products with fewer variations. The number of operators deployed to a cell is not fixed but rather is changed according to the estimated amount of products to be produced in a certain day. Thus, the form of cells frequently changes. The flexibility inherent in cells and the operators' ability to handle multiple work tasks allows the plant to respond to changes in both product models and quantities and to achieve reduction in setup times and inventories and other goals.

The build-to-order (BTO) strategy had been adopted in a PC plant I visited. In accordance with the strategy, the plant produced different PC products (about 20,000 types). The PCs that were made using the one-piece flow production method—so that no products of the same type were manufactured—accounted for 40 percent of the total PCs produced. The PCs that were produced in quantities below ten units accounted for 70 percent of the total. Operators at the plant were typically mobilized into six- or three-worker cells. They worked on complex tasks even as *mizusumashi* workers replenished parts components and conveyed the completed products. In order to help readers to picture these kinds of manufacturing cells, the three-worker/straight-line cell and the six-operator/U-shaped cell are depicted as examples of manufacturing cells in Figure 3.1.

In the PC plant I visited, operators in the three-operator cell(s) were required to perform a broader range of work tasks than those in the six-operator cell(s). When a cell operator had a problem and stopped his or her work, which halted the cell team's production, a nearby operator on the same cell was supposed to assist the colleague in trouble to quickly resume his or her operations. These behaviors allowed the cell team to facilitate the production activities and were called "relay production" in the PC plant. The plant's managers had a plan to extend the practice to relations between cells so that when a cell was in trouble, an operator on the nearby cell could assist the cell to resume its production as soon

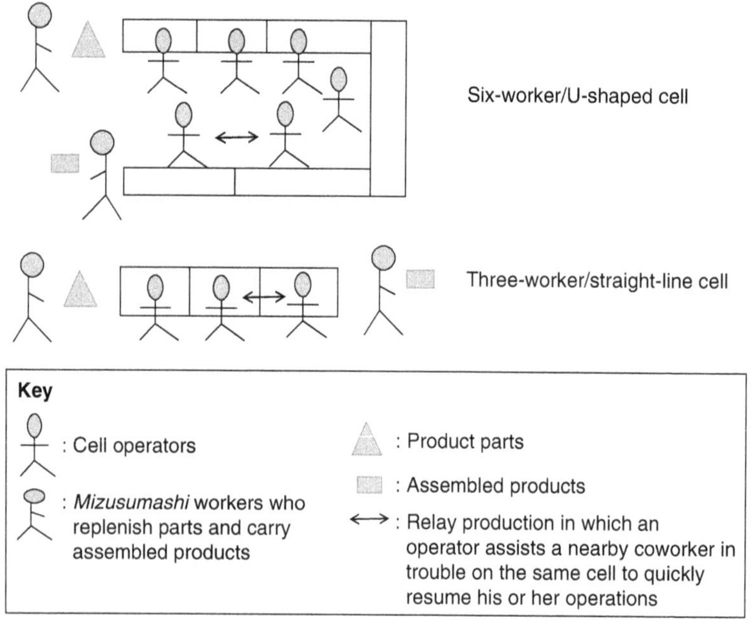

Figure 3.1   Examples of manufacturing cells

as possible. Thus, not only operators' skills but also teamwork allowed for relay production and cell production because these production methods were more team-oriented than traditional mass production.

Thus, cell operators in this PC plant were expected to be multiskilled workers. Managerial employees needed to provide training or education programs to develop the skills of the operators. Job rotation, on-the-job training (OJT), off-the-job training (OffJT), and other education methods seemed to be effective for development of workers' multiskilling abilities.

I also paid visit to a factory that made lighting products, such as fluorescent lamps, and home and office lighting fixtures using fluorescent lamps and light-emitting diodes (LEDs). Operators at this plant, who, like at the other plants using cell production that I visited, were all females, had to be able to handle all of the work tasks required for assembling a lighting product, including wiring, assembling, inspection, and packing. Team leaders checked the skill levels of their respective operators. When team leaders judged that an operator had achieved a targeted skill, this was noted by putting a star-shaped seal on "the multiskilled worker map" (see Figure 3.2). This map showed the skill levels for each of the operators and was posted on a board near the cell lines. One of the requirements for promotion to the position of team leader was to be able to perform all of the required work tasks. I have seen such skill maps in many other Japanese factories both at home and abroad.

In an air conditioner plant I visited, operators were deployed to the cell lines after they had upgraded their skill level on the automated conveyor belt production lines. The plant had training facilities called *kunren dojyo*. This term is composed of the two Japanese words: *kunren* means "training" and *dojyo* means a place or room for practicing judo, kendo, and other traditional Japanese martial arts. The *kunren dojyo*

Name	Ms. A	Ms. B	Ms. C
Wiring	☆	☆	☆
Assembling	☆	☆	
Inspection	☆		
Packing	☆	☆	

Figure 3.2   An example of a multiskilled worker map

facilities were used as an in-house training room to educate operators and develop their abilities to perform multiple work tasks and other capabilities to carry out production jobs. The facilities were given this name with the intention that operators might learn and acquire the knowledge and skills necessary for their current and future work and become well-trained employees, just as judo or kendo athletes hone their skills in *dojyo* facilities. The operators were taught by veteran employees.

The CEO at a copying machine company I visited stressed employment security because he believed that should skilled and knowledge-able operators be fired, it would take too much time to develop and accumulate the same level of skills and knowledge again within the company; he also believed the employees who feel that they may be laid off by a company where layoffs are common would not be motivated to work harder. Thus, he thought that employment security would be effective for developing skilled and committed employees.

Most of the plants I visited hired contingent or nonregular workers such as dispatched or part-time employees. There were those so-called contingent workers at all but one of the plants I visited. Japanese manufacturing companies have hired many contingent workers over the past decades. The percentage of nonregular employees in the Japanese workforce was 20 percent in 1990, but this increased to 35.2 percent in 2011 (*The Japan Times*, February 22, 2012). More than one out of every three Japanese employees is currently nonregular. It is reported that the Japanese electronics industry can be characterized by employment of a large number of contingent workers (Shirai, 2001). It is said that regular workers are responsible for complex and difficult work, such as handling multiple work processes in cell production, while contingent workers are given monotonous and repetitive work tasks, such as those seen in conventional mass production environments (Shirai, 2001). Indeed, at the lighting product plant mentioned earlier, although the number of contingent workers hired there grew year by year, it was the regular workers, as the core employees, who were engaged in cell production.

However, in most of the plants I visited, nonregular as well as regular employees worked on cell lines. Importantly, at some plants, these non-regular employees were not regarded simply as casual workers but rather as "partners" or "support employees." At the PC plant (operated by a manufacturing company) I referred to earlier, regular workers worked together with nonregular employees dispatched from the manufacturing company's subcontractors so that its group companies together could enhance their competitiveness and survive the harsh competition they faced. Both the regular and nonregular employees forged strong ties irrespective of their employment status and seemed to feel part of the same company. A personnel manager and the production managers at the air conditioner plant mentioned earlier said that the contingent workers they hired had high levels of skill and were as skillful as their regular workers. At that plant, nonregular workers were trained to become multiskilled workers. They were not distinguished from regular workers, and they were called support employees, not part-time or dispatched workers or the like. Although managers at the plant expected nonregular employees to become skillful workers by undertaking the education programs provided, they were concerned that these casual workers would move on to rival companies with their acquired skills and knowledge.

In the plants I visited, skillful and knowledgeable workers, irrespective of whether they were regular or nonregular employees, were able to respond flexibly to changes in both product mixes and quantities. By taking advantage of these skillful workers, the manufacturing companies achieved reductions in lead time or throughput time, few or no work-in-process inventory buffers, and improvements in cash flows and capital turnover.

Appropriate incentives

In traditional manufacturing plants where operators are expected to perform specialized, standardized, and repetitive tasks, workers are paid piece-rate wages according to individual-based output so as to improve each operator's productivity (Baron and Kreps, 1999; MacDuffie, 1991). In cell production as well, it has been said that a pay-for-performance incentive system like the piece-rate system is effective because the level of performance achieved by cell production hinges on the skills, knowledge, and capabilities executed by individual operators. In my fieldwork studies, however, I found that there were actually few plants where pay-for-performance systems and other meritocracy-based principles for operators involved in cell production had been adopted. Surprisingly enough, these plants instead stayed with the seniority-based pay and promotion system just like many other traditional Japanese companies, which are known for evaluating employees based on their service length, even though the number of these traditional Japanese companies has decreased over the years. At a copying machine plant I visited, there was no distinction in wages between operators working in cells and those working on traditional conveyor belt lines. Meritocracy-based principles were used at an air conditioner plant that I examined. At this plant, the employees were promoted to higher positions when they achieved their set of targeted goals. These goals were determined in the management by objectives (MBO) framework in which the employees were allowed to set their own goals in consultation with senior employees. Their performance outcomes were evaluated using the "360-degree evaluation method," in which the employees were evaluated by the people around them, including their bosses and colleagues. However, the plant did not establish a meritocracy system because of the introduction of cell production; it had already adopted the system before cell production began.

I could assume that, from a long-term perspective, a seniority-based pay and promotion system, which is closely linked to an employment security policy or lifetime employment system, is necessary in a cell production environment to educate and develop skilled and knowledgeable workers. However, I think that seniority-based pay is not enough to get operators to be committed to work tasks in a cell production environment, where the extent to which cell operators' skills and knowledge are associated with the cell's performance is apparent. In effect, there were some plants with cells I visited that used not just seniority-based pay systems but also several other kinds of incentive system, such as pay for improvement and pay for team performance. In addition, there could be effective nonmonetary or intrinsic rewards in a cell production environment. As I suggested earlier, employment security is effective for developing both skilled and committed employees. Symbolic egalitarianism would also be effective and it comes in several forms, such as no distinction, in terms of uniforms and opportunities to be trained and educated, between regular and nonregular employees: this would motivate all workers engaged in cell production, irrespective of the category of their employment contract, to work harder and exercise consummate skills.

A list of management practices identified in cell production environments

There are several management practices that seem to be relevant to and effective in cell production in terms of opportunities to participate, skills, and appropriate incentives, which are the components of the high-performance work system that Appelbaum and colleagues (2000) assumed was in operation in the manufacturing sector. These management practices may not be common among Japanese manufacturing companies operating with cell production; rather, they may be unique to some of these companies. I can summarize these management practices and provide a list of identified management practices in cell production environments, which is not exhaustive, as follows:

Opportunities to participate:
- empowering cell operators and replenishment workers
- self-managing teams
- line company system
- TQM or TPM
- QC circles
- suggestion systems
- horizontal development of learning (i.e., facilitating knowledge transfer between cells).

Skill enhancement practices:
- employment security
- OJT
- job rotation
- OffJT (e.g., educating employees at *kunren dojyo* facilities)
- developing regular workers into core employees who can perform complex work tasks
- the use of multiskilled worker maps
- the use of nonregular but skilled workers.

Appropriate incentives to motivate employees:
- seniority-based pay
- team-based pay
- pay for improvement
- symbolic egalitarianism in several forms (e.g., treating regular and nonregular employees equally).

It should be noted that some of the management practices listed previously can play multiple roles; for example, job security serves not only as a means to develop multiskilled workers—possibly its primary role—but also as an appropriate incentive.

Opportunities to participate are necessary for teams of cell operators to be flexible to customers' volatility. In the cell production environment, autonomy is achieved by allowing a team of cell operators to have the authority or latitude to operate with the cell; the use of line company system; and so forth. Participation in improvement activities is also important in cell production because cell lines are mutable and not as fixed as mass-production lines and are more likely to evolve into more efficient lines by taking advantage of the suggestions and ideas provided by operators. TQM and suggestion systems help to improve operations in cells. In addition to these "formal" practices, there are also more casual practices or activities to encourage learning in cell production environments, such as the horizontal development of learning (i.e., facilitating knowledge transfer between cells). These practices and activities provide learning opportunities to make cells more efficient and adaptive.

Evidence from Japanese electronics manufacturers shows that it is not the creation of slack resources but the broad range of operators' skills and knowledge and their ability to respond to contingencies—what Koike (1994) called "intellectual skills"—that serve as a buffer to absorb contingencies and uncertainties inside and outside plants. Moreover, in implementing cell production, social skills are important because cell production is a type of team-based production method. As one manager at a plant I visited stated, harmonization among operators is important for the success of cell production. Skill enhancement practices include employment security, OJT, job rotation, OffJT, seniority-based pay, the use of regular workers as core members, and several other practices.

One reason why appropriate incentives are important in a cell production environment is that cell production requires more effort from operators than traditional mass production. The success of cell production is much more dependent on the skills and knowledge of operators than traditional mass production. Appropriate incentives to motivate cell operators to work hard include not only traditional seniority-based pay but also team-based pay, pay for improvement, symbolic egalitarianism in several forms, and other practices. One example of symbolic egalitarianism is treating both regular and nonregular workers equally by providing the latter with the same opportunities to undertake extensive training as the former; this incentivizes nonregular workers to be more committed to their work. Employment security would help companies to get maximum effort from their cell operators as well as to develop their operators' skills and knowledge.

Horizontal and vertical fits involving management practices

As MacDuffie (1995) suggested that the use of a set of HPWPs could achieve a greater level of performance than the use of these management practices in isolation, it is important to adopt a bundle or system of HPWPs and achieve complementarity among them, that is to say, a horizontal fit. There are management practices relevant to cell production: is there coherence among these practices?

I visited two air conditioner plants in Japan that used cell production. In one of these plants, cell production involved employing a set of extensive education and training programs to develop multiskilled workers and TPM activities, including QC circles. This plant achieved higher levels of performance, in terms of lead time, product mix, inventory level, and so forth, than the other one. Apparently, it had adopted a more systematic and planned set of management practices than the other plant, where the managers had a plan to introduce TQM and a formal training system in the near future as a means of implementing cell production. Among the copying machine plants or companies using cell production I visited, the best performing plant had also made more systematic use of management practices centered on the production method.

As the SHRM literature suggests, appropriate management practices or a set of such practices need to be aligned with the company's business or competitive strategies in order to improve company performance. As I explained earlier, this alignment is called the vertical fit, as opposed to the horizontal fit among management practices. Thus, it is necessary to examine a fit between management practices and strategies (or, more precisely, manufacturing strategies) in this research setting. Many of the managers I interviewed told me that cell production had been instrumental in implementing manufacturing strategies, such as high-variety and small-lot production, and agile manufacturing, that is to say, manufacturing quickly according to changes both in product quantities and models. They also said that cell production had been a means of implementing a new business model: the integration of organizations from upstream suppliers to downstream retailers to facilitate quick response to customer needs and shorten delivery time. Furthermore, they suggested that combining SCM and cell production had resulted in a substantial inventory reduction in their plants. These comments suggest that the management practices associated with cell production may be aligned with these manufacturing strategies and, beyond these, with business models or SCM. This alignment would help to boost a cell's performance outcomes.

Cell production and work organizations

Work organizations in a mass production environment are characterized by the 3S's organization principles (specialization, standardization, and simplification) and other traditional management or organization practices such as large organizational buffers, centralization, and separation of conception from execution. Evidence from Japanese cell production has shown a team of cell operators to be a flexible work organization, unlike traditional or bureaucratic ones. Cell operators play key roles when cells respond to changes in the quantities and mixes of products; they are expected to achieve a high standard of productivity and quality while working with such uncertainties.

Galbraith (1973) defined uncertainty as the difference between the amount of information required to perform the task and the amount of information already possessed by the organization. Scholars and researchers in the field of organizational behavior have addressed themes on uncertainty and how to deal with it in individual or organizational ways. Unlike conventional economics, organizational theories assume that a human being is not omniscient and "boundedly rational" (March and Simon, 1958); that is, he or she cannot anticipate everything that might happen in the future and cannot perform complex tasks of optimization except at a very high cost (if at all).

Galbraith (1973) proposed the creation of slack resources (e.g., additional time that the customer must wait, in-process inventory, underutilized man hours and machine time, higher cost) as one way to absorb uncertainty. Slack resources could become a buffer to absorb exceptions, contingencies, and uncertainty, but at the same time, the creation of slack resources reduces performance standards and efficiency. Galbraith then proposed as an alternative strategy the creation of various lateral relations ranging from direct contacts through to matrix organizations. Importantly, he advocated a team as one form of lateral relations and suggested the cellular manufacturing method as an example of a team. Hyer and Brown (1999), scholars in the field of manufacturing, likewise supposed that cellular manufacturing teams could serve as a device to absorb uncertainties. Thus, cell production could be an effective alternative to the use of slack resources.

Evidence from cell production indicates that it is not slack resources but rather flexible work organizations that absorb exceptions, contingencies, and uncertainties inside and outside plants. An organization is defined as a system of coordinated activities or forces of more than two people (Barnard, 1938). By modifying the classic definition of an organization, I would like to argue that a flexible work organization, as seen in a cell production environment, is made up of flexible and adaptive behaviors gained from the people working therein; this corresponds to what Appelbaum and colleagues (2000) called discretionary effort. I would also like to claim that these flexible work organizations can be driven by means of relevant management practices, that is, opportunities to participate, skill enhancement practices, and appropriate incentives to work harder. In conventional mass production, an inventory buffer is utilized to absorb uncertainties or contingencies. Meanwhile, flexible work organizations play a key role in absorbing such contingencies and uncertainties in a cell production environment.

Concluding remarks

In this chapter, I have attempted to examine emerging management and organizational practices in Japan's production front lines that have been introduced as a result of changes in manufacturing systems. Based mainly on my fieldwork at plants that adopted cell production, I identified several management practices that seem to be relevant to and effective for cell production, the new production method. These practices can be distinguished from traditional management practices, as seen in mass production environments, in several respects, that is, in terms of opportunities to participate, skill enhancement practices, and appropriate incentives. Management practices involved in cell production maintain these qualities, which Appelbaum and colleagues (2000) highlighted as components of the high-performance work system. The management practices identified are either common among Japanese plants or unique to a specific one. These practices are important in that they are expected to facilitate a flexible work organization—as opposed to the bureaucratic ones in a traditional mass production environment—that absorbs uncertainties and contingencies inside and outside plants. These management and organizational practices allow for the improvement of operational performance measures, including productivity, quality, lead time or throughput time, sizes of work-in-process inventory, space utilization, and so on. I have argued that these management practices could be congruent with each other and that the use of a set of these practices could be more powerful in affecting performance than any one of these practices in isolation. Thus, it is important to achieve horizontal fit. Furthermore, these management practices are also aligned with specific manufacturing strategies, such as high-variety and small-lot production and agile manufacturing (quick production in response to changes both in product quantities and models). It is important to achieve this vertical fit as well in order to generate high performance.

Before I close this chapter, I can generalize Japanese manufacturers' activities based on arguments I have made so far in this chapter.

I induce and present two tentative propositions on the relations between management practices and performance:

Tentative proposition 1: a set of management practices relevant to cell production is more likely to have a positive effect on manufacturing performance than management practices centered on traditional mass production.

Tentative proposition 2: a set of management practices relevant to cell production is more likely to have a positive effect on manufacturing performance when they are utilized together with high-variety and small-lot production or agile manufacturing strategies than when they are not.

4
Management Practices in Cell Production Environments

Introduction

At the end of the previous chapter, I provided tentative propositions on the relations between management practices and performance based on my studies of Japanese electronics manufacturers. However, I needed to improve my research. More specifically, I needed to make a thorough theoretical and empirical examination of what management practices Japanese manufacturers utilized in a cell production environment and whether the management practices they used mattered. I also needed to expand the number of companies participating in my case studies. This chapter's primary purpose is to generalize and theorize the associations between management practices and manufacturing performance inductively through case study research. I focus on management practices in the area of human resources, that is, HRM practices.

Why HRM practices matter in the cell production environment

Cell production is a new manufacturing method that has been adopted by Japanese manufacturers, especially in the electronics industry, since around the mid 1990s. The number of Japanese manufacturers practicing cell production has been increasing for more than a decade. Japanese manufacturers have even started operating cell production in their overseas manufacturing facilities in recent years. While mass production is still dominant among Japanese manufacturers both at home and abroad, cell production seems to be slowly replacing the conventional manufacturing system.

As I suggested in Chapter 3, there are several reasons why Japanese manufacturers have adopted cell production. First, by utilizing manufacturing cells, they aim to make high-end, not commodity-type, products and deliver them to the Japanese domestic market quickly. By doing so, they wish to continue to operate in Japan while transferring many of the manufacturing facilities to sites overseas where they mass produce commodity-type products. Second, Japanese manufacturers have introduced cell production to reduce work-in-process inventories and shorten manufacturing lead time and consequently improve capital turnovers. Third, they have introduced cell production simply to reduce costs and improve productivity. Fourth, cell production has been adopted as a means of supply chain management (SCM) aimed at linking demand and supply. As these reasons illustrate, Japanese manufacturing companies are looking to build competitiveness or regain the competitiveness lost to their overseas competitors and then improve their manufacturing, and even financial, performance by replacing traditional mass production with cell production.

Conventional mass production relegates manufacturing activities to the status of common, or even mediocre, labor. In a mass production environment, workers perform repetitive and monotonous work and are not put at the center stage of manufacturing activities. Meanwhile, cell production seems to have reinstated the status of production workers, who are expected to play a key role in the new production environment. Thus, cell production is known as a production system that is dependent on people for its success, that is to say, a human-centered production method (Shirai, 2001). Because cell production is supposed to rely on people, Japanese researchers, journalists, and consultants are discussing how to manage the people deployed to cells to ensure the success of cell production. For instance, they posit that training systems aimed at developing multiskilled workers are crucial for the success of cell production. They also argue that a pay-for-performance policy should be adopted, abandoning the seniority-based pay system practiced by most Japanese companies, as each individual operator's efforts are clearly linked to the success of cell production.

These arguments provide us with the impression that the success of cell production hinges heavily on HRM practices. Therefore, to gain an understanding of cell production, a focused study of the HRM practices used is imperative. Not only will such a study provide managers at cell production plants with prescriptions for the success of cell production, but it will also contribute to HRM research generally, especially the field of strategic human resource management (SHRM), which has an interest in examining the relationship between HRM practice and performance. By investigating the HRM practices required for cell production, a study could answer questions in SHRM research such as "What are high-performance work practices (HPWPs) like?" (especially in a manufacturing context).

However, many descriptions of managing people or HRM practices in cell production are "anecdotal," that is, without grounded evidence. Some Japanese scholars and consultants have presented intriguing accounts of the human or organizational and HRM aspects of cell production (e.g., Shirai, 2001; Isa and Tsuru, 2002; Sakatsume, 2002, 2004; Shinobu, 2003; Shinobu and Mori, 2003; Iwamuro, 2004). However, there have been no studies providing systematic statements about these aspects based on rigorous theoretical and empirical research. Thus, I attempt to explore what management practices—in the area of HR—are utilized in the cell production environment and whether the management practices utilized improve the manufacturing performance. To this end, as there is no systematic research on HRM practices for cell production and their effects on manufacturing performance, I conducted case study research and theorized inductively from the cases using the research methodology. I extended and enriched the research I discussed in Chapter 3 by expanding the number of companies or factories participating in my survey and developing my theoretical arguments. HRM is composed of several activities—HRM philosophies, HRM policies, HRM programs, HRM practices, and HRM processes (Becker and Huselid, 1998). In this work, I focus on HRM practices.

Research background

Definition of cell production

I begin by offering a definition of cell production as I did not clearly define it in the previous chapter. Cell production, an alternative to mass production, is employed by Japanese manufacturers, especially in the electronics industry. It is also spreading among other industries, such as the machine tool and the large-scale machine industries. As I discussed in the previous chapter, cell production is said to have evolved out of the U-shaped line production that is utilized in just-in-time (JIT) production environments (Tamaki, 1996). Cell production is popular among Japanese manufacturers, but it is not exclusive to them. An American producer of semicustom heavy machinery for the paper industry, the Langston Company, began what Western practitioners and scholars (e.g., Hyer and Wemmerlöv, 2002) called cellular manufacturing in the late

1960s. As their similar names suggest, cell production in Japan has much in common with cellular manufacturing in the Western Hemisphere, although the former is typically used in parts assembly plants and the latter in parts-processing or metal-making plants. Thus, the cellular manufacturing used in US and European manufacturing plants may also be an original form of cell production. In this type of operation, a team of operators is responsible for all of the work tasks required to complete a family of products. This production method is an alternative to the job shop production method, which is driven by a functionally organized production unit in charge of a single operation, for example, milling, drilling, and soldering. Cellular manufacturing is not just characterized and enabled by the physical layout of production equipment: people are central to the manufacturing system (Hyer and Wemmerlöv, 2002). Human factors, such as multiskilling ability and the presence of visual controls, promote the success of cellular manufacturing.

Similarly, Shirai (2001) regarded Japanese cell production as a production method that is dependent on people, especially their motivation and skills, for its success. Simply put, it is a human-centered production method. People play central roles in both cell production and cellular manufacturing, yet how committed a group or team of operators, not individual workers, is to work is crucial in these production environments. Hyer and Wemmerlöv (2002) suggested that cellular manufacturing is sometimes synonymous with terms such as "group production," "modules," or simply "teamwork"—although one-operator cells are sometimes used in cellular manufacturing plants. They argued that it is possible to have cells without teamwork and teamwork without cells; however, a cell that entails teamwork or vice versa is more powerful and effective than a cell or teamwork alone.

It can be difficult to define a team or a group. Hackman (2002) identified four essential features of "real" work teams: team tasks; clear boundaries; a clearly specified authority to manage the teams' own work processes; and membership stability over a reasonable time period. As Hackman pointed out, authority or autonomy is an important aspect of any team; it is said to be the most distinctive aspect of cell production. The Japanese management scholar Shinobu, who argued that cell production originated in team production, Lean Production System, and flexible manufacturing system (FMS), stressed the importance of autonomy in her definition of cell production:

A [manufacturing] cell is composed of machines, equipment, and a team of operators who is allowed a certain amount of discretion in handling the entire work processes assigned to the team; it is autonomous enough to be regarded as a self-sufficient unit. A set of such cells independent but connected to each other is the cell production system.

Shinobu (2003: 104)

She went on to define the line production system and to make clear the difference between the two production systems:

The line production system is composed of [equipment and] individual operators who have less discretion than their cell operator counterparts; it is highly integrated [under the control of managerial employees off the line] compared to the cell production system.

Shinobu (2003: 104)

Taking into consideration the previous descriptions and definitions of cell production and similar manufacturing methods such as U-shaped line production and cellular manufacturing, to put it simply, cell production could be regarded as a kind of team-based production method stemming from the Toyota Production System (TPS). However, in order to differentiate the production method and conventional mass production more clearly, I propose to define cell production as *a human-centric production method where operators are expected to work closely with each other, be highly committed, and exercise their skills and knowledge to the maximum.* This definition might suggest that cell production has reinstated the status of production workers, which had been relegated to that of common and even mediocre laborers. By a "cell," "cell line," or "work cell"—terms often heard at plants carrying out cell production—I mean a production workplace that comprises operators (usually a small number) and machines arranged in a U-form, a straight line, or other forms. Cell production is also the production method operated using such cells. When Japanese people working at cell production plants talk about cell production, by cells they mean biological cells because cell lines are changed or change occasionally like living biological cells. Thus, cell in the phrase "cell production" connotes biological cells, not prison cells. Practitioners and researchers in the field do not simply use the word "cells," but instead sometimes use the phrase "manufacturing cells" lest the layperson should have an image that cell production workplaces are like prison cells.

SHRM and cell production

As mentioned earlier, cell production is not just related to the physical layout of production equipment—people are central to the manufacturing method. The human or organizational and HRM aspects of cell production can be analyzed using certain organizational or HRM theories. For example, the socio-technical systems (STS) approach might help to explicate human behaviors and effective management practices involved in cell production (Trist and Bamforth, 1951; Emery and Trist, 1960). However, this approach places too much emphasis on "responsible autonomy" as one of the organizational aspects of a technological system; to enhance our understanding of a given technological system, it would be necessary to pay attention to all of its human or organizational aspects, including autonomy and opportunities to participate. More importantly, this approach has a major interest in the social and psychological consequences of technology, such as employee satisfaction and working life. In addition to these outcomes, it is important to examine manufacturing or operational performance because the manufacturing method of cell production has been introduced with the intention that it can improve lead time, inventory level, and other elements of manufacturing performance and ultimately build and sustain competitiveness, not improve the working conditions of employees.

In sum, the STS approach might be useful for investigating one HR aspect (i.e., the responsible autonomy of cell production), but it might not be sufficient for examining the comprehensive HRM aspects of cell production and, more importantly, whether and how these HRM aspects are associated with manufacturing performance. Thus, in my work, I use insights or perspectives gained from the SHRM literature rather than the STS approach. The SHRM literature addresses not just autonomy but also other human and organizational aspects, including team activities, skills, knowledge, and commitment, all of which seem to be related to cell production. In addition, it provides the perspectives by which it is possible to delineate the relations between management practices and performance, as I explain in more detail further.

Using the resource-based view (RBV) of the firm found in the strategy literature, SHRM theorists posit that HPWPs represent a source of intangible and firm-specific resources, such as skills, knowledge, desired behaviors or attitudes, and so on. These resources create value but are difficult to imitate because HPWPs are socially complex and intricately linked in such a way that makes it difficult for competitors to copy them (Wright, Dunford, and Snell, 2001).

Based on such an assumption, three perspectives have been developed in the SHRM research (Delery and Doty, 1996; Dreher and Dougherty, 2002). The first is the universalistic perspective. Researchers taking this perspective argue that there are particular HRM practices that generate high performance across organizations, and these practices are called "best practices." For example, Pfeffer (1998) proposed a set of seven HRM practices as best practices: employment security; the selective hiring of new personnel; self-managed teams; remuneration contingent on organizational performance; extensive training; reduced status distinctions; and information sharing.

The second perspective is the contingency perspective. Theorists taking this perspective state that individual HRM practices should be consistent with the specific behavioral requirements mandated by organizational conditions, such as strategies and technology. According to the contingency perspective, HPWPs are dependent on those organizational conditions and an organization is likely to gain high performance if it achieves a fit between its strategies, structures, technology, and so forth and its management practices. Thus, the terms "the contingency perspective" and "the fit perspective" are used interchangeably. As such, this perspective seeks to achieve the alignment of focused management practices with strategies, technology, and other organizational conditions: in other words, to maximize the "vertical fit."

The third perspective is the configurational perspective. This posits that unique and often complex HRM patterns or systems enable an organization to effectively achieve its goals. Such terms as "system" and "bundle" are key words when using this perspective. This perspective seeks to maximize the horizontal fit, as opposed to the vertical fit stressed in the contingency perspective, by employing a set of coherent management practices that complement each other, not just any one of these practices in isolation. The configurational perspective assumes that the greater the number of management practices used, the better the outcomes. To use Staw's expression, firms must "throw the kitchen sink at the problem" (1986: 47) in order to achieve their desired results. By integrating the contingency and configurational perspectives, it follows that firms must employ a system of HRM practices that are aligned with the behavioral requirements mandated by organizational conditions in order to achieve superior performance.

Thus, given that there are the three perspectives in the SHRM literature and that there are several management practices to be considered when evaluating HPWPs, I must be careful in exploring the management practices involved in successful cell production. Of the several studies conducted in the field of SHRM research, the work done by Appelbaum and colleagues (2000) was again the starting point for my case study research on HRM practices required for cell production, just as it was in my prior work detailed in the previous chapter, because their work focused on the high-performance work system used by US steel, apparel, and medical electronic instruments manufacturers and provided a better theoretical and empirical foundation for my studies on HRM practices in cell production environments. By drawing on Appelbaum and colleagues' work where they presented the management practices relevant to the manufacturing sector, scholars can confirm whether those management practices can in fact be effective when studying manufacturing organizations. I suppose that according to the universalistic perspective, the models of the high-performance work system proposed by Appelbaum and colleagues present relevant and even effective management practices across manufacturing companies in general, irrespective of manufacturing systems used. According to the contingency perspective, however, the effectiveness of the management practices presented by Appelbaum and colleagues is expected to differ depending on the manufacturing systems or methods used. Drawing on their work, as the first step in my case study research, I explore the effective management practices in cell production environments according to the universalistic, rather than the contingency, perspective.

As I explained in the previous chapter, Appelbaum and colleagues argued that effective high-performance work systems require three basic components: opportunities for substantive participation, in other words, autonomy achieved by participating in self-managing teams, off-line problem-solving activities, and so on; appropriate incentives for motivation; and skill and selection policies that guarantee an appropriately skilled workforce. They posited that it is through the effective elicitation of discretionary efforts that HRM practices positively influence a plant's performance. Discretionary efforts are expected to mediate the relationship between a high-performance work system and a plant's performance. Discretionary efforts mean the contributions of workers above and beyond what is called for in their job descriptions. HRM practices that promote and sustain autonomy, skills, and motivation are necessary to elicit discretionary efforts from workers.

Research questions

Drawing on work of some Japanese researchers and consultants who discussed the human or organizational and HRM aspects of cell production as well as on Appelbaum and colleagues' work, I next present research questions on relevant and effective management practices in cell production environments and the impacts of these management practices on manufacturing performance, followed by my case study research.

Autonomy

As traditional STS scholars have argued, autonomy is a crucial organizational aspect of manufacturing work environments. I would like to use the term "autonomy" rather than other words with a similar meaning, such as worker participation, because the meaning of the term "autonomy" is inclusive of the meanings of these similar words. Autonomy is related to job enrichment—which means that operators are allowed to make supervisory or managerial decisions that were previously made by supervisors or technicians. Appelbaum and colleagues argued that one important feature of high-performing work organizations is autonomy, characterized by self-managing teams, quality control (QC) circles, and so on. STS theorists have argued that autonomy can affect employees' motivation (Trist and Bamforth, 1951; Emery and Trist, 1960; Berggren, 1992). Likewise, some Japanese scholars and consultants have placed an emphasis on cells as autonomous or self-contained work units. For example, Shinobu (2003) and Shinobu and Mori (2003) argued that autonomy is a distinguishing aspect of cells. They mentioned that a cell is so self-sufficient as to bear responsibility for a broad range of work tasks, from arranging work processes, maintaining equipment, and setting production schedules to contacting customers and suppliers, since an autonomous cell is expected to act adaptively or flexibly in the face of contingencies outside as well as inside a plant. Management practices that promote autonomy are expected to be necessary when operating with cell production and to be in place in cell production workplaces. Therefore, I put forward the following research question:

Research Question 1: Are the HRM practices centered on autonomy important in implementing cell production?

Skills

Appelbaum and colleagues argued that HRM practices that help to upgrade skills and knowledge, which are also part of the high-performance work system defined by scholars, are adopted by high-performing manufacturing companies. Shirai (2001), a Japanese researcher, likewise stated that one HRM aspect of cell production is the development of multi-skilled workers; this is because cell production operators are responsible for handling multiple work processes and are accountable for the outcomes as a team, whereas mass production operators are each assigned to a limited range of work tasks and typically committed to individual-based tasks. Other Japanese researchers, for example, Kumazawa (2004), suggested that cross-training programs and job rotation are necessary to facilitate the development of multiskilled workers and thus ensure the success of cell production. These arguments in prior studies allow me to present the second research question:

Research Question 2: Are the HRM practices that help to upgrade operators' skill levels vital to the implementation of cell production?

Motivation

Appelbaum and colleagues mentioned that appropriate incentives to motivate employees to work harder or management practices that can serve as these incentives allow manufacturing companies to outperform their competitors. Likewise, Japanese researchers and consultants have argued that incentivizing workers to work harder is significant in cell production environments. For instance, Iwamuro (2004) discussed the importance of highly motivated operators to cell production. One of the reasons why this is important is that the working pace on a manufacturing cell is determined by the willingness as well as the abilities of an operator to perform her or his job; thus, how strongly each operator in the cell is motivated to carry out his or her job is directly linked to the cell's outcomes. Meanwhile, as the working pace on an automated mass production line is sometimes determined by the speed set by the conveyor belt, operators on the line are not motivated to make products faster than this speed even if they could do so. Thus, it has been suggested that rather than the outdated seniority-based pay system that has been traditionally espoused by Japanese companies, meritocracy-based wages or a pay-for-performance policy should be utilized in parallel with the introduction of the cell production system (Noguchi, 2003). These practices related to motivation, particularly performance-based pay, are expected to be common among cell production workplaces. These arguments lead me to ask the following:

Research Question 3: Are the HRM practices centered on motivation, especially a pay-for-performance policy, important to the implementation of cell production?

Impacts of HRM practices on manufacturing performance

Appelbaum and colleagues found that a system of HRM practices that enhance autonomy, skills or knowledge, and motivation affects plant performance measures such as productivity and quality. Iwamuro (2004), a Japanese cell production consultant, also suggested that cells can improve manufacturing performance measures such as cost and lead time and even financial performance measures such as capital turnovers, cash flows, sales, and net profits. He went on to argue that knowing how to manage people is vital to the success of cell production and the improvement of manufacturing outcomes. Thus, Japanese researchers, consultants, and journalists have discussed the impact of managing people on performance, but not one of them has empirically examined whether the use of HRM practices involved in cell production can in fact yield superb performance in manufacturing cells. Among the numerous relevant performance measures—quality, cost, and delivery time, that is, the so-called QCD manufacturing performance measures—are the outcomes indicators I focus on in my work. This is because these manufacturing outcomes are considered to be significant not only for cell production plants but also for manufacturing companies (Hyer and Wemmerlöv, 2002). The units of analysis for this study are manufacturing cells or the teams of operators in them, not plants or enterprises. Attention needs to be paid to the manufacturing outcomes corresponding to the unit of analysis, that is, focused cells. Based on the arguments developed previously, I ask the following question:

Research Question 4: Does the use of HRM practices involved in cell production affect the QCD manufacturing performance measures for the focused manufacturing cells?

Methods

I chose to conduct case study research. This research methodology is aimed at finding facts inductively and then building propositions by examining cases (Eisenhardt, 1989; Yin, 2003). The reason why I decided to conduct case study research was that there was no existing literature representing a formal proposition on the comprehensive HRM aspects of cell production and the relations between management practices and performance in cell production environments. I visited 20 plants in Japan that employed cell production (until the time when I had completed my work upon which this chapter is based). These plants made a wide range of products, such as PCs, copy machines, printers, air conditioners, lighting products, electrical appliances, electronic components, game consoles, machine tools, large-scale machines, and automotive parts components. I had the opportunity to go on a plant tour at all of the plants that participated in my survey. Of these 20 plants, I selected 16 plants where sufficient evidence could be gathered for my case study research. I selected multiple cases in an attempt to generalize findings from my case study research (Eisenhardt, 1989).

In this case study research, I used direct observations, interviews, archival records, and public documents as sources of evidence. In addition to these sources, I handed out questionnaire sheets at a few plants and collected hard evidence on management practices, manufacturing systems, and other associated issues. Among these sources of evidence, the interviews were particularly important because the respondents provided deep insights into, and intriguing views on, various aspects of cell production, including technological characteristics, organizations, and cell operator management. The respondents included plant managers, personnel managers, production managers, and other people in charge of cell production.

Before entering the field sites, I constructed interview protocols, that is to say, a set of question items that an interviewer plans to ask interviewees, and used them as an interview guide when visiting plants. The interview guide was designed to ask questions not just on issues centered on management practices but also on every aspect of cell production, including production volume, product items, manufacturing strategies, workforce, the history of cell production, cell forms, organizational structures, and the role of support staff. This was because I wanted to gain an insight into cell production without overlooking factors affecting manufacturing performance that were separate to management practices, an independent variable of interest in my work. Although, in principle, I interviewed according to the interview guide, the interviews were open-ended so that I could discover facts and pieces of information that I had not expected to find or simply encourage interviewees to talk a lot.

Every time I visited a plant, I modified the contents of some of the question items in order to make them clearer. I also eliminated the question items that I had found to be irrelevant in the last interview. Meanwhile, I added new questions to the question list on the interview guide as I discovered new and interesting facts each time I visited field sites. Thus, I did not ask all of the respondents the same questions.

After visiting field sites and gathering data and information, I made my field notes while my memories were fresh so that I could review them and compare cases (i.e., manufacturing cells or plants) in the future based on documented facts. I exchanged my opinions and impressions with graduate students I had asked to participate in field research as multiple investigators in order to avoid biased assessment. These students also recorded interviews and documented observations.

Results: Relevant management practices

Overview

In addition to HRM practices that enhance skills and motivation, HRM practices that promote interdependence and continuous improvement were also found to be important to cell production. Meanwhile, autonomy and its related management practices were not as essential to cell production as expected. Table 4.1 represents a list of HRM practices—although not an exhaustive one—required for cell production, each of which is expected to meet the behavioral requirements (single or multiple) of a cell production environment. Case study research confirmed that these management practices affected QCD manufacturing performance. It should be noted that the HRM practices in Table 4.1 could constitute what I will argue is the "perfectly-tapping-potentiality" HR system.

Relevant management practices in cell production environments

Autonomy and HRM practices

Based on the evidence from the case study research, the level of cell autonomy was actually not as high as I had assumed. Cell operators were assigned some supportive and administrative tasks, such as inspection and maintenance, but in many cases, they were not allowed to set production schedules, directly contact suppliers and customers, select team members, and so on. Before mass production was replaced by cell production, operators had not been allowed to set their working pace; instead, conveyer belts had determined how fast operators should assemble product parts. Even after the introduction of cell production, cell operators were not allowed to determine their working pace; only production engineers had the right to do so. It was assumed that one-operator cells were self-managing in that operators in these cells can control their own work pace (Hyer and Wemmerlöv, 2002). In fact, the case study found that even operators in the one-person cells were not allowed to determine the pace of their own work. It was evident that cells were not as self-managing as generally supposed. It seemed that the level of autonomy in each work team did not dramatically change even after the introduction of cell production.

There were particular reasons why the cells were not as autonomous as expected. For example, in some plants, trust between employees and managers was lacking. Managers assumed that production workers did not have the capabilities required to do jobs involved in cell production. They were concerned that not just a limited number of workers,

Table 4.1 Relevant HRM practices in cell production environments

HRM Practices	Behavioral Requirements					
	Multiskilling ability	Motivation		Interdependence		Continuous improvement
		basic work needs	higher-level work needs	task interdependence	goal interdependence	
Staffing: internal labor market oriented						
high percentage of regular workers	√					√
Training: aimed at multiskilling and problem-solving abilities						
OJT for training multiskilled workers	√					
systematic training for multiskilled workers	√					
within-plant qualifications to facilitate multiskilling ability	√		√			
industrial engineering (IE) education						√

Work design: team-based							
one-team task					√	√	
line company system	√					√	
off-line improvement activities							√
promoting inter-group	√						
competition							
horizontal learning between cells							√
Participation in decision making: great opportunities for continuous improvement activities							
suggestion system							√
direct contact with R&D staff							√
Incentives: meeting both basic and higher-level work needs							
seniority-based pay		√	√				
praising and publicizing				√			
targets achieved to satisfy							
need for achievement							

Notes: The check mark symbol (√) in the table represents the ability of an HRM practice to meet a behavioral requirement of a cell production environment.

but also all of the people working in the plants would be affected and that the plants would descend into chaos if cell operators were allowed to set production schedules or to change the schedules already set by production managers at will. At those plants, manufacturing cells, as a team of operators, were not as autonomous as assumed for this very reason.

Another reason might be that autonomy is not as powerful a motivator as assumed. No one I interviewed at the field sites said that autonomy was linked to motivation as STS theorists have argued. This corroborates the assertion made by Adler based on his case study of New United Motors Manufacturing Inc. (NUMMI)—then a joint venture between General Motors Corp. and Toyota Motor Corp. and now the factory of the Silicon Valley-based electronic car maker, Tesla Motors Inc.—that "autonomy is not a critical motivating characteristic of jobs" (1993: 174).

I do not deny the importance of autonomy just because it does not appear to be so important in cell production environments. The amount of autonomy operators are allowed is greater in cell production environments than in mass production environments. Even though cell operators were not allowed much discretion in most of the plants I visited, they did participate in improvement activities such as QC circles and total productive maintenance (TPM) activities, although how often or to what extent they took part in these activities varied from plant to plant.

Skills and HRM practices

At most of the plants I visited, cell operators were expected to become multiskilled workers because they were required to handle a broader range of work tasks in their cells than they had done on the mass production lines. For example, at a plant making electrical appliances, automated mass production lines 100 meters (approximately 91 yards) long had previously been run, but now cells composed of around five operators were responsible for handling all of the tasks in the cells. In a copying machine plant, operators had been in charge of a limited range of work tasks on long mass production lines that were driven by automated conveyor belts, but since the introduction of cell production, the plant's production workers tackled many challenging tasks; for example, workers attempted to assemble many complicated parts components on their own. As a result, very talented operators were able to handle all of the work processes—made up of 600 work tasks and taking around three hours—by themselves. A manager at the plant said, "At first, I did not think that they [the talented operators] could assemble all of the parts components by themselves. But, in fact, if they tried, they could. Now, I think that people have more capabilities or potential than I expected." Meanwhile, in the same plant, as operators worked more than they did before cell production was introduced, they felt more fatigued from their work when operating in cells.

The plants I visited did have ways to develop multiskilled workers. For example, by undertaking on-the-job training (OJT), cell operators could learn how to do the work tasks assigned to them from more skillful and veteran workers or their seniors. Managers provided systematic cross-training programs, and the skill levels required to perform certain jobs were clearly defined and current skill levels and target skills were shown to each operator working in the cells. Operators participating in the programs were expected to upgrade their skill levels step by step according to the skills or multiskilled worker map. In the copying machine plant I previously referred to, managers developed a within-plant or in-house qualification system designed to encourage cell operators to become multiskilled workers. If operators were recognized as having a certain skill level, they were awarded a corresponding qualification. The most talented operators at the plant, who were acknowledged as having the highest skill levels, were awarded the highest qualification ranking, and this award was regarded as highly prestigious by people working within the plant. They were promoted to the rank of cell leader and, what is more, presented with a badge stating that she or he was a most talented operator. The most talented workers wore the badge on their uniforms and worked with a sense of pride. When I toured the workplaces, it appeared that these workers were extolled and regarded as "charismatic operators" by their colleagues at the plant. The most praised cell operators were invited to a French restaurant near to the company's headquarters by the company's chief executive officer once a year and had the opportunity to attend a dinner with the CEO. In that sense, the within-plant qualification system was not just part of a training system; it also served as a nonmonetary incentive and had a motivating effect on operators. It seemed to satisfy the employees' higher level work needs, namely, their need for self-esteem. In addition to these ways of promoting multiple skills, from the long-term perspective, hiring a high percentage of regular workers—in other words, internal labor market oriented staffing—helped to develop multiskilled workers because the regular workers whose employment was secure could be trained to become multiskilled workers.

In this way, regular workers were trained to become skillful or multiskilled workers and to work in cells. Unskillful nonregular workers were also deployed to work in cells at most of the plants I visited. Among the nonregular workers were subcontracted workers from affiliated companies, dispatched workers from personnel agencies, and part-time workers and other contingent workers whose working status was unstable. As far as I could observe, the majority of the nonregular workers were dispatched workers from personnel agencies. Cell production plants and other Japanese factories make, terminate, or renew contracts with dispatched workers indirectly through personnel agencies, which was a growing industry in Japan in the early 2000s (Fu, 2012). In most plants I visited, nonregular workers were rarely expected to become skillful and multiskilled workers although, as I mentioned in Chapter 3, I witnessed some plants where nonregular employees were as skillful as regular ones.

Thus, HRM practices whereby skillful workers are trained and developed are not necessarily important and relevant in all cell production environments. At a PC plant I visited, contingent workers were assigned to cell lines after taking a mere two-day training program off the production lines. At a game console plant, managers tried to develop "skill-less" or de-skilled cell lines where anybody could easily assemble parts components and manufacture products and where workers were not asked to acquire a high level of skills. Like at other plants, unskilled contingent workers were hired by this factory so that the plant could respond to changes in demand and become more efficient. When demand increased, unskilled nonregular workers were hired, and when demand decreased, their contracts were terminated; in a sense, they were literally contingent or casual workers. In general, unskillful contingent workers were deployed to cell lines composed of a large number of operators where the operators were responsible for a limited range of assigned work tasks. They manufactured products with simple designs, that is, products with a high level of "modularity," for example, PCs and game consoles (Baldwin and Clark, 1997). These products were seemingly complex, but actually they were designed to be built easily with a few similar components in the same way that Lego blocks are assembled.

Motivation and HRM practices

Most of the plants I visited still maintained a seniority-based pay system. A few plants had a pay-for-performance policy, but they had already adopted this policy prior to the introduction of cell production. Only one plant had introduced a pay-for-performance policy at almost the same time it started cell production. I could assume that seniority-based pay, which is linked to the lifetime employment system espoused by Japanese firms, is suitable for developing skilled workers from the long-term perspective. More importantly, I could also assume that existing conventional reward systems are established enough to be regarded as institutionally legitimate by Japanese companies (Scott, 1995). Thus, it might have been difficult for the plants I visited to transform their reward or evaluation systems.

Interestingly, competition among cells in terms of cost, output, and so on caused rivalry among the cells and encouraged cell operators to work harder. At some of the participating plants, inter-group competition had been intentionally created by the managers, although the cell operators were not aware of this fact. It seemed that not only seniority-based pay but also inter-group rivalry helped to motivate cell operators to work harder.

In addition to seniority-based pay and inter-group competition, managers at the plants I visited emphasized other means to motivate cell operators. For example, managers at some plants endeavored to praise and recognize operators' efforts and contributions—whether nontrivial or trivial—so that they could satisfy operators' higher level work needs (e.g., their need for achievement and/or self-esteem) and then motivate them to work harder. They posted operators' achievements on a board near the cell lines to publicize them because they assumed that the amount of effort operators contributed had a direct effect on cell performance. Meanwhile, even if operators on a conventional mass production line were motivated, they were not able to affect performance since the pace of work was controlled by conveyor belts. As suggested before, within-plant qualifications were not just part of a training system; they also had a motivational effect on cell operators. These qualifications satisfied employees' higher level work needs, such as the need for self-esteem. Thus, one way or another, managers made meticulous efforts to motivate cell operators.

HRM practices emerging from case study research

As I continued my case study research, behavioral and HRM aspects important to cell production emerged that I had not previously imagined. These HRM practices were associated with interdependence and continuous improvement.

Interdependence and HRM practices

As mentioned earlier, a multiskilling ability is a behavioral requirement in the implementation of cell production. Workers in a manufacturing cell who are dexterous enough to handle multiple work processes are assigned interdependent tasks and are responsible as a team for the consequences. A multiskilling ability, that is, the ability to handle multiple work tasks, allows and facilitates interdependence among cell operators. Alternatively, interdependence, which is inevitable in implementing team-based production such as cell production, requires the employees to have the ability to perform multiple work tasks. Here, interdependence is concerned with what Wageman (1995) and Van der Vegt, Emans, and Van de Vliert (2001) called "task interdependence" and "goal interdependence."

In the days of the supremacy of mass production in Japanese manufacturing landscapes before cell production was widely used, some operators assembled parts components quickly while others worked slowly. This was because those operators' jobs were characterized by the division of labor and operators focused on a limited range of assigned work tasks. As a result, idle time, or the time operators spent doing nothing on the line, increased and work-in-process inventory took place on the lines. It was found that the smaller the range of work tasks assigned to individual operators, the greater the subsequent idle time and volume of work-in-process inventory. Naturally, no idle time or work-in-process inventory occurred in one-operator cells. Some of the managers I interviewed, referring to a result of the division of labor on the lines, told me that conventional mass production aimed to achieve "partial optimality." On the contrary, in the plants I visited, operators in a cell were required to address a wider range of work tasks and to be interdependent on or harmonize with each other due to the essential quality of cell production: team production. Cell operators, as a team, were supposed to handle the entire work processes assigned to it, not just their individual work tasks. These team-based production activities allowed the cells to improve line balancing or to reduce work-related idle time on lines (i.e., to shorten lead times), and to reduce the volume of work-in-process inventory. At times, cell operators were required to help adjacent workers on the same cell who were having trouble so that they could achieve and sustain line balancing and consequently reduce lead time and work-in-process inventory. Work in the cells was more interactive and cooperative than that on the lines. As such, each operator in a cell was required to exercise her or his efforts toward achieving the cell's goals, not just his or her individual goals. According to some of the managers, cell operators were asked to achieve "total optimality" so that they could make their cells more efficient, as opposed to partial optimality on the line.

As demonstrated earlier, interdependence is significant in cell production environments because this production method is team-based. The quality of teamwork exercised by cell operators affects manufacturing lead times and work-in-process inventories or vice versa. Cell operators improve manufacturing performance by addressing a wide range of work tasks and working interdependently with or helping each other in the same cell. Wageman (1995) and Van der Vegt, Emans, and Van de Vliert (2001) called this working situation "task interdependence." What is more, cell operators are responsible not only for their own work tasks but also for the consequences—Wageman (1995) and Van der Vegt, Emans, and Van de Vliert (2001) called this "goal interdependence."

One of the HRM practices used to enhance task interdependence is one-team tasks, where one cell's members work interdependently to achieve their tasks and are held accountable for the outcomes as a team. HRM practices facilitating goal interdependence include not only one-team tasks, but also a control system called the line company system, which I explained in detail in the last chapter. Cells controlled by the line company system are treated as "pseudo mini profit centers" like a business unit. Supervisors in charge of these cells are regarded as "presidents," just like a business unit's president. In one sense, the line company system also serves as a means of encouraging people to work harder. It should be noted that the system is considered to be associated with opportunities to participate or autonomy; here, I designate it as a management practice for interdependence because autonomy is not that relevant to cell production.

Continuous improvement and HRM practices

By improvement I mean what Argyris and Schön (1978) called "double-loop learning," that is, detecting and correcting problems without changing basic assumptions and values. Continuous improvement activities are those activities that rank-and-file workers engage in that will last, not stop after a while. In cell production environments, operators learn, and continue to learn, how to reduce costs, improve quality, shorten lead times, and so forth. They also attempt to make their cells more efficient through continuous improvement activities. As Appelbaum and colleagues (2000) suggested, employees' participation in off-line improvement activities, such as QC circles, could be regarded as part of the autonomy achieved because continuous improvement activities can be initiated and facilitated by allowing operators to take part in such activities and, furthermore, administer them on their own initiative. However, I assume that continuous improvement is a phenomenon separate from autonomy by taking into consideration its significance in terms of its effect on the success of cell production. In addition, continuous improvement is concerned with continued learning—which is essential to running cell production—while autonomy is not necessarily associated with learning (Huang, Rode, and Schroeder, 2011). Therefore, in my work, I would like to treat continuous improvement as a behavioral dimension different from autonomy.

One reason why continuous improvement is important to cell production is that cell lines are mutable, like living biological cells, and not as fixed as mass-production lines; they are more likely to transform into more efficient methods by taking advantage of the suggestions and ideas provided by cell operators. A Japanese cell production researcher, Sakatsume (2004), argued in his article that the impact of continuous improvement after introducing cell production is significant.

Continuous improvement is supported and enhanced by HRM practices, including off-line improvement activities, for example, QC circles, total quality management (TQM), and suggestion systems. In addition to these "formal" practices, there are "informal" practices or daily activities that encourage continuous improvement, such as the "horizontal development of learning" where operators exchange know-how and solutions not only with coworkers in the same cell but also with operators in other cells. Furthermore, in some of the plants I visited, operators offered ideas to improve product design by making direct contacts with research and development (R&D) staff visiting the shop floor or even by attending concurrent or simultaneous engineering projects across different departments in the plants. At these plants, operators were expected to acquire a higher level of skills, such as problem-solving skills required for improvement activities. Thus, they took industrial engineering (IE) and QC classes off the job. These highly skillful and knowledgeable operators were usually the regular workers, which indicates that internal labor market oriented staffing was important to developing these people.

Results: Relationships between HRM practices and manufacturing performance

Multiskilling ability, motivation, interdependence, and continuous improvement are all necessary for the implementation of cell production. They are also the behavioral requirements that need to be met to ensure the success of cell production. If certain management practices meet the behavioral requirement(s) and focused cells improve their manufacturing performance in terms of quality, cost, and delivery time, it could be said that these HRM practices affect these QCD manufacturing performance indices concerning the cells. Given such reasoning is permitted in explaining the relationships between HRM practices and manufacturing performance in cell production environments, next I provide three representative cases showing that these relationships can be confirmed. Here, the cost performance measurements are concerned with labor productivity (output/operators) and the level of the work-in-process inventory. The quality performance measure represents, as a percentage, all of the products manufactured in the cells that were not defective. The delivery time performance measure means manufacturing lead time or throughput time. I visited the plants between 2004 and 2006 and thereafter conducted my case study research based on the evidence gained from these visits. I do not disclose the real names of the plants in the cases because I promised the managers at the plants that participated in my survey that their identities would be kept confidential. I therefore named the three case-study plants plant A, plant B, and plant C.

Case 1: Plant A's cells producing electronic devices

Overview

Plant A was operated by a medium-size manufacturing company. It produced electronic devices for digital cameras that were supplied to Japan's leading electronics companies. Cell production started at the plant in 2001 in order to transform it into a more efficient factory that could compete against overseas competitors, in particular Chinese manufacturers. At that time, developing employees' multiskilling ability was a significant behavioral requirement for plant A. Therefore, plant A's managers made the utmost efforts to develop skillful people. These efforts finally led to the success of cell production. However, with a digital camera manufacturer, one of plant A's major customers, transferring its production facilities to China, cell lines at plant A were being transferred to the affiliated Chinese plants.

Multiskilling ability and HRM practices

When plant A started cell production, workers were not used to performing certain tasks in the cells because they had been accustomed to performing tasks on mass production oriented assembly lines, and this was the reason why managers started education aimed at developing multiskilled workers. Unskillful workers learned work tasks from cell leaders through OJT.

Interdependence and HRM practices

After the introduction of cell production, the jobs performed by the workers at plant A changed from individual-based to team-based jobs. At that time, not all workers reached the skill level required to be multiskilled workers. Consequently, the cells did not succeed. As operators expanded the range of their skills and performed team-based jobs, they started to feel responsible for the tasks assigned to their team, not to themselves. They also began pursuing the goals of total, not partial, optimality and maximizing output as a team of operators.

Continuous improvement and HRM practices

Under the suggestion system at plant A, workers were obliged to provide solutions to problems. More interestingly, as they handled multiple work processes, they came to understand their colleagues' tasks, the problems associated with them, and how to prevent these problems. This helped to increase improvements to the work done in the cells. In addition, since taking part in cell production, the operators had definitely increased their quality awareness. This heightened quality awareness also helped to improve operations in the cells and thus the manufacturing outcomes.

Motivation and HRM practices

When plant A had operated using mass production lines with conveyor belts, even if workers made great efforts, their efforts or contributions did not affect the line's performance because they had been engaged in, and focused their attention on, highly limited and individual-based work tasks. However, in the new work environment, where a few people worked in a cell, not only their individual efforts but also their integrated efforts as a team were clearly linked to cell performance. Thus, in order to motivate operators to work harder, it was imperative to satisfy not just the employees' basic work needs (e.g., getting more wages) but also their higher level work needs (e.g., their need for their achievements to be recognized).

The managers at plant A attempted to praise and encourage the workers who contributed to cell performance as far as possible and to avoid finding fault with them so as to satisfy their need for recognition. This encouragement helped to motivate operators to accept the challenges posed by their new tasks in the cell production environment, such as addressing multiple work tasks. Operators wanted even the processes involved in their work achievements to be recognized. Thus, even if cell operators did not achieve target goals, managers still recognized their efforts. Plant A's managers also attempted to satisfy their operators' need for achievement in different ways (e.g., by posting operators' achieved goals on a board near the cell lines). By letting operators know that their targets had been achieved, managers were able to satisfy these higher level work needs.

Manufacturing performance measures

Compared to the outcomes achieved previously using mass production lines with conveyor belts, the manufacturing performance of the cells in plant A improved significantly. Productivity (output/workers) increased 163 percent, manufacturing lead time was shortened by 66 percent, and work-in-process inventories decreased by 13 percent. In addition, compared to the same benchmark when mass production lines were used, 40 percent less work space was utilized. The managers believed that the operators' quality awareness had increased. The HRM practices used after the introduction of cell production addressed the behavioral requirements of the new work environment. Thereafter, the manufacturing performance of the cells improved. Thus, I could say that these management practices helped to ensure the success of cell production and improve manufacturing outcomes. However, as plant A's principal customer, a digital camera manufacturer, was shifting production facilities to China, the cells at plant A were being transferred to the affiliated Chinese plants so that they could be operated near to the customer.

Case 2: Plant B's cells producing electronic devices

Overview

Plant B was operated by a manufacturing company that was a spin-off of a major Japanese electronics company. In addition to plant B, the manufacturing company owned other factories at home and abroad. Plant B produced parts components and manufactured electronic devices for PC manufacturers and even its own original electronic products that were designed inside the plant. Its cell lines were introduced in 2000, and its cell operators assembled these parts and products. The managers at plant B had not intended to employ cell production; it was simply the manufacturing method they happened to come up with and develop while pursuing an optimal production method for the build-to-order (BTO) strategy. Unlike other plants, therefore, plant B's engineers and even its workers built their original cell lines without any advice from consultants familiar with cell production. The manufacturing company running plant B competed against major global companies that manufactured in large-lot sizes, such as South Korean, Chinese, and Taiwanese manufacturers. Facing such competitive threats, the manufacturing company designated plant B as the mother plant to the affiliated overseas plants located in East Asian countries and expected the plant to play a vital role among the group factories at home and abroad. Plant B's cell lines served as experimental "pre-production lines," to use the words of one manager, or pilot run lines so that the overseas plants could smoothly commence manufacturing products in large-lot sizes. Because plant B's cell operators manufactured the latest products in small-lot sizes, they occasionally worked together with R&D staff and were asked to offer their suggestions and ideas to them. Non-Japanese production workers from the affiliated overseas plants were dispatched to plant B and taught how to operate and run manufacturing cells. In this manner, plant B served as the mother plant to the overseas affiliated manufacturing companies and strived to transfer new manufacturing methods, including cell production, to them and to educate foreign nonmanagerial and managerial employees sent from these companies.

Multiskilling ability and HRM practices

Plant B had a systematic training program for developing multiskilled workers. Skills were graded according to their complexity and difficulty and skill levels were clearly defined. Target skill levels were given to individual operators. By participating in the program, workers were expected to achieve their target skill levels and to upgrade their skill levels step by step.

Interdependence and HRM practices

Plant B adopted the line company system. Each cell bore responsibility for quality, cost, delivery time, and so on, which were linked to plant-level profits and losses. In that sense, the system allowed goal interdependence between operators in a cell. However, cell operators were not evaluated based on their cell's performance. The line company system was used for the purpose of education rather than personnel appraisal.

Continuous improvement and HRM practices

After introducing cell production, the managers at plant B were able to find out who made which products as workers' names were shown on the products made by the operators. This practice was performed under the line company system. As a result, the operators' sense of responsibility for quality increased, and this resulted in a significant improvement in product quality.

The parent company that owned the manufacturing company that operated plant B, a major Japanese electronics company, and the group companies, one of which was the manufacturing company, were known for their high standard of product quality and for improvement activities that promoted high quality production. Among these group companies and factories, plant B was best known for its quality-enhancing activities and its enthusiasm for these improvement activities. Employees at plant B participated in off-line improvement activities through QC circles. Operators did not always offer useful ideas, and the number of ideas they provided was not unlimited. In order to encourage the operators to provide more ideas, they were allowed to take classes in IE and QC along with the engineering staff at the in-house training room called the "Techno-School."

Cell operators at plant B had direct contacts with R&D staff members visiting the shop floor and gave their suggestions and ideas on how they could manufacture products more easily from the perspective of manufacturing workers. A close working relationship between cell operators and R&D staff members was crucial for plant B because the plant was the mother plant to the affiliated manufacturing companies abroad. The cell lines were pilot run lines and experimental lines at the mother plant to the affiliated plants mass-producing overseas. The suggestions and ideas offered by plant B's cell operators facilitated these pilot run lines. Know-how was then subsequently transferred to the overseas affiliated plants, enabling them to build new cell lines and mass production lines smoothly and quickly.

Motivation and HRM practices

The managers at plant B understood how important it was to motivate workers when implementing cell production. Both leaders and operators studied the significance of teamwork and of work or jobs by reading books on these subjects together so that they could motivate themselves. Even if operators did not achieve targets, managers took great care of and encouraged poor-performing workers by announcing higher levels of performance than the cell had actually achieved. The managers attempted to intentionally facilitate competition or rivalry among cells in order to motivate cell operators to work harder, although the cell operators were not aware of this fact.

Manufacturing performance measures

Plant B had seen its manufacturing lead time and work-in-process inventory improve since cells were employed. In particular, the cells at plant B achieved a higher level of product quality compared to cells at the group companies' plants. The management practices associated with cell production seemed to help improve these manufacturing outcomes. The cells played the critical role as pilot-run production lines and made a significant contribution to the mission of plant B as the mother plant. Managers and engineers were developing the latest high value-added products that its global competitors could not emulate, and these were shipped to the Japanese domestic market so that plant B could continue to produce using manufacturing cells and to maintain its manufacturing activities in Japan; otherwise, they would have had to close the plant and move the manufacturing facilities to somewhere overseas where they could enjoy the low-cost advantage.

Case 3: Plant C's cells manufacturing PCs in large-lot sizes

Overview

Plant C was operated by a manufacturing company wholly owned by one of the major Japanese electronics companies which was on a par with the parent company of the manufacturing company operating plant B; it made PCs. Cell production began at the plant in 1997. This plant had the cell lines for both small- and large-lot manufacturing. The large-lot production cell lines were longer than the small-lot production cell lines and looked like mini mass-production lines. All of the operators in the large-lot manufacturing cells were nonregular workers whose skills were limited; these cells were more cost advantageous than common cells.

Multiskilling ability and HRM practices

The large-lot manufacturing cells did not require a higher level of skills; therefore, all of the workers in these cells were nonregular workers, mainly ones who were dispatched from personnel agencies or subcontracted manufacturing companies. Before they were engaged in the assigned tasks in the cells, they took a mere two-day training program to obtain the skills required to complete the tasks. Average cells consisted of around ten nonregular workers. Even if the unskilled nonregular workers voluntarily quit their jobs, replacements—also unskilled nonregular workers—could easily be found and mobilized within or outside the plant.

Interdependence and HRM practices

Operators were not allowed to help colleagues in trouble nearby in the same cell.

Continuous improvement and HRM practices

Cell operators were not allowed to troubleshoot; supervisors or technicians bore this responsibility.

Motivation and HRM practices

The managers at plant C had a plan to promote even contingent workers to the position of leader if they were excellent workers. They suggested to temporary staff agencies that excellent contingent workers should be paid more. These attempts were one of the ways the managers tried to motivate nonregular workers in large-lot manufacturing cells.

Manufacturing performance measures

Since introducing cell production, plant C had improved the level of inventory and work space utilization. However, this improvement was due to the efforts of managers and engineers. Cell operators cut costs only because the cell lines were designed to manufacture PC products with a few variations in large-lot sizes.

What can be learned from the three cases?

The three cases suggest the importance of the use of relevant management practices in cell production environments and that these practices are associated with manufacturing performance in a cell production environment. The case of the cells at plant A revealed that since the introduction of cell production as an alternative to mass production, several problems had been encountered with the cells. Most of these problems were to do with human or organizational factors, including skill levels, interdependence, and motivation. They also concerned the behavioral requirements for driving cell production. To meet these behavioral requirements, managers at plant A utilized numerous management practices, including training for multiskilled workers, team-based and interdependent jobs, and several incentives to satisfy employees' work needs. These efforts eventually allowed for the success of cell production, which in turn led to an improvement in manufacturing performance. It was evident that the management practices utilized were associated with manufacturing outcomes (e.g., productivity).

The case of plant B's cells also demonstrates that as pilot-run production lines at the mother plant to the affiliated overseas plants, the cells performed well, particularly in the area of manufacturing quality, and that these outcomes were the result of the use of relevant HRM practices, such as QC circles, direct contacts with R&D staff, IE education, and so forth.

The large-lot production cell lines at plant C were aimed at enlarging manufacturing capacity. The cell lines seemed to be "mini mass-production lines." I hardly perceived the extensive and intensive use of HPWPs, as seen in plants A and B, in these cells at plant C. The effect of the cells was a reduction of costs. This was achieved in such a way that a relatively high number of operators in the cells manufactured commodity types of PC products with a few variations in large-lot sizes. This type of mass-producing cells might be transferred to countries where labor costs are low. Indeed, at other plants I visited, these cells were later transferred to overseas plants.

These three cases indicate that the decision to use HRM practices affects the manufacturing performance of cells. It is apparent that the use of relevant HRM practices improves not only cost but also quality and delivery time in cell production environments. If plants A and B had not adopted these HRM practices, their cells would not have achieved superior performance in these areas. Although extensive and intensive use of management practices was irrelevant to the large-lot production cell lines at plant C, these cell lines achieved cost reduction through enlarging production capacity and enjoying the economy of scale. Such "quasi" or "pseudo" cells would be less dependent on operators' skills, knowledge, and teamwork, and management practices to facilitate these human factors than "real cells," and it would not cost a lot to develop operators in these cell environments. Despite the advantages, these mass-producing cells could be transferred to overseas plants in countries with low labor costs, just as conventional mass production lines have been.

Discussions

My case studies revealed many facts about Japan's cell production in terms of HRM practices. In this section, I discuss these findings using the three perspectives from the SHRM literature: the universalistic, contingency, and configurational perspectives.

From the universalistic perspective

My case study research identified the behaviors and knowledge or skills required in implementing cell production and the HRM practices that can meet these behavioral requirements. The required behaviors and knowledge or skills are multiskilling ability, task and goal interdependence, motivation (by satisfying basic and higher-level work needs), and continuous improvement. As Table 4.1 shows, there are numerous management practices that meet the behavioral requirements and are thus relevant to the cell production environment. These management practices are similar to, and more comprehensive than, what Appelbaum and colleagues (2000) proposed as parts of the high-performance work system in their studies of American manufacturing companies. Thus, the management practices identified in my work might be relevant and effective across manufacturing industries and even across countries. From the universalistic perspective, these practices might be universally effective in the manufacturing sector worldwide.

From the configurational perspective

My case study research showed that some managers (e.g., the ones at plants A and B) attempt to fully elicit and utilize the capabilities and skills of people to ensure the success of cell production, whereas others (e.g., the managers at plant C) try to develop "skill-less" or de-skilled cell lines where people are hardly expected to exercise their capabilities or skills and their teamwork. The managers at plants A and B tried to adopt as many of the HRM practices shown in Table 4.1 as possible whereas plant C's managers did not. Thus, it appears that some managers attempt to employ as many relevant management practices as possible in order to harness employees' potentialities as much as possible while others do not. There are no one-size-fits-all management practices for all cell production environments, and yet the management practices I identified seem to converge into two HR systems. Based on these findings, and according to the configurational perspective, I would like to propose two HR systems that would be central to the manufacturing sector in general. The first one is an HR system whereby managers attempt to tap employees' work potentialities as much as possible, as the managers at both plant A and plant B did with their set of management practices. I would like to call this the "perfectly-tapping-potentiality HR system." Elements of this system are constituted by the management practices shown in Table 4.1. This HR system would be similar to both the commitment system proposed by Mossholder, Richardson, and Settoon (2011) and the high-performance work system proposed by Appelbaum and colleagues (2000). Yet, it is also an HR system that is unique to the manufacturing sector and affects rank-and-file workers in this sector, as opposed to the commitment system that could be used more widely in both manufacturing and nonmanufacturing industries. It is also, as I suggested earlier, more comprehensive than Appelbaum and colleagues' notion of the high-performance work system.

The second HR system is one whereby managers intentionally or unintentionally attempt to limit employees' potentialities to perform advanced work, as plant C's managers did through their set of management practices. I would like to call this the "imperfectly-tapping-potentiality HR system." This system would be similar to the compliance system proposed by Mossholder, Richardson, and Settoon (2011). Yet, this proposed HR system is different from the compliance system for the same reason that the perfectly-tapping-potentiality HR system is different from the commitment system.

I shall compare the two HR systems in the light of staffing, training, work design, participation in decisions, and incentives, each of which is considered to be a key dimension in HRM practices (Mossholder, Richardson, and Settoon, 2011). Table 4.2 presents the two HR systems for the manufacturing sector, possibly across countries. I discuss the two HR systems in more detail further.

The emphasis in the perfectly-tapping-potentiality HR system is on the internal labor market where regular workers play a vital role as core members of the company. Under this system, training aims to develop the multiskilling and problem-solving abilities of employees, mainly the regular ones. The knowledge and skills that employees develop in the internal labor market would be unique to the company(ies) involved and difficult for competitors to imitate and would thus become a competitive advantage. Work processes are designed to be team-based in such a way that tasks are assigned to a team of operators rather than to individual

Table 4.2   Two HR systems for the manufacturing sector

Imperfectly-Tapping-Potentiality HR System	Dimensions in HRM Practices	Perfectly-Tapping-Potentiality HR System
emphasis on external labor market	staffing	emphasis on internal labor market
provision of less extensive training so that workers can perform only simple and monotonous work tasks	training	provision of extensive training so that operators can perform multiskilling and problem-solving tasks
individual-based	work design	team-based
limited participation in decision making	participation in decision making	limited participation in decision making, except for continuous improvement activities
satisfying only basic work needs	incentives	satisfying both basic and higher-level work needs

operators, and workers are expected to achieve the assigned task as a team. As a result, operators are interdependent on each other and collectively responsible for the consequences. Operators' participation in decision-making might be more limited in the manufacturing context than generally assumed because allowing them considerable discretion might sometimes interrupt operations. However, their participation in continuous improvement activities, such as QC circles and other learning opportunities, is an exception: workers are encouraged to generate and suggest ideas in these improvement activities. By taking advantage of ideas and suggestions from workers, managers are more likely to build efficient manufacturing systems than they would otherwise have done. Incentives are given to operators in order to satisfy both their basic and higher-level work needs. The ability of managers to build an HR system whose components are congruent with each other leads to the achievement of horizontal fit.

The imperfectly-tapping-potentiality HR system has facets that are different from those of the perfectly-tapping-potentiality HR system. It puts emphasis on the external labor market where the majority of the workforce comprises nonregular or casual workers (e.g., temporary workers dispatched from employment agencies or subcontracted manufacturers, and part-time workers). Typically, these nonregular operators are rarely expected to perform multiskilling and/or problem-solving work tasks. Thus, in the imperfectly-tapping-potentiality HR system, training is less extensive than it is in the perfectly-tapping-potentiality HR system; for example, operators in plant C only had to take a two-day training program before they were mobilized to the cell lines. Work processes are designed to be individual-based so that the operators who are not educated to handle a broad range of work tasks on the lines can focus just on their own work tasks. Thus, operators in the imperfectly-tapping-potentiality HR system are not as interdependent on each other as their counterpart operators in the perfectly-tapping-potentiality HR system. Operators' participation in decision-making is limited. Also, they typically do not attend continuous improvement activities. Instead, managers and/or engineers take responsibility for continuous improvement in the imperfectly-tapping-potentiality HR system. Incentives are used to satisfy only the basic work needs of operators.

Both of these HR systems would affect manufacturing performance, yet, generally speaking, the perfectly-tapping-potentiality HR system would be more likely to improve all of its indices than the imperfectly-tapping-potentiality HR system would.

From the contingency perspective

I suggested earlier that, in general, the perfectly-tapping-potentiality HR system is more effective than the imperfectly-tapping-potentiality HR system. However, I assume that the effects of each the two systems might vary depending on the manufacturing strategies adopted. I now discuss the contingent relations of the two systems with manufacturing performance based on the findings of my case study research and according to the contingency perspective in the SHRM literature.

My case study research revealed the two types of manufacturing strategies in cell production environments. It also confirmed that two different HR systems each aligned with the respective manufacturing strategies, suggesting the achievement of vertical fit. One of the two manufacturing strategies seeks to make products with large variations in small-lot sizes by means of cells in which a small number of operators work. This type of cell represents a typical cell or a real cell. The products manufactured using this strategy are generally high value-added products for delivery to the Japanese domestic market. This manufacturing strategy corresponds to that adopted at plants A and B. The perfectly-tapping-potentiality HR system is expected to align with this strategy, and the vertical fit achieved is likely to generate a high standard of manufacturing performance in terms of quality, cost, and delivery time. Figure 4.1 depicts the relationships between this HR system and manufacturing performance, contingent on the manufacturing strategy.

The other manufacturing strategy aims at making products with a few variations in relatively large-lot sizes—compared to those of the manufacturing strategy using real cells—by means of cells in which a larger number of operators work. Such cells resemble traditional mass production lines and can be called pseudo or quasi cells. The products manufactured in these cells are typically commodity types of products. This manufacturing strategy is similar to that adopted in plant C. The imperfectly-tapping-potentiality HR system is expected to fit this manufacturing strategy, and the vertical fit achieved is likely to improve only cost performance through enjoying the economy of scale. If I were permitted to go further and expand my arguments, I would suppose that this HR system would be more relevant to traditional mass production with conveyor belts than any other production methods.

Propositions

Based on the arguments I have made so far, I can induce and generalize the associations between management practices and manufacturing performance from my case studies of Japanese manufacturers. Further,

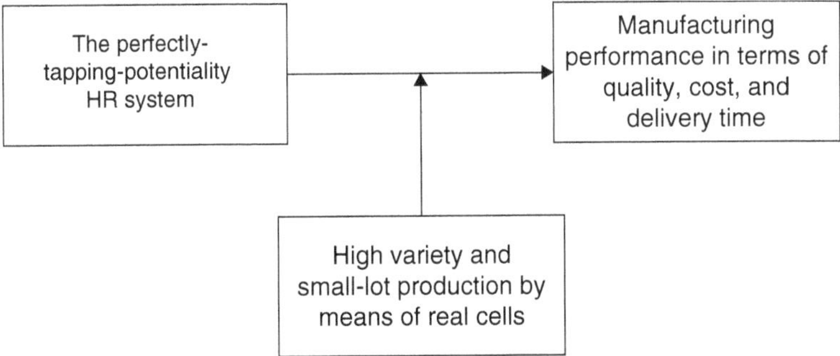

Figure 4.1   The relation between the HR system and manufacturing performance, contingent on the manufacturing strategy

I present my proposition on the direct relation according to the universalistic perspective.

Proposition 1: a system of management practices facilitating multiskilling ability, teamwork, motivation, and continuous improvement, that is to say, the perfectly-tapping-potentiality HR system, is associated with manufacturing performance in terms of quality, cost, and delivery time.

According to the contingency perspective, I can also present the contingent or moderated relation, as shown in Figure 4.1.

Proposition 2: the relation between the perfectly-tapping-potentiality system and manufacturing performance varies as a function of the manufacturing strategy, that is, high variety and small-lot production by means of real cells. More specifically, the HR system is more likely to improve manufacturing performance with the manufacturing strategy than without it.

Limitations and future work

In my work, I have answered the question "why" focused management practices are significant by identifying the behavioral requirements needed to run cell production. I have also sought to answer the question of "what" focused management practices are significant by attempting to identify relevant and effective management practices in cell production environments. Furthermore, I have answered "whether" these management practices do in fact affect manufacturing perform-ance by collecting soft evidence.

However, I was unable to examine "how much" these management practices affect manufacturing performance. Case study research can-not address this kind of question (Yin, 2003). This is one limitation of my work demonstrated in this chapter. By performing survey-type research and statistical analyses, scholars can answer these questions. My work also sought to explore the management practices central to cell production. Although I have supposedly identified the effective-ness and relevance of management practices across the manufacturing sector, I still needed to verify the efficacy of these practices irrespective of the manufacturing methods adopted. By taking into consideration these limitations, I had to improve my work: this was my next project.

5
Management Practices and Manufacturing Performance

Introduction

Based on the findings of my case study research on Japanese manufacturers engaged in cell production, in the previous chapter, I attempted to generalize their manufacturing activities and presented propositions on the relations between management practices and manufacturing performance. In spite of my efforts to explore these relations using case study research, my work had limitations: (1) the inability of case study research to assess how much these management practices affected manufacturing performance and to estimate the effects and (2) the lack of hard evidence in my work to validate the efficacy of identified management practices irrespective of the manufacturing system or strategies adopted.

In order to respond to the issues left outstanding from the previous chapter and to develop my work, in this chapter, I theorize and hypothesize the relations between management practices and manufacturing performance and empirically test the hypotheses by drawing on hard or quantitative evidence collected from 77 production teams at 20 Japanese manufacturing companies. I theorize and build hypotheses based on the strategic human resource management (SHRM) literature. This work not only identifies the effects of the management practices adopted and carried out by Japanese manufacturers but also attempts to fill the gaps or chasms in the studies in the SHRM literature, that is, the questions that still remain unanswered despite a large body of empirical work supporting the central thesis in the literature: "human resource management (HRM) matters." In this manner, this research makes a contribution to the development of the field as well as to the area of Japanese businesses studies. I begin by delineating the gaps, such as the fact that little is known about the exact impacts of these practices, in the next section.

Unfilled gaps in the SHRM literature

In general, the empirical studies to date have supported the proposition of SHRM scholars (e.g., O'Reilly and Pfeffer, 2000) that certain HRM practices, known as high-performance work practices (HPWPs) or high commitment HRM, generate high performance. Nevertheless, several issues concerning the research on HRM practices and performance remain unresolved. The first concerns measuring HRM practices. In conducting such research, scholars (e.g., Arthur, 1994; Osterman, 1994; Huselid, 1995; MacDuffie, 1995; Guest et al., 2003) typically ask an HRM manager or executive for information or data on the proportion of the firm's employees covered by particular HRM practices. They do so even though, as Ichniowski et al. (1996) suggested, he or she may have limited knowledge of what is going on in or behind the scenes in the workplace. Arthur and Boyles (2007) argued that a large number of prior works on SHRM research have centered on the more abstract level of HRM policies or programs, as stated by HRM managers, rather than on HRM practices as they are actually implemented by people. SHRM research can stand on firmer ground by capturing and assessing actual practices rather than stated policies (Wright and Boswell, 2002).

The second issue concerns the choice of performance indicators. SHRM research differs from traditional HRM research in that it focuses on organizational or corporate performance rather than individual outcomes (Becker and Huselid, 2006). Among the corporate performance measures scholars have preferred to select are return on equity (ROE), return on assets (ROA), Tobin's q, sales, net profits, and other financial and accounting performance indices. The linkages between HRM practices and such company performance measures are remote. Thus, Becker and Huselid (1998) supposed that there are mediating variables between them, such as labor turnover and productivity. As the process through which HRM affects performance is long, its impact on performance becomes progressively weaker. Guest (1997) argued that this is because, in addition to HRM, other factors might affect performance outcomes. Thus, the use of outcome indicators that are relevant to, and correspond to, HRM practices is recommended in SHRM research; estimating the impact of HRM on performance accurately would be facilitated more by using these indicators than by not using them.

The third issue concerns the contingency perspective in the SHRM literature. In building hypotheses on HRM-performance associations, scholars use the perspective that assumes that the relationships between HRM practices and performance vary depending on organizational conditions, including strategies, business segments, and technology. However, only a limited number of empirical studies have supported this view (e.g., Batt, 2002).

To address these issues as yet unresolved, I examine the relations between HRM practices and manufacturing performance by using evidence from Japanese manufacturers in the electronics industry. More specifically, I collected evidence from both the assembly lines and cells at these factories. Following Johnson's (2005) usage, in my work I call a mass production line an assembly line, a manufacturing line, or simply a line. Meanwhile, I also call a cell production line an assembly cell, a manufacturing cell, or just a cell. The collection of data from both mass production and cell production will make it possible to estimate not only the impacts of focused HRM practices irrespective of the manufacturing methods employed, but also the differences in the impacts depending on the adopted manufacturing methods.

Theoretical backgrounds and hypotheses

The concept of HRM

Guest (1997) insisted that in examining HRM–performance relations, scholars first and foremost need a theory about HRM to enhance an understanding of these relationships. In accordance with this HRM scholar's advice, I begin by addressing some issues related to the concept of HRM, including the level of abstraction, and what precisely the HRM practices that will boost performance are.

HRM is defined as a set of employee management activities (Bohlander, Snell, and Sherman, 2001), although, as yet, no consensus has been formed as to what constitutes these HRM activities (Boselie, Dietz, and Boon, 2005). HRM revolves around its philosophy, principles, policies, programs, and practices (Becker and Gerhart, 1996; Becker and Huselid, 1998; Huselid and Becker, 2000; Bowen and Ostroff, 2004; Arthur and Boyles, 2007). The philosophy and principles of HRM are defined as the beliefs and values that shape employee management activities, and they concern corporate culture. HRM policies and programs represent an organization's stated intentions regarding employee management activities. The term "HRM practices" means actual and operational HRM programs and policies and any employee management activities that are implemented in practice by people. HRM policies or programs are more abstract than HRM practices as the former are not as actual and observable as the latter (Boselie, Dietz, and Boon, 2005). Conversely, HRM practices are more to do with operations than HRM policies and programs. HRM philosophy is, by definition, at the most abstract level in terms of being observed and experienced by workers. Thus, the notion of HRM can be classified in terms of "the level of abstraction," which Colbert (2004) defined as the level of abstract thoughts and constructs under consideration. The level of abstraction differs from the notion of the level of analysis. The level of analysis can be defined as the structural level of a theoretical construct; a construct can be at the individual-, group-, organization-, industry-, or other unit level.

Recognizing the level of abstraction of HRM provides important implications, both theoretical and methodological (Wright and Boswell, 2002). For example, HRM policies and programs are not necessarily implemented; consequently, there may be a gap between them and HRM practices. Thus, it is methodologically important to capture and assess HRM practices when conducting empirical SHRM research. Despite the importance of HRM practices, scholars have often failed to capture them. As Huselid and Becker (2000) suggested, this is because they have used question items that included a mix of policy and practices. It is also because SHRM scholars have asked an HRM manager or executive to estimate the percentage of those who were covered by, or directly experienced, particular HRM practices.

As a means of addressing these methodological issues and of correctly assessing HRM practices, I focus on assembly cells and lines, not on companies or even on plants, in my work in the hope that this will allow me to capture what actually goes on behind the scenes. My study is not the first one that has ever tried to capture HRM practices implemented by rank-and-file workers. For instance, Appelbaum and colleagues (2000) studied management practices in US manufacturing plants. Overall, however, these scholars did not assess HRM practices themselves, but rather manufacturing methods. In addition, their model stressed commitment, job satisfaction, and other worker outcomes, not manufacturing performance, as its outcome variables. Likewise, some other previous studies that explored HRM practices had an interest in the question of whether the use of management practices is related to worker outcomes such as commitment and labor turnover rather than in manufacturing or financial performance (e.g., Dore, 1973).

Some scholars (e.g., Pfeffer, 1998) have designated a certain HRM practice, such as job security or symbolic egalitarianism, as a high-performance work practice or best practice. They argued that these management practices are likely to improve company performance and subsequently generate high performance. As yet, however, there seems to be no agreement on what HPWPs are exactly. Thus, scholars have selected the HRM practices deemed to be relevant to their research frameworks or settings (Boselie, Dietz, and Boon, 2005). In line with such prior work, I also decided to investigate management practices relevant to my research setting, the manufacturing sector. By conducting the inductive or case study research described in Chapter 4, I identified management practices that I supposed to be relevant and effective across the manufacturing sector, in particular in cell production or other team-based production methods. As I mention later in this chapter, I developed questionnaire items based on these identified HRM practices. These practices can meet the behavioral requirements of the work environments under consideration: the ability of operators to perform multiskilling tasks; task and goal interdependence and teamwork; operators' basic and higher-level work needs; and continuous improvement. In the last chapter, I called a set of the coherent management practices the perfectly-potentiality-tapping human resource (HR) system. Taking into consideration the relevant and effective management practices I identified in my case study research on Japanese manufacturers, I build and test my hypotheses on the relations between management practices and manufacturing performance.

SHRM research differs from traditional HRM research in that the former emphasizes the system of HRM practices as a solution to business problems rather than individual HRM practices in isolation (Becker and Huselid, 2006). The review by Boselie, Dietz, and Boon (2005) found that 46 of the 104 articles on SHRM that had demonstrated empirical research employed such a configurational or system perspective. In the hope of identifying the overlapping and mutually reinforcing effects of multiple management practices, the scholars who adopted the configurational perspective aggregated and averaged or even multiplied the values on a set of questionnaire items that informants, for example, HRM managers, responded to (MacDuffie, 1995). They then evaluated the effects of a set, system, cluster, bundle, or configuration of HRM practices on performance. Similarly, I too adopt this perspective and seek to evaluate the impact of the system of HRM practices rather than of any of these management practices in isolation.

Choice of performance indicators

As Guest (1997) argued, in addition to a theory about HRM, a theory about performance is also needed to conduct HRM-performance research. It is important to at least take stock of the performance measures selected when examining the relationships between HRM and performance. Becker and Huselid (2006) pointed out that besides its emphasis on the role of the system of HRM practices, SHRM research differs from traditional HR research because it focuses on organizational- or company-level performance rather than individual-level performance. Boselie, Dietz, and Boon (2005) found that financial performance measures were treated as corporate performance in half of the 104 empirical SHRM articles they reviewed, with profits being the most common measure followed by various measures of sales. Boselie, Dietz, and Boon (2005) argued that in many articles, there was a tacit recognition that financial measures are the best indicators of organizational success and sustainability.

However, there are also factors that can mediate between HRM practices and financial performance (Guest, 1997). In SHRM research, it is assumed that improved performance is achieved through people and that HRM practices are used to improve HRM or worker outcomes, such as commitment, skill and ability, and team flexibility (Guest, 1997). It is expected that only when a high level of HRM outcomes is achieved will operational performance, including productivity, quality, and labor turnover, be improved and that this will translate into better financial performance. As stated earlier, as the effect of HRM practices is distant from the targeted outcomes, it becomes progressively weaker because other factors may intervene and affect the process (Guest, 1997). Such intervening factors include corporate culture, organizational structure, IT, market fluctuations, oil prices, financial dexterity, and marketing campaigns. Thus, as Boselie, Dietz, and Boon (2005) argued, in building and testing HRM-performance models, the use of outcome indicators located near to where HRM practices are implemented is theoretically more plausible and makes it methodologically easier to connect HRM and performance than performance measures distant from the effects of management practices, such as financial performance.

The review conducted by Boselie, Dietz, and Boon (2005) found that the most popular operational (not worker) outcome immediately connected to HRM practices was employee turnover or leaving rates; this indicator was used in 26 articles they reviewed. Turnover is indeed an important indicator, but it is less important in countries that traditionally enjoy a low rate of labor turnover, such as Japan, although these days, the number of Japanese workers voluntarily leaving jobs is increasing. Relevant dependent or outcome variables may vary depending on the particular context, such as nations, industries, and types of technology used. Thus, selected outcome variables must be meaningful for the context in which the focused companies are embedded (Becker and Gerhart, 1996). Relevant outcome variables also vary depending on whether selected outcome variables correspond to management practices as independent variables in terms of the level of analysis (Becker and Gerhart, 1996); for example, if management practices at a team level are focal independent variables, it is recommended that performance outcomes at the same team level are selected as dependent variables.

Thus, when selecting my work's outcome variables, I take into account the proximity of management practices to dependent or outcome variables, the meaningfulness of the outcome variables adopted, and the agreement at the level of analysis between management practices and outcome variables. Accordingly, I select manufacturing performance required for focused manufacturing teams engaged in traditional mass production or cell production as the performance indicator in my work. More specifically, the manufacturing performance indicator was composed of the following elements: quality (lower product defects), reduction in work-in-process inventory, productivity (product quantities made per worker), and reduction in lead time (the time it takes to make a product, or throughput time). These indicators represent quality, cost, and delivery time (QCD) manufacturing performance measures. They are strategically significant for manufacturing companies.

It is noted that, as MacDuffie (1995) argued in his research on the world automobile industry, QCD manufacturing performance indicators can be compatible with, or even complementary to, each other. For example, a reduction in work-in-process inventory can be achieved along with, or through, a reduction in lead time or vice versa.

As I argued earlier, I emphasize the effect of a set of management practices rather than the effect of individual ones and attempt to assess the effect of a system of management practices. An HR system—which corresponds to the perfectly-tapping-potentiality HR system argued in the previous chapter—is constituted of management practices that seek to develop multiskilled operators, to encourage their teamwork, to enhance their continuous improvement activities, and to motivate them to work harder. The manufacturing performance measures, as dependent variables, in my model are reduction in work-in-process inventory, lead time, quality, and productivity. Assuming that the greater the value attached to respective management practices on the questionnaire, the stronger the effects exercised by them, I make the following hypotheses on the direct relations between the HR system (I referred to earlier) and respective manufacturing performance measures:

Hypothesis 1a: the system of HRM practices is positively associated with reduction in work-in-process inventory.

Hypothesis 2a: the system of HRM practices is positively associated with reduction in lead time.

Hypothesis 3a: the system of HRM practices is positively associated with quality.

Hypothesis 4a: the system of HRM practices is positively associated with productivity.

The contingency perspective

Three perspectives have been developed in the SHRM literature: the universalistic, the contingency, and the configurational (Delery and Doty, 1996; Dreher and Dougherty, 2002). The universalistic, or "best practice" perspective posits that a certain HRM practice or set of practices allows for high performance across organizational conditions, that is, an organization's strategies, structures, technology, and the like. Because the aforementioned hypotheses 1a, 2a, 3a, and 4a predict the impacts of HRM practices on manufacturing performance regardless of the type of manufacturing method adopted, it could be said that these hypotheses are built on the universalistic perspective. Underlying the contingency perspective is the assumption that HRM practices generate high performance when they are in alignment with organizational conditions. The configurational perspective is used to capture not a single effect of individual HRM practices but the overall effect of a set of these practices. Although SHRM research has employed these perspectives and has, in general, demonstrated the impact of HRM practices, only a few instances of prior empirical work found support for the contingency perspective (e.g., Batt, 2002).

The data set used in this research came from assembly lines as well as cells. By taking advantage of this, I can attempt to prove the efficacy of the contingency perspective by designating the technical aspects of manufacturing cells and lines as a moderator or the second variable that might affect the effect of management practices on manufacturing performance. This would also prove my claim that identified management practices are supposed to be relevant and effective across manufacturing settings.

Conventional assembly lines are typically used to mass produce using automated conveyor belts, the symbolism of the line. A large number of unskilled operators, whose jobs are narrowly defined, are deployed on these lines so that the effects of the division of labor and subsequent production efficiency can be maximized. Meanwhile, assembly cells are typically used to perform high-variety and small-lot production or agile manufacturing (flexible production in response to changes in both the products' models and amounts caused by unpredictable consumer demand). They are operated by a smaller number of skilled operators, with the machines and equipment arranged in U-shape, T-shape, straight line, circle, or other cell configurations.

In order to capture the technological differences between cells and lines and to explore any interactive effect between HRM practices and a cell and a line, I conceptualize the technical aspect encompassing the two manufacturing methods as the manufacturing configuration. By using this construct, I try to capture not only the layouts of the machines and equipment but also product volume and variety and other issues involved in manufacturing strategies. I define the manufacturing configuration as a continuum with real cell and traditional mass production line at opposite ends because, as my case studies showed, manufacturing lines have been transformed into manufacturing cells. Thus, cell production is considered to be an alternative to mass production. Various forms of cell and line—real cell (Hyer and Brown, 1999), quasi or pseudo cell, a mixed or "compromised" form of a cell and a line, a mixed-flow line (on which a batch or mix of variant products is flowed and manufactured one after another), and a typical conventional mass production line—lie somewhere on this continuum. Since a cell is a manufacturing configuration that is dependent on workers for its implementation and success, a system of HRM practices like the perfectly-tapping-potentiality HR system is more likely to harness employees' potentialities and generate a high standard of QCD manufacturing performance when it is exercised along with a manufacturing configuration that is more similar to a cell than to a line. Assuming that as the greater the value attached to manufacturing configuration on the questionnaire, the more similar the manufacturing configuration is to a cell, I propose the following interaction or moderated hypotheses:

Hypothesis 1b: the system of HRM practices has a positive interactive effect on reduction in work-in-process inventory with the manufacturing configuration in such a way that the association predicted in Hypothesis 1a is stronger when the manufacturing configuration is more similar to a cell than to a line.

Hypothesis 2b: the system of HRM practices has a positive interactive effect on reduction in lead time with the manufacturing configuration in such a way that the association predicted in Hypothesis 2a is stronger when the manufacturing configuration is more similar to a cell than to a line.

Hypothesis 3b: the system of HRM practices has a positive interactive effect on quality with the manufacturing configuration in such a way that the association predicted in Hypothesis 3a is stronger when the manufacturing configuration is more similar to a cell than to a line.

Hypothesis 4b: the system of HRM practices has a positive interactive effect on productivity with the manufacturing configuration in such a way that the association predicted in Hypothesis 4a is stronger when the manufacturing configuration is more similar to a cell than to a line.

Methods

Research design and sample

In order to collect data and to test the hypotheses, I asked Japan-based manufacturing companies in the electronics industry to participate in survey research centered on their manufacturing technology, management practices, and manufacturing performance. The companies that agreed to participate in the survey research were asked to respond to the questionnaire items I developed. When conducting HRM-performance research like my survey research, a methodological issue that might have serious consequences arises when a single respondent fills out questionnaire items on both management practices and performance measures (Becker and Gerhart, 1996). In such a case, the respondent is inclined to answer questions on HRM practices positively if his or her organization's performance is superior or negatively if the performance is poor. In this manner, the correlation coefficients between the two variables might be inflated by the respondents' bias. In order to address this issue, I developed two different types of questionnaire sheets (in Japanese), one for managers and one for team or group leaders. The managers were in charge of the manufacturing or assembly section, and they received reports from their subordinates, that is, the group leaders. The managers were asked to respond to the questionnaire items centered primarily on manufacturing performance and manufacturing technology (configurations). The group leaders were responsible for cells or lines; thus, in some plants, they were also called cell or line leaders. They were asked to respond to the questionnaire items centered primarily on HRM practices concerning their production teams. These team leaders would be what Huselid and Becker (2000) called "key informants," in that they were more knowledgeable about the management practices that were actually implemented than any other people, even the operators who were actually engaged in production operations under the leadership of the group leaders. However, as my case study in the previous chapter revealed, most operators are nonregular workers, such as dispatched, temporary, and part-time workers and the like, and have no lengthy experience of, and little knowledge about, their current jobs. Accordingly, dyads consisting of a manager and a leader responded to the questionnaire items and assessed management practices, manufacturing performance, and other topics involved in their production teams. Managers and leaders were asked to return the completed questionnaire sheets to the people I had asked to supervise my survey at their companies (e.g., personnel in charge of general affairs). Then, the survey supervisors mailed the questionnaire sheets to me. It should be noted that the unit of analysis in my work is a production team or the cell or line on which it operates, not a plant or a company. The English version of the questionnaire items is presented in the Appendix at the end of the book; I am using this for my survey research in English-speaking countries, which is currently in progress.

I collected data from the autumn of 2006 through to the beginning of 2007. I did not randomly distribute questionnaire sheets to companies by mail, a technique used in many previous studies. I contacted the managers at the plants that I had previously visited for my case study research and asked them to participate in the questionnaire-based survey research. Although this method of data collection may cause a response bias (Ichniowski et al., 1996), it was necessary because this survey required a great deal of involvement by the participating companies; numerous manager–leader dyads were required to fill out many and various questionnaire items on the focused cells or lines they were in charge of. Although commitment to this kind of survey research might be burdensome not only for managers and leaders but also for their companies, I thought that my survey would not be successful without such commitment from participating companies and their employees. I expected that the companies that had participated in my case study research would agree to participate in this questionnaire-based survey and cooperate with my research, hence my decision to ask them to participate in the survey. As a result, ten of the companies I had contacted before agreed to participate in this survey. This number was not enough to perform statistical analyses, and therefore I had to expand the sample size. Thus, I asked companies with which I had no previous contact to participate in my survey. As a result, an additional

10 companies agreed to participate in the survey, making 20 companies in total.

All of the participating companies could be categorized generally as "electronics manufacturers" according to the industrial classification system widely used in Japan. This system was developed by the Tokyo Stock Exchange (TSE), Japan's largest bourse. However, these companies made a variety of products, such as PCs, printers, copier machines, air conditioners, lighting products, wireless communications equipment, heating appliances, refrigerators, automated teller machines (ATMs), electronic components for digital cameras, PCs, and so forth as well as industrial equipment such as motors, breakers, and transformers. Most of the production teams surveyed were engaged in product assembly, but some of the teams performed metal-making or parts-processing work tasks.

The companies had multiple affiliated plants. Some of the participating companies were cooperative enough to get some plants operated by them to participate in my survey. Accordingly, it should be noted that the number of participating companies does not coincide with the number of participating plants.

Many of the participating companies had transferred production facilities outside Japan; they had built production bases and were operating factories in areas such as China and Southeast Asia. However, I focused on their Japan-based plants to remove or control for any cultural or national factors that might affect my statistical results (I examine the effect of different national environments later in this book).

Table 5.1 provides information on the survey participants. Twenty companies and their 23 affiliated plants participated in the survey. Some of the participating companies were well known for their efforts to transform their outdated manufacturing methods that were no longer competitive into cell production, thereby recapturing competitiveness and rejuvenating themselves. These efforts have sometimes been reported in the Japanese media. Seventy-seven manager–leader dyads from these participating companies completed two types of questionnaire sheets. Accordingly, 77 production teams constituted the cases or observations used for the subsequent statistical analyses. The number of participating leaders (77) was larger than that of their manager counterparts (43) because managers were typically responsible for more than one production team and thus for more than one subordinate (leader).

Although 77 questionnaires were completed and returned, 75 leaders actually responded; there are two reasons for this: (1) one manager in company 6 simultaneously oversaw a production team as a leader and (2) a leader in company 16 was in charge of two different production

Table 5.1 Information of survey participants

Company Codes	Plants	Manufacturing teams	Managers	Leaders
company 1	1	22	11	22
company 2	1	4	2	4
company 3	1	1	1	1
company 4	1	3	2	3
company 5	1	3	1	3
company 6	1	4	1	4[a]
company 7	1	4	1	4
company 8	1	1	1	1
company 9	1	1	1	1
company 10	1	1	1	1
company 11	1	1	1	1
company 12	1	1	1	1
company 13	1	2	2	2
company 14	2	5	5	5
company 15	1	4	1	4
company 16	1	2	1	2[b]
company 17	1	2	2	2
company 18	3	6	5	6
company 19	1	1	1	1
company 20	1	9	2	9
Total Number	23	77	43	77[c]

Notes:
[a] In company 6, a manager was also responsible for a production team at that company as its leader at the same time. Therefore, at that company one manager and three leaders actually participated.
[b] In company 16, a leader was in charge of two different production teams at the same time. Therefore, at that company one leader actually participated.
[c] For the two previous reasons, a total of 75 leaders actually participated.

teams at the same time. These two cases were not excluded from the sample because these cases were considered to reflect a reality in production front lines, and 75 cases or observations would not have been large enough to perform statistical analyses with the sample size.

Of the 77 cases, 22 were from company 1. The results of the data analyses might be disproportionately affected by these 22 cases. However, I decided to use the data from this company along with the data from other companies because the unit of analysis in my work is a production team or a cell or a line, not a plant or company. Even in the same plant, some production teams can generate superior performance while others cannot. Indeed, when conducting my case study research, I found that there were differences in outcomes between production teams that were caused largely by their work environment, which was constituted by manufacturing technology and management practices. In order to examine the effects of companies or plants on production teams, I performed multilevel random coefficient regression analyses in which production teams (level 1) were nested within the companies (level 2). The results revealed that the second-level companies did not affect the manufacturing performance of production teams. Of course, I would need to assess the plant- or company-level effects more correctly in the future.

A sample size of 77 may seem small for performing statistical analyses and estimating parameters. When I started this survey, I found that it was difficult to conduct this type of survey research in Japan by collecting data, especially hard evidence, from Japanese electronics manufacturers. They were reluctant to disclose data because they faced formidable competition from rivals around the world. They were also concerned that competitors might exploit any data released. Thus, even some of the companies that I had visited for the case study rejected my request that they participate in the survey research. Given such difficulties in collecting data in those days, let alone these days when competitive environments have become much more severe, I decided to base the statistical analyses on the 77 cases.

Variables

Criterion variables

I used productivity, work-in-process inventory, lead time, and quality as my criterion or dependent variables. For several reasons, I adopted a five-point Likert scale to measure both these performance indicators and the predictors and controls. One reason was that the participating electronics companies manufactured many different categories of products (e.g., PCs, copier machines, and electronic components), and this made it difficult to apply the same benchmarking criteria (e.g., the absolute number of products assembled) to all of the production teams surveyed; for example, PC production workers would typically manufacture far more products than copying-machine production workers. Another reason was that the extremely severe competition in the electronics industry made the participating companies and their managers concerned that their manufacturing outcomes and other data obtained in my survey might be exploited by their competitors. As a result, some of the managers were reluctant to provide raw data on manufacturing performance and other outcomes and activities. Therefore, managers were asked to evaluate the manufacturing performance of the production teams they were in charge of by means of a five-point Likert scale. They were asked to assess the current performance of focused production teams by making comparisons with (1) the current performance level of other teams within the same plant, (2) the level of the same performance indicator of an average production team that had made the same type of products within the same plant about five years earlier, and (3) the "average" level of the corresponding performance indicator in the same industry. Each performance index (e.g., productivity and quality) was an aggregated, averaged value for a set of several question items. The internal consistency reliabilities (Cronbach's α) of all performance indices were high—.80 for productivity, .83 for work-in-process inventory, .83 for lead time, and .75 for quality—and so these indices were used as the criterion variables. A higher value in each of the performance measurements represents superior performance: for the productivity variable, it represents a higher level of performance; for the work-in-process inventory variable, a smaller inventory level; for the lead time variable, a shorter lead time; for the quality variable, a higher standard of quality; and for the productivity variable, a higher level of productivity.

Independent variables

I developed the questionnaire items on management practices so that they would fit my research framework, that is, manufacturing settings, and capture the management practices that I had found in my case study research to be relevant and effective across the manufacturing sector, as other scholars have done in their research (e.g., Appelbaum et al., 2000; Batt, 2002). Bearing these management practices in mind, I produced 24 question items on HRM practices. The questionnaire items sought to capture management practices concerning multiskilling training, teamwork or interdependence, continuous improvement activities, and motivation. HRM practices were assessed on a five-point Likert scale by the leaders. Responses ranged from 1 ("strongly disagree") to 5 ("strongly agree"); for details, see the Appendix. The question items included six items on multiskilling training (or skill enhancement training), five items on teamwork, seven items on improvement activities, and six items on motivation. I performed a confirmatory factor analysis by using the Statistical Analysis System (SAS) Covariance Analysis of Linear Structural Equations (CALIS) procedure with maximum likelihood (ML) estimation in order to test the four-factor model and to demonstrate construct validity. Overall fit statistics for the four-factor model were not favorable (χ^2 = 471, df = 246, p < .0001; GFI = .65,

RMSEA = .11) because the sample size was not large enough, compared to the number of indicator variables used to perform a factor analysis (Brown, 2006). Then, following Youndt et al. (1996), I performed a within-block confirmatory factor analysis for the respective blocks of HRM practice in order to verify construct validity with a small sample size, although this methodology cannot be guaranteed to provide an assessment of unidimensionality (Koufteros, 1999). Although all of the results were unfavorable, they were much better than the results of the four-factor model: multiskilling training (χ^2 = 23.49, df = 9, p < .01; GFI = .91, RMSEA = .14); teamwork (χ^2 = 24.49, df = 5, p < .005; GFI = .88, RMSEA = .22); improvement activities (χ^2 = 61.19, df = 14, p < .0001; GFI = .83, RMSEA = .21); and motivation (χ^2 = 9.10, df = 9, p < .45; GFI = .96, RMSEA = .01). Thus, I averaged the values for management practices for respective cases (i.e., production teams) by each of the four blocks. The correlations among the four blocks of HRM practices were all significant. As for all 24 indicators, the Cronbach's α was high at .91. Accordingly, I attempted to capture the whole effect of HRM practices using an additive, not a multiplicative, approach; I therefore aggregated and averaged all 24 question items' values. The additive approach is not only conceptually but also empirically better than the multiplicative because it does not reduce the index value to zero when a single HR practice is absent from an HRM system (Youndt et al., 1996).

Moderator variable

Manufacturing configuration was the moderator by which I attempted to explore whether and how much the second variable moderated relations between manufacturing performance and management practices. The managers were asked to assess the technological aspects of the cells or lines under their supervision not only in terms of their shape (i.e., layouts of machines on cells or lines) but also in terms of issues related to manufacturing strategies (i.e., lot size, varieties of product items or models, and frequency of change in production volume and product items). This assessment was made using five question items on a five-point Likert scale. I averaged the values of these five question items (Cronbach's α = .61) and used this average to capture manufacturing configuration. A manufacturing configuration with a greater value represents a manufacturing method closer to a manufacturing cell, while a manufacturing configuration with a lower value depicts a manufacturing method that is closer to a manufacturing line. To explore the interactive effect between the system of HRM practices and manufacturing configuration, the product term of these two variables was used in the models seeking to find the effect.

Control variables

I used three control variables expected to affect manufacturing activities in the models, and the controls were assessed on a five-point Likert scale by the managers. *Mizusumashi* was selected as the control variable to test hypotheses 1a, 1b, 2a, and 2b. As already explained in Chapter 3, *mizusumashi* replenishment workers are expected to correctly and promptly pick up a variety of parts components and supply them to production teams on time. Thus, they are supposed to be a key enabler in shortening lead time, thereby reducing work-in-process inventory, or vice versa. They typically belong to the replenishment section, not the assembly or production section. A higher value in *mizusumashi* means that the managers who participated in the survey felt more satisfied with the timely and appropriate supply of parts components or materials by *mizusumashi* replenishment workers. *Pokayoke* (meaning "mistake proof" in Japanese) was selected as the control variable for the quality models (to test hypotheses 3a and 3b). *Pokayoke* tools or equipment can prevent product defects in cells or lines and consequently enhance quality by taking such measures as halting wrong operations or activating an alarm if a minor human error occurs in a cell or line. Production operators could conceivably design and prepare *pokayoke* tools on their own, but in general, these tools are designed and set up by production engineers. A greater value in *pokayoke* means that participating managers felt more satisfied with their *pokayoke* mistake-proofing equipment and tools. Production volume was used as the control variable for the productivity models (to test hypotheses 4a and 4b). A higher value for production volume means that the current weekly-based production volume is larger than that of previous weeks.

In addition to the three control variables described previously, I used manufacturing performance measures as control variables because, as I suggested earlier, these are considered to be complementary with each other. I also used employees' attitudes toward manufacturing activities, which I refer to as line (or cell) culture, as a control variable. Employee attitudes or workplace cultures are known to affect work outcomes (Schein, 1985). Production workers' proactive attitude toward change, in particular, is needed to implement flexible production systems, such as the Toyota Production System (TPS), and to enhance manufacturing performance (Liker and Hoseus, 2008). Thus, I developed questionnaire items on workers' attitudes. Leaders were asked to respond to them on a five-point Likert scale. I averaged the values of these five questionnaire items (Cronbach's $\alpha = .75$) to produce the line culture index.

Results

To test the hypotheses, I carried out hierarchical moderated (interactive) regression analyses. I entered the controls in the first step and manufacturing configuration in the second step. The model in the first step was the baseline model for subsequent analyses. To examine the effect of the system of HRM practices, I entered the index in the third step. To test the interaction hypotheses and to estimate the interactive effect between system of HRM practices and manufacturing configuration, I entered their product term in the fourth and final step. The analyses were conducted for each of the dependent variables. In examining the interactive effect, I followed the advice of Cohen et al. (2003): that is, I mean-centered the predictors in such a way that both the independent variable of system of HRM practices and the moderator variable of manufacturing configuration were expressed in deviation form by subtracting their mean values from their original ones in order to avoid multicollinearity between the independent and moderator variables and their product term. The descriptive statistics, including means, standard deviations, correlations, and reliabilities, are presented in Table 5.2. Given that the sample size (77) was not large, I considered regression coefficients at a probability level of less than .1 significant.

Table 5.3 shows the regression results of testing hypotheses 1a and 1b. As model 3 shows, system of HRM practices was unrelated to work-in-process inventory ($\beta = 0.37$, n.s.). Consequently, I did not find support for Hypothesis 1a. As model 4 shows, as opposed to Hypothesis 1b, system of HRM practices and manufacturing configuration did not have an interactive effect on work-in-process inventory ($\beta = -0.36$, n.s.). Thus, I did not find support for Hypothesis 1b either.

Table 5.4 shows the regression results of testing hypotheses 2a and 2b. As model 3 shows, system of HRM practices had a significant effect on lead time, but the relation was negative ($\beta = -0.30$, $p < .05$). Thus, the results did not yield support for Hypothesis 2a. Nonetheless, model 4 indicates the presence of an interactive effect between system of HRM practices and manufacturing configuration ($\beta = 0.35$, $p < .01$). In order to increase an understanding of this interactive relation, I plotted the interactive effect with manufacturing configuration closer to a cell defined as a three standard deviation above the mean and manufacturing configuration closer to a line defined as a three standard deviation below the mean. This definition was meaningful for capturing a manufacturing configuration's resemblance to a real

Table 5.2 Means, standard deviations, correlations, and reliabilities[a]

Variables	Mean	s.d.	1	2	3	4	5	6	7	8	9	10
1. Production volume	2.96	1.07										
2. *Mizusumashi*	2.79	0.71	.14									
3. *Pokayoke*	2.92	0.68	−.04	.59**								
4. Line culture	3.12	0.57	−.03	.22+	.08	(.78)						
5. Manufacturing configuration	3.30	0.67	−.18	−.14	−.10	.08	(.61)					
6. Productivity	3.35	0.68	.27*	.40**	.46**	.01	−.31**	(.80)				
7. Work-in-process inventory	3.22	0.91	−.02	−.20+	−.23*	−.01	.32**	.11	(.83)			
8. Lead time	3.44	0.64	.34**	.33**	.29*	−.02	−.26*	.70**	.25*	(.83)		
9. Quality	3.34	0.68	.28*	.50**	.28*	.00	−.14	.37**	.07	.52**	(.75)	
10. System of HRM practices	3.13	0.55	.12	.22+	−.09	.73**	.13	−.01	.06	−.13	.03	(.91)

Notes:
[a] $n = 77$. Internal consistency reliability coefficients (Cronbach's α) appear on the diagonal.
+$p < .10$
*$p < .05$
**$p < .01$

Table 5.3   Results of regression analysis for work-in-process inventory[a]

Predictors	Model 1	Model 2	Model 3	Model 4
Constant	2.23** (0.82)	1.77* (0.76)	2.55** (0.92)	2.93** (0.95)
Mizusumashi	–0.45** (0.17)	–0.44** (0.15)	–0.45** (0.15)	–0.41* (0.15)
Lead time	0.47* (0.23)	0.51* (0.21)	0.59** (0.21)	0.67* (0.22)
Productivity	–0.01 (0.21)	0.11 (0.19)	0.08 (0.19)	–0.03 (0.21)
Quality	0.10 (0.18)	0.09 (0.17)	0.06 (0.17)	0.02 (0.17)
Line culture	0.11 (0.17)	0.05 (0.16)	–0.19 (0.23)	–0.26 (0.23)
Manufacturing configuration		0.55** (0.14)	0.52** (0.14)	0.53** (0.14)
System of HRM practices			0.37 (0.24)	0.42[+] (0.25)
System of HRM practices × manufacturing configuration				–0.36 (0.27)
ΔR^2		.15	.02	.02
F for ΔR^2		14.56**	2.21	1.80
R^2	.15	.30	.32	.34
Overall model F	2.66*	5.07**	4.74**	4.42**

Notes:

[a]n = 77. Values in parentheses are standard errors.

[+]$p < .10$

[*]$p < .05$

[**]$p < .01$

cell or to a conventional mass production line, although one deviation is conventionally used in providing such a definition (Cohen et al., 2003). Figure 5.1 shows that system of HRM practices has a positive relation with lead time when a manufacturing configuration closer to a cell is adopted, whereas this relation is negative when a manufacturing configuration closer to a line is adopted. Thus, Hypothesis 2b was supported.

Table 5.5 shows the regression results of testing hypotheses 3a and 3b. As model 3 shows, system of HRM practices had a positive effect on quality (β = 0.35, $p < .10$), which means that Hypothesis 3a was supported, although the effect was marginal. However, as opposed to Hypothesis 3b, model 4 shows no presence of a joint effect between system of HRM practices and manufacturing configuration (β = –0.23, n.s.). Thus, Hypothesis 3b was not supported.

Table 5.6 shows the regression results of testing hypotheses 4a and 4b. As model 3 shows, against the prediction of Hypothesis 4a, system of HRM practices did not have a positive effect on productivity

Table 5.4 Results of regression analysis for lead time[a]

Predictors	Model 1		Model 2		Model 3		Model 4	
Constant	0.41	(0.42)	0.42	(0.42)	–0.30	(0.50)	–0.70	(0.50)
Mizusumashi	0	(0.08)	0	(0.08)	0.02	(0.08)	0	(0.08)
Work-in-process inventory	0.11*	(0.05)	0.14*	(0.06)	0.16**	(0.05)	0.17**	(0.05)
Productivity	0.54**	(0.08)	0.50**	(0.08)	0.48**	(0.08)	0.54**	(0.08)
Quality	0.28**	(0.08)	0.27**	(0.08)	0.27**	(0.08)	0.28**	(0.08)
Line culture	–0.02	(0.08)	–0.01	(0.08)	0.18	(0.12)	0.24*	(0.11)
Manufacturing configuration			–0.11	(0.08)	–0.10	(0.08)	–0.11	(0.07)
System of HRM practices					–0.30*	(0.12)	–0.34**	(0.12)
System of HRM practices × manufacturing configuration							0.35**	(0.13)
ΔR^2			.02		.03		.03	
F for ΔR^2			1.93		5.58**		7.13**	
R^2	.58		.60		.63		.66	
Overall model F	20.40**		17.55**		19.92**		17.01**	

Notes:
[a]$n = 77$. Values in parentheses are standard errors.
$^{+}p < .10$
$^{*}p < .05$
$^{**}p < .01$

($\beta = 0.20$, n.s.). Thus, Hypothesis 4a was not supported. As model 4 indicates, system of HRM practices and manufacturing configuration had a statistically significant interactive effect on productivity ($\beta = -0.53$, $p < .01$), but the product term had a negative sign as opposed to the positive sign predicted by Hypothesis 4b. I depict the interaction in Figure 5.2, with manufacturing configuration defined in the same way that I did earlier. The figure reveals that system of HRM practices is positively related to productivity when a manufacturing configuration closer to a line is used but negatively related to productivity when the manufacturing configuration employed is more similar to a cell. According to this result of the regression analysis, the capabilities and skills of operators can be utilized better on lines rather than in cells. In this sense, and contrary to the widely held belief, the manufacturing configuration that is dependent on people is not a cell but a line, at least in this productivity model.

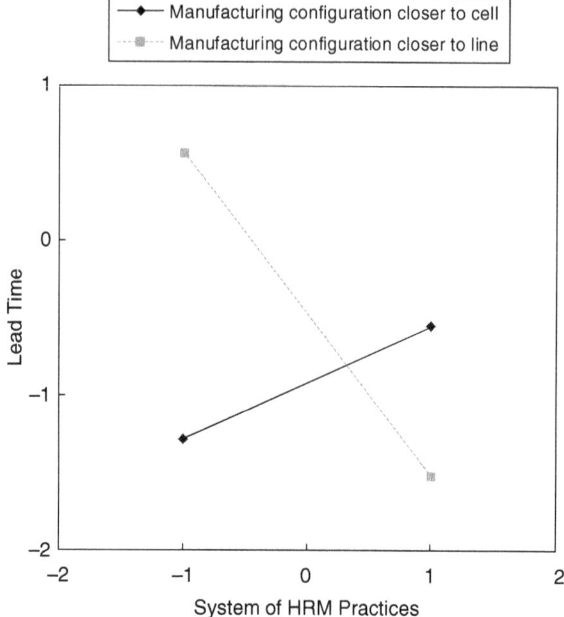

Figure 5.1 The relation between system of HRM practices and lead time as a function of manufacturing configuration

Discussion

Most of the hypotheses, except for Hypothesis 2b and Hypothesis 3a, were not supported, and the results seem to be somewhat discouraging. By taking stock of the results, however, I might be able to gain deep insights into the relations between management practices and manufacturing performance and to present a new point of view in the SHRM literature. I therefore conducted additional analyses. I even conducted follow-up research by visiting some of the companies that had participated in the survey and interviewing questionnaire respondents and other people in charge of HRM and manufacturing. I interpret and discuss the results based on these efforts further.

First, I interpret the results for the work-in-process inventory models. System of HRM practices had neither an additive effect nor an interactive effect with manufacturing configuration on work-in-process inventory. To further examine the relations between HRM practices and work-in-process inventory, I performed additional analyses by "unbundling"

Table 5.5   Results of regression analysis for quality[a]

Predictors	Model 1		Model 2		Model 3		Model 4	
Constant	1.29*	(0.60)	1.29*	(0.60)	1.95**	(0.63)	2.21**	(0.72)
Pokayoke	0.14	(0.11)	0.14	(0.12)	0.20	(0.12)	0.19	(0.12)
Work-in-process inventory	−0.01	(0.08)	−0.01	(0.09)	−0.02	(0.09)	−0.04	(0.09)
Productivity	−0.05	(0.15)	−0.05	(0.15)	−0.12	(0.15)	−0.18	(0.16)
Lead time	0.54**	(0.15)	0.54**	(0.15)	0.61**	(0.15)	0.66**	(0.16)
Line culture	−0.01	(0.12)	−0.01	(0.12)	−0.26	(0.17)	−0.30	(0.18)
Manufacturing configuration			0	(0.12)	−0.02	(0.12)	0	(0.12)
System of HRM practices					0.35+	(0.19)	0.39*	(0.19)
System of HRM practices × manufacturing configuration							−0.23	(0.20)
Δ R^2			0		.04		.01	
F for Δ R^2			0		3.53+		1.29	
R^2	.28		.28		.32		.33	
Overall model F	5.68**		4.66**		4.64**		4.24**	

Notes:
[a]$n = 77$. Values in parentheses are standard errors.
+$p < .10$
*$p < .05$
**$p < .01$

system of HRM practices and designating manufacturing configuration as a mediator, not a moderator. Specifically, I explored whether there were indirect effects of parts of the HRM system (namely, multiskilling training, teamwork, improvement activities, and motivation) on work-in-process inventory and whether those effects occurred via manufacturing configuration. I did so because manufacturing configuration had a significantly positive effect on work-in-process inventory across all models (as seen in model 2 through model 4 in Table 5.3) and it also had a positive co-relation with multiskilling training, described as the averaged value of six questionnaire items on that type of training (the result is not shown in this book). First, I regressed manufacturing configuration on each part of system of HRM practices (i.e., each of the four blocks of HRM practices)—among them multiskilling training—simultaneously. The results showed that only the regression coefficient of multiskilling training was significant ($\beta = 0.38$, $p < .05$). Second, to recheck the results, I obtained the partial correlation coefficients of those predictor variables

Table 5.6   Results of regression analysis for productivity[a]

Predictors	Model 1		Model 2		Model 3		Model 4	
Constant	0.79	(0.49)	0.79	(0.43)	1.25*	(0.61)	1.61**	(0.58)
Production volume	0.01	(0.05)	0.01	(0.05)	0	(0.06)	0.03	(0.05)
Lead time	0.73**	(0.11)	0.68**	(0.11)	0.73**	(0.12)	0.74*	(0.11)
Work-in-process inventory	–0.04	(0.06)	0	(0.07)	–0.02	(0.07)	–0.05	(0.06)
Quality	0	(0.09)	0	(0.09)	0	(0.09)	–0.05	(0.09)
Line culture	0.03	(0.10)	0.04	(0.10)	–0.09	(0.15)	–0.16	(0.14)
Manufacturing configuration			–0.13	(0.09)	–0.14	(0.09)	–0.08	(0.09)
System of HRM practices					0.20	(0.16)	0.24	(0.15)
System of HRM practices × manufacturing configuration							–0.53**	(0.15)
ΔR^2			.01		.01		.07	
F for ΔR^2			2.03		1.50		11.65**	
R^2	.49		.50		.51		.58	
Overall model F	13.67**		11.89**		10.48**		12.40**	

Notes:
[a]$n = 77$. Values in parentheses are standard errors.
[+]$p < .10$
[*]$p < .05$
[**]$p < .01$

with manufacturing configuration. Again, only the partial correlation coefficient of multiskilling training was significant ($pr = .25$, $p < .05$). Third, I regressed work-in-process inventory on multiskilling training, adjusting for other variables, that is, the control variables, manufacturing configuration, and parts of the HRM system other than multiskilling training. The result showed that multiskilling training was not directly related to work-in-process inventory, which indicates that multiskilling training has an entirely indirect effect on work-in-process inventory via manufacturing configuration (Cohen et al., 2003). However, this is just a limited way to examine the indirect effect. In order to examine the indirect effect or a mediating role of manufacturing configuration more rigorously, other methods, for example, the procedure provided by Baron and Kenny (1986), are needed to confirm the indirect effect. Furthermore, theoretical foundations are needed to empirically test the indirect effect. Nevertheless, based on my experience at field sites,

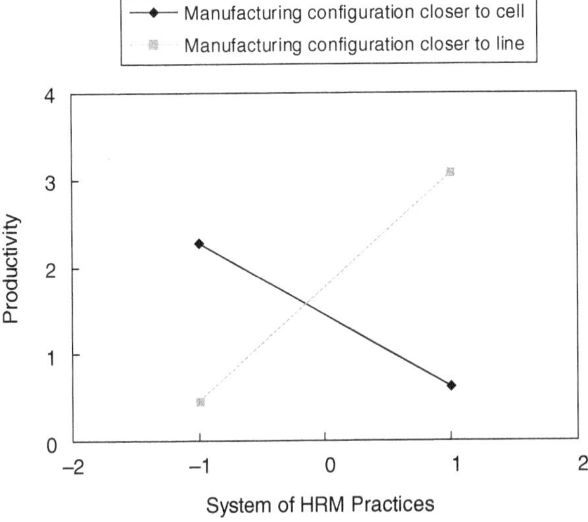

Figure 5.2 The relation between system of HRM practices and productivity as a function of manufacturing configuration

I believe that manufacturing configuration could also serve as a mediator through which multiskilling training affects work-in-process inventory.

Second, I consider the results for the lead time models. System of HRM practices was related to reduction in lead time, but the relation was negative, which means that less use of a system of HRM practices can shorten lead time. I learned one way to shorten lead time from my follow-up research: by limiting work processes assigned to operators while shortening a cycle or "takt" (meaning "bar" or "beat" in German) time, a period within which each operator is supposed to perform a certain work task. This method seems to be old-fashioned management with an emphasis on division of labor and may fit long assembly lines better than cells. Although HRM system did not have a direct and positive effect on lead time, it did interact with manufacturing configuration. The relation between system of HRM practices and lead time was positive when a manufacturing configuration closer to a cell was employed and negative when a manufacturing configuration closer to a line was adopted. This may prove that managing workers whose work tasks are limited according to takt time in order to shorten lead time does fit manufacturing lines rather than cells.

Third, I interpret the quality model results. As hypothesized, the use of system of HRM practices caused a high standard of quality, but it did not have an interactive effect along with manufacturing configuration. This means that whatever manufacturing configurations are employed, HRM practices are likely to affect quality outcomes. That is, the result supports only the universalistic perspective that a system of HRM practices can improve quality despite the manufacturing configurations adopted or irrespective of whether cells or lines are used. The manufacturing configurations employed do not affect the relations between management practices and quality. Indeed, when I asked a production manager about quality while visiting an electronic device manufacturer for follow-up research, he replied, "In terms of quality, it does not matter whether cells or lines are adopted." This comment reflects the previous result.

Finally, I consider the results of the productivity models. System of HRM practices did not have an additive or direct effect on productivity. As the production manager mentioned before put it, "In the stage of designing products, engineers devise products that are easy for operators to assemble;" engineers can design products in such a way that every worker, whether skillful or not, can assemble products with few difficulties. Consequently, even unskilled and nonregular workers can be assigned to lines or cells after receiving a few days' training. They become more productive as they perform less complicated work tasks. Engineers and production managers are more involved in production process nowadays than they were before, and they thus can increase productivity and other performance measures.

Although system of HRM practices did not have an additive effect, along with manufacturing configuration, it had an interactive effect on productivity. However, this effect was negative, contrary to the prediction of Hypothesis 4b. As long as productivity was the performance indicator selected, the manufacturing configuration that was actually dependent on people was not manufacturing cells but rather lines. This result indicates that the activities and skills of line operators were not as mediocre as I had supposed. At a PC plant I visited in the autumn of 2007 for follow-up research, assembly cells—which had been the dominant manufacturing configuration when I visited the plant for case study research in 2004—had been replaced by assembly lines, which again became the standard manufacturing method at the plant just as it had been before the introduction of cell production in 1997. However, the assembly lines that were reintroduced were not just long lines that used conveyor belts; they were operated on the principles of just in time (JIT). Workers, especially line leaders, were required to acquire a higher level of problem-solving skills and to be more committed to work tasks than they had been when assembly cells had been dominant at the plant. As a result, productivity had improved. It may be that a system of

HRM practices is likely to raise productivity when used in tandem with assembly lines that are driven by JIT principles.

Theoretical and practical implications

These results have both theoretically and practically significant implications. First, they imply that the relationships between HRM practices and manufacturing performance are not straightforward and may even be tenuous. This is because direct, moderated relations differ depending on the manufacturing performance indicators selected; they are also generally weak. This situation is the case even when these linkages are close compared to the distant relations between HRM practices and company performance. It has been said that the linkages between HRM practices and a company's performance remain a "black box," even though many SHRM scholars have endeavored to explore these relations (Gerhart, 2005; Becker and Huselid, 2006). In order to unpack the black box and increase our understanding of those linkages, it is crucial, as Becker and Huselid (2006) argued, to examine the relationships between HRM practices and the direct, or at least proximal, outcomes that will, in turn, translate into company-level performance (e.g., net profit, ROE). However, the results of my survey research indicate that these close relations between HRM practices and manufacturing performance are not straightforward, and may even be tenuous, despite their proximity; in fact, their linkages may be more complex than they appear to be.

Second, the results imply the limits of HR's strategic impact (Becker and Huselid, 2006). System of HRM practices was associated with quality and had a positive interactive effect on lead time. However, system of HRM practices or its product term with manufacturing configuration did not affect all manufacturing performance measures. The results imply that the impact of HRM practices may be not as strong as I—and other SHRM scholars—expected. These results should encourage those scholars (e.g., Cappelli and Neumark, 2001) who question the impact of HRM practices on performance to be even more skeptical of it. These results notwithstanding, HRM practices had something to do with manufacturing performance, as seen not only in the results for the supported hypotheses but also in the results for the unsupported productivity hypothesis, which found that use of management practices mattered more in a mass production environment than in a cell production environment. As discussed later, HRM still matters, particularly for manufacturing companies and their managers.

Third, the results should make management practitioners, particularly in the manufacturing sector across countries, aware of, or make them reconsider, the importance of managing people. Managers in manufacturing companies, especially those in charge of manufacturing operations, sometimes overstress the technological aspects of manufacturing systems and overlook the human and HRM aspects. The results suggest that these managers should pay more attention to HRM issues if they want to improve manufacturing performance; for instance, this research found that system of HRM practices and manufacturing configuration combined to create a synergistic effect on lead time. Many manufacturers, both US and Japanese, have transferred manufacturing functions to overseas facilities located in countries with low labor costs (O'Toole and Lawler, 2007), where they engage in mass production operations. If managers working for these manufacturers hope to continue production at home, they will need to make both HRM practices and manufacturing techniques more sophisticated. This research could help managers who are struggling to improve their manufacturing competitiveness.

Limitations and future directions

Although this research has provided some findings on the relationships between HRM practices and manufacturing performance, it has some limitations. First, this research was conducted in the context of Japanese manufacturing sites and excluded other national and cultural contexts. It is well known that Japanese workers are culturally collectivist and that Japanese companies are characterized by an internal labor market (Dore, 1973). Japanese electronics manufacturers are currently introducing and operating cell production even in countries overseas such as China. I have suggested the limits of HR's strategic impact, but these statements may have to undergo change as a result of using data from overseas as well as from Japan and performing the analyses again using this research framework. Second, I used the same single measurement approach in this research and, as a consequence, I may not have obtained robust results. If I had used additional methods, I may have obtained different results. To obtain robust results and consistent findings, I will also need to adopt multiple measurement approaches and improve this research. Third, the sample size used to perform the statistical analyses described in this chapter was small. Thus, I may not have found support for several of the hypotheses I proposed. Therefore, I could develop this research by enlarging the sample size. I had to improve this research keeping these limitations in mind: this was my next endeavor.

Part II
Transforming Workforce and Organizational Cultures of Japanese Companies

6
Japanese Firms' Workforce and Cultures in Transition

Introduction

Organizational culture is bound to an organization, and is even more tenacious than organizational structures, strategies, management practices, and other organizational phenomena. The reasons for this are that organizational members are affectively committed to their organizational culture, and that people consider getting their work done at their workplaces as customary. If a person attempts to change a traditionally accepted way of work bolstered by organizational culture, other members will endeavor to prevent such an attempt. Another reason for this is that organizational culture is largely affected by and closely associated with the national culture in which organizations are embedded, which is more stable and slower to change than organizational culture. Due to the tenacity of organizational culture, organizational cultures of Japanese companies are expected to not have considerably changed over the past two decades since the collapse of the Japanese bubble economy in the early 1990s, not to mention over the decade or so since the turn of the century, the focal period of this book.

Organizational culture by definition is more stable than other organizational phenomena, such as organizational structures and business strategies, but it is less stable than national culture. Indeed, recently, some parts of organizational culture in Japanese companies have been gradually transforming, as I demonstrate in this chapter. Thus, herein I explore these cultural transformations from the perspective of cultural diversity, that is, the extent to which an organization is heterogeneous as a result of the presence of subcultures. Diversity is one of the extensively discussed issues these days in the area of management studies. However, although this new management topic has been discussed by corporate executives, journalists, and scholars extensively and intensively in the Western Hemisphere, Japan and other Asian countries have not engaged in such analysis.

Is diversity the new landscape of Japanese workplaces?

In their book that sought to explore new American workplaces, O'Toole and Lawler (2007) stated that diversity is the new corporate landscape. This statement underscores the fact that the workforce within a country or company has become more diverse than before in terms of gender, nationality, race, religion, and sexual orientation. I identify this situation as "workforce diversity." Furthermore, and more importantly, from the perspective of both management theorists and practitioners, diversity at work is considered a source of competitive advantage (Cox, 1993). Thus, it affects net profits and bottom lines (Jayne and Dipboye, 2004; Svyantek and Bott, 2004).

In recent years, I have had opportunities to attend conferences and meetings where globally renowned chief executive officers (CEOs) have spoken about their companies' management philosophies and policies as well as the current challenges facing their companies, such as globalization and environmental sustainability. I was particularly impressed by their emphasis on diversity or heterogeneity among the challenges while playing down conformity or homogeneity. For instance, A. G. Lafley, CEO of Procter & Gamble (P&G) Co., spoke about the importance of diversity and how the US consumer-products giant achieved diversity (Lafley, 2007). He stated that around 40 percent of leaders in the corporation were from outside the US and that 35 of the top executives hailed from a dozen countries such as Tanzania and Portugal. Nearly 40 percent of the P&G managers were women, and one of them was president of P&G's business in Greater China. Furthermore, the CEO stated that P&G's diverse organization, in terms of not only ethnicity and gender but also career experiences, leadership styles, and thinking styles, was more capable of understanding consumers from all walks of life than demographically and culturally homogeneous organizations would be. P&G is just one example of many US and Western companies that have become diverse. The statement given by O'Toole and Lawler (2007) that diversity is the new corporate landscape suggests that Western workplaces have become more diverse than ever before and that diversity has become a business standard or norm for many Western companies.

Given that diversity is the new corporate landscape in the Western Hemisphere, what is diversity inside Japanese companies? Homogeneity traditionally prevails over heterogeneity in Japanese business contexts. Japanese companies are traditionally well known for their culturally homogeneous organizations or strong culture, which has been considered to be a source of their strength (Deal and Kennedy, 1982). However, among Japanese businesses, there is a growing, but slow trend, compared with that of their Western counterparts, toward workforce diversity, as Japanese workplaces are becoming diverse in terms of nationality, career, gender, age, and disability. Thus, Japan's corporations and their top managers have stressed diversity in recent years, even though the number of Japanese companies that value diversity is far fewer than that of their Western counterparts.

Nissan Motor Co., best known as Nissan, is among the small number of diversity-oriented Japanese companies. Carlos Ghosn, CEO of Japan's second largest automobile company, prioritizes diversity as one of the managerial challenges. His philosophy is reflected in one of Nissan's principles, diversity. Nissan was on the verge of bankruptcy in the late 1990s, and like other Japanese companies struggled to survive the financial woes that followed the collapse of the Japanese bubble economy. However, only two years after the charismatic Carlos Ghosn took over the automotive manufacturer's top position in 1999, Nissan regained competitiveness and emerged from near-bankruptcy, and posted a substantial operating profit of $2.3 billion. This is how Nissan achieved a "V-shaped recovery." One innovation that Ghosn introduced to restore competitiveness and boost the V-shaped recovery was creating cross-functional teams involving talented young people from different functions, such as marketing, procurement, manufacturing, and planning, and striving to solve problems more effectively. The people in the cross-functional teams were heterogeneous in terms of not only their job backgrounds but also their nationalities. Moreover, Nissan achieved diversity by increasing the number of not only general female employees but also female managers. Such effort is rare in a Japanese business context, where male employees traditionally dominate Japanese workplaces, particularly managerial positions.

I had the opportunity to attend a meeting where Okuda Hiroshi, the former CEO of Toyota Motor Corp., Japan's and the world's largest automobile company (when I was writing this chapter) and Nissan's rival Japanese car manufacturer, spoke about his management philosophy. He mentioned that homogeneity or similarity was no longer a source of competitive strength, and therefore, Toyota took advantage of diversity. He went on to state that, while nurturing diversity, his company had to overcome its negative consequences, for instance, loss of social solidarity built on homogeneity, by making Toyota employees world-wide share its corporate culture.

Against this backdrop of a burgeoning trend of homogeneous Japanese companies transforming into heterogeneous ones and the lack of research on the new Japanese business landscape, in this chapter, I attempt to explore the workforce diversity within Japanese companies. I develop concepts and theories built on literature about organizational culture. Specifically, I treat workforce diversity as a proxy of cultural diversity, although workforce diversity is not exactly cultural diversity. Furthermore, I attempt to explore not only the situation of workforce or cultural diversity but also the causes of the phenomenon and its effects on organizations. Therefore, apart from examining Japanese companies and their workforce diversity and organizational culture, I attempt to demonstrate a new framework to study diversity issues by drawing on the organizational culture literature.

Theories on organizational culture

Strong culture and the single-culture perspective

Organizational culture emerges and develops as organizational members interact and cooperate with each other. There are various definitions of this organizational phenomenon: meanings, interpretations, or frames of reference shared by organizational members; "a pattern of basic assumptions" (Schein, 1985) that lies beneath, and affects, not only behaviors but also values of organizational members. The phenomenon can be described in more than one way: for example, organizational culture as an invisible or intangible structure as opposed to an organizational structure as a visible or tangible structure. No consensus seems to have been reached on the definition of organizational culture. Despite the lack of a consensus on its definition, by "organizational culture," I mean a general term that embraces any concept scholars in the category define as organizational culture, including beliefs, values, norms, attitudes, meanings, customs, assumptions, and other aspects of organizational life that are shared by people working together and distinguish focused organizations from others. So how does organizational culture work? For instance, when interpreting or understanding events or information in organizations, people are affected by organizational culture (Weick, 1996).

In the early 1980s, when organizational or corporate culture emerged as a new, popular theme in management research, scholars seemed to assume that it represented strong culture, a term forged by the pioneering scholars in the field, Deal and Kennedy (1982). Strong culture is one shared by all or most people in an organization. It is synonymous with what Frost et al. (1985) called "homogeneous culture," "dominant culture," "organization-wide culture," and the like. This nomenclature indicates that organizational culture is a single culture, a monolithic organizational phenomenon. Because such a single or strong culture is shared by the majority of organizational members, it expresses an organization's core value.

The perspective in the literature about organizational culture that views it as a strong or single culture is called the integration or single-culture perspective, as noted by Martin (2002), one of the outstanding scholars in the area. According to this perspective, an organization is characterized by a strong culture wherein a single core value is dominant and organizational members are integrated underneath the umbrella of that value. Because a strong culture eliminates values not in accordance with the core value, the concept of strong culture is interchangeable with that of homogeneous culture.

High performance is attributable to a strong culture, and there are some reasons for that relationship (Kotter and Heskett, 1992). Organizational members are committed to organizational goals because personal goals can be identified with organizational ones in the context of a strong culture. A strong culture motivates people to work harder, for instance, because they simply like that culture. Even if there is no bureaucratic control, those who work in an environment of strong culture can act autonomously and work independently because they know their company's goal very well and even share implicit and tacit meanings of everyday operations with each other. Consequently, overhead costs can be reduced. From the standpoint of organizational performance, a strong or homogeneous culture is expected to affect organizational efficiency—the ratio of output to input—as an aspect of organizational performance elaborated on by Kast and Rosenzweig (1985). That is because (1) people affected by strong culture work passionately and generate a high standard of productivity; (2) it takes less monitoring and overhead costs to run an organization by means of strong culture than by bureaucracy; (3) a company with highly committed employees owing to a strong culture can build strong unity among the employees, thereby maintaining a low rate of labor turnover and absenteeism; and (4) accordingly, a company characterized by strong culture can recoup investments in educating and developing the people working there.

Subculture and the multicultural perspective

In addition to the integration or single-culture perspective illuminated before, there is another perspective in the literature about organizational culture: the differentiation or multicultural perspective (Martin, 2002). To what extent organizational culture is shared by people in an organization differs depending on organizations; at some organizations, culture is shared by a large number of organizational members, while at others it is not. This fact suggests that organizational culture is not a monolithic organizational phenomenon and that there are cultural fault lines within organizations. The culture shared by a specific group of people in an organization is a subculture in the organization or an organizational subculture. Caution should be exercised when understanding the meaning of subculture. A subculture is not an antonym of a "superior" or "superordinate" culture suggesting an organizational culture at the higher level of an organization. Rather, it is opposite to a dominant culture or organization-wide culture; thus, the culture of an administrative division is a subculture from the perspective of an organization-wide culture. The construct of subculture suggests that it is part of the company-wide culture. An organization's cultural diversity represents the extent to which the organization is heterogeneous as a result of the presence of subcultures. Some organizations can be characterized by greater cultural diversity than others. Organizations with a strong or homogeneous culture would have a lower level of cultural diversity, whereas organizations with many, heterogeneous subcultures would maintain a higher level of cultural diversity.

The bases on which organizational subcultures are formed include organizational structure, technology, products, organizational layers, tenure, and labor unions (Schein, 1985). These could be categorized as within-organization bases. Subcultures formed on these bases are unique to the organization and are "organizational," in that they are literally organizational subcultures. Meanwhile, some subcultures stem from outside organizations; the bases that facilitate the formation of such subcultures could be categorized as outside-organization ones, and they include occupations, professions, gender, ages, education, nationality, races, and religions (Sackman, 1997; Martin, 2002). Subcultures formed on outside-organization bases are shared among people not only within a given organization but also across several organizations; in that sense, such subcultures are trans-organizational. For example, professional cultures are shared among professionals such as engineers, computer programmers, accountants, and lawyers across organizations (Bloor and Dawson, 1994). Thus, precisely speaking, subcultures stemming from outside organizations are not organizational subcultures but "[sub] cultures in organizations" (Martin, 2002: 164–165).

Subcultures can be nested or structured inside an organization- or company-wide culture. Organizational subcultures can also cross each other. For example, consider a company's manufacturing department that consists of two sections, assembly and press. The cultures of the sections are nested within the higher level or the "parent" culture, that is, the culture of the manufacturing department, and hence can be regarded as subcultures inside the manufacturing culture. However, from the perspective of the corporate culture, or the company-wide culture, the manufacturing department's culture can also be seen as a subculture in tandem with the cultures of other departments of the same company (e.g., sales). The department-based cultures can be considered to be beneath the higher-level culture, in this case, the managerial culture held by top management. This suggests that there are hierarchy-based cultures inside the hypothetical organization. This culture at the top of organizations is also a subculture in terms of the corporate culture. Therefore, department-, section-, and hierarchy-based cultures can be regarded as subcultures and structured within the corporate culture. Such subcultures as religious beliefs can be shared horizontally across an organization's departments and vertically across its hierarchy.

In a nutshell, in addition to homogenous or dominant culture, there exist various subcultures in organizations. Thus, according to the multicultural perspective, organizations can be seen as "a nexus where a variety of cultural influences come together within a boundary" (Martin, 1992: 111). Paraphrasing the expression, one could describe an organization's cultural situation as a "nexus of subcultures."

Organizational subcultures exercise their effects and influence the dominant culture of a given organization (Martin, 1992). If subcultures support, complement, or enhance the dominant culture, they are called "enhancing subcultures." As members of enhancing subcultures assimilate into the dominant culture, the two kinds of cultures are barely different from each other by nature. On the contrary, if subcultures run counter to the values and beliefs shared and supported by the majority of people in an organization, namely, the dominant culture, they are called "countercultures." Naturally, countercultures are different in character from the dominant culture. Some subcultures are neutral and neither support nor resist the dominant culture. From a different angle, they can be viewed to be indifferent to the dominant culture. Such subcultures are called "orthogonal subcultures" in the sense that the subcultures go in neither the same direction nor the opposite direction of the core values of the organization.

On one hand, because countercultures oppose the dominant culture, they are likely to reduce the effect of a strong or homogeneous culture, that is, organizational efficiency. On the other hand, countercultures provide a counterbalance to a strong culture in which organizational members are blind to the environment around the organization and cannot change strategies; in other words, they are trapped into "strategic myopia" (Lorsch, 1986). Figuratively speaking with the metaphor provided by Pascale (1990), when a strong culture sometimes swings the pendulum, that is, the organization's decision making and activities to an extreme pole, countercultures allow the pendulum to swing back to the opposite pole. In such a way, organizational subcultures, particularly countercultures, can strike a new balance and enhance organizational adaptability, another aspect of organizational performance proposed by Kast and Rosenzweig (1985): the ability of an organization to adapt to its surrounding environment. This is the crucial effect of subcultures on organizations. It is expected that the greater the cultural diversity, the more likely it is that organizational adaptability can be achieved.

Another rationale behind the power of cultural diversity to allow organizations to be innovative and adaptive is that the diverse knowledge or perspectives stemming from various subcultures can combine to enrich the knowledge base and create new knowledge within the organizations (Nonaka, Toyama, and Hirata, 2008), ultimately leading to an improvement in net profits and profitability. More specifically, those who constitute subcultures are likely to bring new perspectives, insights, practices, leadership styles, knowledge, and so forth into their company. This would be more likely to take place when a larger number of such diverse people are hired and, furthermore, allowed to assume managerial positions.

Employment systems and organizational culture

Japan's traditional management system and strong culture

While the consequences or outcomes of cultural diversity in organizations have been earnestly argued, their antecedents or causes have not received so much attention, although it has been suggested that increased globalization, a changing labor market (e.g., a massive influx of immigrants into the labor market), and legislation (e.g., affirmative action) have impacted cultural diversity in organizations (Cox, 1993). A mix of these environmental factors surrounding companies can affect cultural situations within them and promote or impede their cultural diversity. From the perspective of management theorists and practitioners, however, it would be more important to focus on and explore effects of managerial factors, by which companies and their managers can directly affect cultural diversity, rather than those of environmental factors on the formation and development of cultural diversity. Thus, in this section, I attempt to explore what cultural diversity inside Japanese companies looks like and how it is affected by management practices or employment systems.

Three decades ago, when Western managers had little knowledge of how the Japanese managed their companies, Ouchi (1981) studied Japanese management and companies in his best-selling book *Theory Z*. In the book, he presented his ideas on how management or employment systems can affect organizational culture. He conceptualized different types of organizations that might originate in different national cultures: Type J organizations, epitomized by Japanese companies; Type A organizations, evident in American companies; and Type Z organizations, which have characteristics of both Type J and A organizations. At the time when Ouchi published his book, IBM Corp. and Hewlett-Packard Co. were examples of Type Z eclectic organizations. He asserted that Type J and Z organizations possess the organization-oriented employment system, as proposed by Jacoby (2005), in which a strong culture is more likely to be formed than inside Type A organizations. In such organizations or companies, high job security for the employees over a long period is guaranteed—from the time of joining the company through reaching retirement age. In return for job security, employees dedicate their efforts to the company and its goals. The employees whose jobs are guaranteed are evaluated, and their career growth along the organizational ladder is ensured, according to their tenure or seniority. Their positions or status are promoted and pay levels increased in proportion to their tenure with the current employer. Since the tenure is proportional to age, there is no significant difference in payment and status within the organization between employees of approximately the same age. Furthermore, there is little difference in payment even between top management and general employees. Therefore, this type of organizations tends to dislike such distinction between employees and instead value egalitarianism. The employees not only master skills specific to the organization where they are destined to commit their entire working lives but also respond to conforming pressure to assimilate the values and beliefs of the organization. If they did not function in this manner, they would be ostracized by their colleagues. This accelerates their absorption of their company's value. Naturally, the employment system driven by organization-based principles can help to develop organizational culture and enable sharing the culture by people throughout the organization. The organizational culture is a strong or homogeneous culture, which constitutes the organization's competitive strength (Deal and Kennedy, 1982).

Thus, the cultural situation inside traditional Japanese companies can be characterized by the homogenization of the workforce and organizational culture. Managerial positions are occupied by male employees with long tenure in the companies, and therefore share the organization's core value with their colleagues. Similar backgrounds shared by people working together in the company can cause and accelerate the homogenization of the workforce and organizational culture. The employees usually have the same national origin, and this similarity helps to further homogenize Japanese companies' organizational culture. Importantly, the employees and their attributes can largely affect the organization's core value in such a way that the employees personify the culture of the old generation, masculine or male culture, such as proposed by Hofstede (1980), and ethnocentric culture. The organization's core value(s) affected by the majority of employees in turn can likely become its mainstream and dominant culture throughout the organization. Figure 6.1 illustrates the traditional cultural situation in Japanese companies.

This cultural situation can allow the development of a strong culture and appears to be desirable for companies. However, it might cause backlash. That is, even if the managers and management teams who

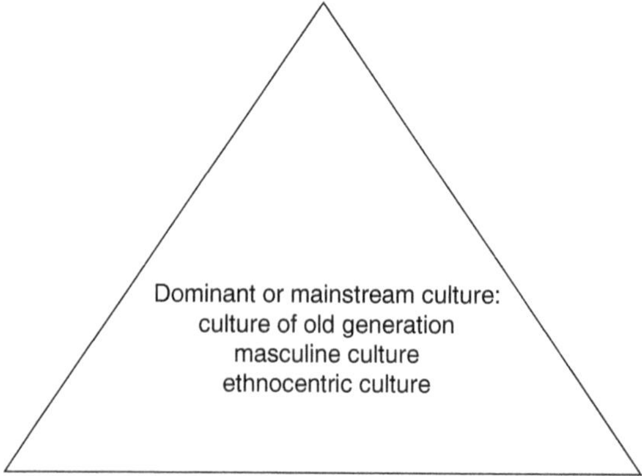

Figure 6.1   The traditional cultural situation inside Japanese companies

work in monolithic and homogeneous cultures strive to formulate new strategies and deliver new products, they may not be able to conceive innovative or breakthrough ideas in the homogeneous working environment.

Japan's emerging management system and cultural diversity

Traditionally, Japanese enterprises have utilized systems such as the seniority system, lifetime employment, job rotation, and on-the-job training. The employment system in Japanese organizations still remains much more organization oriented than that in their US counterparts. Yet, in recent years, they have emulated some of the management practices of US companies, for example, by instituting a performance-based pay policy and outsourcing the workforce because of pressure from investors and intense global competition or simply because it is a "fad" (Cappelli, 1999; Jacoby, 2005). Consequently, Japanese companies are said to be progressing in the opposite end on the continuum of employment system; that is, they are tending toward a market-oriented system these days (Jacoby, 2005).

Corporations that have replaced a traditional organization-oriented employment system with a market-oriented one no longer have a "psychological contract" between employers and employees, an implicit expectation between them that, while employers guarantee employees' job security in return for contributions the employees have made toward achievement of the companies' goals, the employees will continue to be loyal or committed to the companies as long as the employers ensure the security of the employees' jobs (Cappelli, 1999). In corporations that have adopted a market-oriented employment system, employers make little investment in educating and training people to acquire the skills necessary to perform their jobs. Rather, they prefer to outsource the workforce, for instance, to personnel agencies, so that they can respond to fluctuations in product or service demands or because they simply want to avoid costs of having regular workers, such as health insurance and other benefits. The employees are evaluated not on the basis of seniority but on their abilities or capabilities to perform their assigned work tasks, and their capabilities and abilities are benchmarked against those outside the company or on the labor market. The employers cannot, or do not intend to, guarantee their employees' jobs and future. Meanwhile, the employees do not intend to continue their careers till the retirement age at a single corporation; they wish to increase their value in the labor market, that is, "employability," by honing their skills by themselves. Often, they are ready to leave their corporations and shift to others that provide more attractive jobs and opportunities. The company itself recommends that employees enhance their employability and live without any dependence on the company. It is not a shared value or corporate culture but an explicit contract that unites people in such corporations under the market-oriented employment system. A strong culture is difficult to develop under such a system.

Unlike companies under an organization-oriented employment system, where people with similar demographics, careers, and backgrounds work together, at companies driven by a market-oriented employment system, people with varied backgrounds come together. However, is it possible that various organizational subcultures emerge and develop at such companies? People with different backgrounds might not always work together and interact at the same section or workplace. However, they could bring new values, insights, leadership styles, philosophy, and the like to the current companies, which are different from or even opposed to their companies' cultures. These new values can cause a "chemical reaction" in the corporate culture and spawn subcultures within the company. They might strike a chord with a group of employees and be accepted by them, which causes the formation of a subculture within the company. In any event, a market-oriented employment system is more likely to cause diversity at work and cultural diversity than an employment system driven by organization principles.

Figure 6.2 represents an emerging cultural situation inside Japanese firms as a result of their adopting market-oriented management practices. I elaborate on such a situation in a hypothetical company by focusing on the administrative organization, not the operative organization. The company's CEO has been recently recruited to hold his current position. The CEO is not bound to the company's status quo or culture, and thus has begun to replace organization-oriented management practices with market-oriented ones. He has promoted talented employees to higher ranks in the organization, irrespective of their ages or tenure, such as managerial positions that used to be occupied by older male employees with the same national origin. Old generations, and masculine and ethnocentric cultures used to be the dominant and mainstream culture in the company, as seen in Figure 6.1.

Now, younger people who have spent only three to five years or less with the corporation, female employees, non-Japanese employees, and job hoppers have begun to occupy managerial positions and constitute the company's administrative organization. These newcomers have brought new values and ways of thinking into the company. They have begun to spawn new cultures in the company, that is, youth culture,

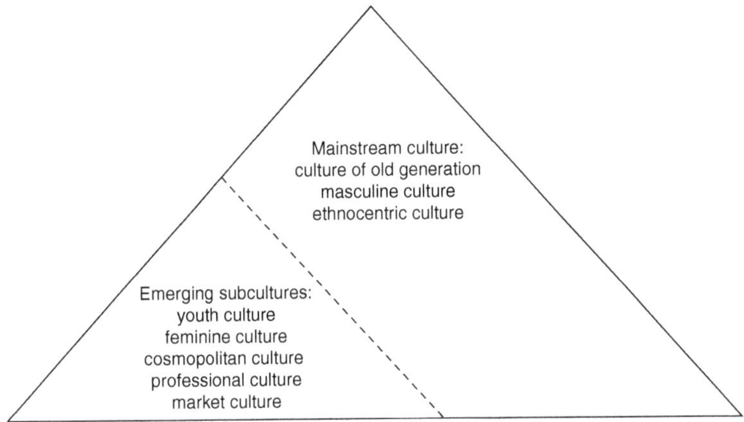

Figure 6.2   An emerging cultural situation inside Japanese companies
Notes: Cultural boundary is represented by the dotted line.

feminine or female culture, cosmopolitan culture brought by non-Japanese employees with global views, and market and professional culture introduced by job hoppers. Kerr and Slocum (1987) elaborated on the concept of market culture. Consequently, the old generation, and masculine and ethnocentric cultures might still remain the mainstream cultures in the company, but they are no longer influential. Instead, a new and emerging subculture could become powerful enough in the company to affect the mainstream culture and eventually change the corporate culture. As Figure 6.2 shows, a cultural boundary might arise between the dominant or mainstream culture and a set of emerging subcultures in the company. It is expected that the managers and managerial teams with varied backgrounds, which would cause cultural diversity, would come up with more innovative strategies or ideas than people of similar backgrounds. Cultural transformation as seen in the story of the hypothetical company is in fact taking place at some Japanese workplaces: for example in Nissan.

Cultural fault lines within Japanese companies

I have suggested a cultural boundary in Japanese companies' administrative organizations. This is also apparent in Japanese operative organizations.

Japanese companies traditionally are well integrated, and solidarity among employees is particularly strong among Japanese rank-and-file workers. Japanese production workers value teamwork, collectivism, unity, and harmony. However, the situation inside Japanese operative organizations is changing.

Japanese manufacturers have outsourced the workforce to personnel staffing agencies over past years so that they can carry out flexible production or curb personnel costs. This indicates that such Japanese companies have placed more emphasis on a market-oriented employment system rather than an organization-oriented one. As a result, the majority of the rank-and-file workers at Japanese manufacturing plants are not regular workers but nonregular, for instance, temporary workers dispatched from personnel agencies or subcontracted manufacturers and other contingent workers. Although managers at Japanese manufacturing plants attempt to instill in such casual workers, for example, the plant policy or manufacturing practices, generally the workers are indifferent or unwilling to accept them. Nonregular workers' jobs are not secure unlike those of regular employees as core members, thus broadening the gap between regular and nonregular employees and strengthening the cultural boundary between the two different categories. Managers at some Japanese manufacturing plants strive to reduce distinctions between regular and nonregular employees, such as symbolic differences (e.g., uniform colors between the two groups), to prevent the occurrence of cultural fault lines. Such cultural fault lines are detrimental to team solidarity and morale, which can reduce organizational efficiency. These situations involving current Japanese companies suggest that cultural diversity is not a panacea for achieving organizational goals and targeted profits. It has its downsides along with the upsides. One downside involves organizational instability as a result of lost organizational solidarity. Thus, as some diversity scholars (e.g., Milliken and Martins, 1996) have suggested, cultural diversity can be "a double-edged sword" for Japanese and Western companies.

The traditional and emerging types of organizational culture in Japan

So far in this chapter, I have explored organizational culture in transition in Japanese companies in terms of what I have termed "cultural diversity." Japanese companies—at least some of them—have become more diverse in terms of their workforce as they have replaced organization-oriented management practices, whereby they have intentionally or unintentionally pursued the development of a strong culture, with market-oriented practices. Those who formerly did not make up the majority in Japanese companies, such as females, younger people, job hoppers, and non-Japanese individuals, have started to hold managerial positions and constitute subcultures in the companies. As subcultures, these individuals can affect mainstream cultures embodied by the typical types of Japanese managerial employees, such as older male employees who have spent a long time with their current employer since being hired for the job after graduating from schools, usually prestigious Japanese universities, for example, the University of Tokyo. Although young people, female managers, job hoppers, and the like are not exactly representative of cultural diversity, they could hold values, beliefs, and attitudes different from those of traditional Japanese companies and challenge the dominant culture.

Cultural diversity is expected to allow organizations to be adaptive to changing environments and be innovative. This is because those who constitute subcultures can bring new perspectives and knowledge to their current workplaces. Empirical tests are required to verify whether and how much cultural diversity in Japanese companies can actually affect innovation or financial performance. Japanese companies' cultural diversity would not necessarily be a panacea; it has a downside as well. Specifically, cultural diversity can cause cultural fault lines in organizations and hurt organizational integrity and efficiency previously achieved through the homogenization of organizational culture. Japanese workplaces are experiencing this same phenomenon nowadays. Table 6.1 summarizes organizational cultures at Japanese traditional and emerging workplaces caused by different employment systems and the cultural consequences.

Concluding remarks

My study not only explores the organizational culture of Japanese companies but also generalizes relationships among organizational culture, its antecedents, and consequences, irrespective of whether the company is Japanese. More specifically, it presents a process through which a certain type of employment system, characterized as either organization oriented or market oriented, can affect organizational efficiency or adaptation via homogenous or heterogeneous culture. The types of management practices or employment system companies utilize affect the nature of their organizational cultures or determine whether they are homogeneous or heterogeneous. In the case of Japanese companies, the organization-oriented employment system has traditionally homogenized their organizational culture. However, they are currently experiencing a situation

Table 6.1 Employment systems, organizational cultures, and the cultural consequences at Japanese workplaces

Traditional Japanese workplaces	Workplaces	Emerging Japanese workplaces
Organization-oriented employment system: lifetime employment seniority-based pay internal promotion the use of tacit knowledge such as company-specific skills generous fringe benefits	**Employment system**	Market-oriented employment system: short-term employment performance-based pay outsourcing personnel the use of explicit contracts emphasis on employability
homogenous culture strong culture culture's lesser diversity	**Organizational culture in terms of the homogeneous and heterogeneous nature**	heterogeneous culture multiple subcultures culture's greater diversity
organizational efficiency high productivity strong unity among employees organizational rigidity	**The cultural consequences**	organizational adaptability innovation cultural fault lines among employees lost social solidarity

in which their use of a market-oriented employment system heterogenizes their organizational culture. The strong culture developed within Japanese companies has been a source of their strength and competitiveness because it integrates employees into the company's core value. As a result, organizational efficiency is expected to be enhanced. Although culturally diverse organizations might lose their cultural integration, cultural diversity can enhance such organizations' abilities to be adaptive to the new environment and be innovative, which would ultimately lead to improvement in their bottom lines. I generalize the relationships among organizational culture, its antecedents, and consequences as follows: employment system determines the nature of organizational culture— whether the organizational culture is homogeneous or heterogeneous— and then, the determined nature affects organizational performance, that is, the organization's ability to be efficient or adaptive, more specifically productive or innovative.

I conclude this chapter by mentioning the study's limitations and my future work. First, I did not clarify how specific subcultures, for example, market culture and professional culture, are associated with organizational adaptability. Second, I ignored the possibility that an employment system might interact with cultural diversity to affect companies' performance. I limited the employment system's role to an antecedent of cultural diversity. I had to examine its role as a moderator that might affect relationships between organizational diversity and companies' performance. Third, I did not consider organizational outcomes other than organizational efficiency and adaptability, for instance, financial outcomes such as profitability and stock prices. Fourth, I did not examine how one can mitigate cultural diversity's negative effects and then gain more from cultural diversity. Fifth and more importantly, I did not examine whether and to what extent cultural diversity is actually associated with companies' performance using evidence from Japanese companies. I had to provide the formal hypotheses of the associations and empirically test them on the basis of hard evidence from Japanese companies. My future research was to develop my study demonstrated in this chapter by taking these limitations into consideration.

7
Workforce Diversity's Consequences in Japan

Introduction

In the last chapter, I attempted to provide a glimpse of how Japan's traditionally homogeneous workplaces are transforming into demographically and culturally diverse ones. However, one of the issues left to be addressed was to build formal hypotheses regarding cultural diversity and to empirically test them using hard evidence from Japanese companies. To address this issue, in this chapter, by treating workforce diversity as a proxy for cultural diversity, I assess its positive and negative consequences in Japan. More specifically, I test whether and to what extent cultural diversity affects net profits and voluntary labor turnover drawing on a sample of 976 Japanese firms. I argue and theorize on the basis of my work demonstrated in the preceding chapter.

A slow, but growing trend among Japanese businesses toward workforce diversity

In his inaugural speech US President Barack Obama described his country as a patchwork, referring to its diversity of religions, values, and beliefs, and voiced the strength of the nation's culturally diverse society. Diversity is not only a phenomenon of a country or society but can also represent the nature of an organization or a company. Diversity is the new corporate landscape (O'Toole and Lawler, 2007), and at the present time, organizations are more heterogeneous than before. Importantly, in terms of management practice and theory, it is believed that diversity at workplaces is a source of competitive advantage (Cox, 1993), and that it affects net profits, or bottom lines (Jayne and Dipboye, 2004; Svyantek and Bott, 2004). Not only management scholars but also journalists (e.g., Vedantam, 2007) have voiced the fact that firms can benefit from diversity at work.

Meanwhile, diversity at work is not necessarily considered to be a panacea for all business problems. Studies (e.g., Williams and O'Reilly, 1998) have found that diversity has a negative effect on group outcomes and is sometimes associated with turnover. This implies that diversity has both advantages and disadvantages and can be a "double-edged sword" to firms.

Most previous work has been conducted in the US, a country that is a "patchwork" of various cultures, using President Obama's words. The question of whether diversity has a large impact on business activities and performance in traditionally homogenous East Asian countries and areas, including China, Taiwan, and South Korea, remains to be answered. China is, of course, a diverse society where multiple ethnic groups live. However, Chinese as well as other East Asian companies are less diverse than their Western counterparts. Among the East Asian companies, Japanese firms in particular are well known for the homogenization of their values and culture. Deal and Kennedy (1982) wrote about the phenomenon in their classic book, titled *Corporate culture*. Business leaders and scholars from around the globe have believed that Japanese companies' cultural homogenization and strength is a source of their competitive advantages, as suggested by Peters and Waterman, the co-authors of *In search of excellence* (1982), one of the world's best-selling business books of all the time.

Japanese firms' cultural homogenization stems from the nation's ethnic similarity that has been generated and enhanced not only by the nation's geography, being surrounded by seas, but also by the government's traditional policy of closing the door to foreign workers. However, Japanese companies are being pressured to employ people with diverse cultural backgrounds to tap their capabilities and compete in global markets (Kitazume, 2010). Japanese employees, particularly in managerial positions, are traditionally homogeneous in terms of not only nationality and ethnicity but also gender, tenure, and careers. Japanese managers are typically older male employees who have served only their current companies since the beginning of their working lives immediately after graduating from college.

One reason for this similarity is the nation's geography and the government's policies. In addition to such environmental factors, this cultural homogenization has been enhanced by Japanese companies' unique organization-oriented employment system, and labor markets internally developed by means of this system. However, facing increasingly fierce global competition, Japanese companies cannot avoid replacing traditional management practices with newer ones and utilizing personnel who are capable regardless of their age, gender, and careers. Accordingly, some Japanese companies are eager to accommodate diversity within their organizations and utilize it as a business resource. For example, Nissan Motor Co., Japan's second largest automotive manufacturer, has increased the number of non-Japanese as well as female managers to tap such diversities, since Carlos Ghosn, Lebanese Brazilian-born CEO of the company, took over the current position. Fast Retailing Co., Ltd.—the operator of Uniqlo, the world clothing retail chains—is another innovative Japanese company that seeks to embrace and take advantage of diversity (Yanai, 2011).

However, except for innovative Japanese companies such as Nissan and Fast Retailing, the majority of Japanese companies still have a workforce characterized by its homogeneity in terms of characteristics such as nationality, race, gender, tenure, and careers. In general, workforce diversity in Japanese companies is still limited, compared with that in their Western counterparts. Nevertheless, there is a slow, but growing trend among Japanese businesses toward workforce diversity, as a new corporate landscape is emerging. This ongoing situation could have positive and negative consequences on Japanese companies, as predicted by prior research on diversity. The purpose of my study in this chapter is to empirically examine workforce diversity's positive and negative consequences in Japan, more specifically whether and how much it affects net profits and voluntary labor turnover. I theorize on grounds of studies on organizational culture and treat workforce diversity as a proxy for cultural diversity. I test the hypotheses on the basis of disclosed data from 976 Japanese companies.

This study will contribute to the existing research on diversity management by examining the consequences of workforce diversity drawing on evidence from Japanese firms. It will also complement the previous research on organizational culture in which the multicultural perspective or approach to heterogeneous culture was proposed, but the researchers in the area have not demonstrated the theoretical applications or conducted empirical research on the basis of the perspective. Moreover, this study will provide practical contributions by testing the hypotheses on the basis of evidence from Japanese corporations and organizations, where homogeneity traditionally prevails over heterogeneity. The results can provide information to Japanese managers regarding whether workforce diversity would affect their companies as well, and if so, then how should they address diversity issues.

Theoretical development

Theoretical background

Globalization focuses on differences between people from different countries; on the other hand, workforce diversity addresses differences among people within given countries and the companies there (Robbins and Judge, 2009). By workforce diversity, I mean the phenomenon where organizations are or become diverse in terms of member demographics (e.g., gender, race, nationality, and age), careers, tenure, religion, disability, and sexual orientation. In this manner, diversity centers on factors such as gender, race, nationality, age, tenure, education, disability, religion, and sexual orientation (Robbins and Judge, 2009). Diversity can be found at several levels: individuals, groups, and organizations. Individual-level diversity concerns intrapersonal diversity, implying the extent to which an individual has various functional backgrounds. For example, some people have experience in production, R&D, accounting, or personnel, while others have experience only in sales (Cannella, Park, and Lee, 2008). Group-level diversity is concerned with the extent to which a particular group is diverse in terms of race, gender, and functional background, or how many people within a group are included in some diversity category or other. Organizational-level diversity involves questions such as "What percentage of an organization's members is affiliated with a certain demographic category or another?" Many previous studies have focused on group-level diversity (e.g., Ely and Thomas, 2001), irrespective of the fact that all three levels need to be considered.

Williams and O'Reilly (1998) reviewed past diversity research. According to them, previous studies on diversity were built largely on social categorization, similarity/attraction, and information/decision making. They classified types of empirical diversity studies in terms of laboratory or field studies, and found that the majority of them were field studies.

Numerous empirical studies have been conducted, especially at the group level. Such studies have produced mixed results on the relationships between diversity and its outcomes (Williams and O'Reilly, 1998). Some studies concluded that groups can benefit from diversity, as scholars expected, while others found that diversity had no effect on group performance. Other studies found that diversity had a negative effect on group outcomes and that it was sometimes associated with turnover. There are plausible reasons for these inconsistent results: different researchers used different dependent variables in their studies, and researchers empirically tested their hypotheses by adopting various dependent variables such as problem-solving, communication, creativity, conflict, task performance, and turnover (Pelled, 1996). Thus, the studies' results may vary depending on the dependent variables chosen. The difference in results may also be because researchers did not pay much attention to the relevant second or moderator variable that could affect the relationships between diversity and group performance. Such relationships are conditional on a moderator, such as task requirements or personality. The most significant reason, Pelled (1996) suggested, is that previous studies on diversity were atheoretical, lacking theoretical foundations. The management scholar went on to argue that to date, there had been no theory to adequately explain both the upsides and downsides associated with diversity.

Theoretical foundations

I treat workforce diversity as a proxy for cultural diversity and draw on theories and perspectives from the literature on organizational culture as this work's theoretical foundations. This is because organizational culture and cultural diversity are organization-level phenomena and the literature has more potential to address workforce diversity at an organization level than approaches taken by previous studies on diversity, most of which examined group-level diversity. According to theories and perspectives from the organizational culture literature, as argued later, females, young people, job hoppers, and other new categories of Japanese managers can constitute subcultures in Japanese firms. Thus, in my approach, I could treat these parts of the workforce as subcultures and develop theories relevant to the Japanese context.

In addition to the popular integration or single-culture perspective, the literature concerning organizational culture presents a differentiation or multicultural perspective (Martin, 2002). Not all organizations are characterized by a single or dominant culture; in other words, not all organizations are culturally homogeneous. Some organizations are characterized by the ubiquity of subcultures, which are defined here as organizational cultures shared by a particular constellation of people in an organization. Such organizations are culturally diverse or heterogeneous in the sense that they include various subcultures. This cultural situation is what I call cultural diversity. By this, I mean the extent to which an organization is heterogeneous as a result of the presence of subcultures. An organization could be seen as "a nexus where a variety of cultural influences come together within a boundary" (Martin, 1992: 111). By extending the view, the cultural situation inside a company could be regarded as a "nexus of subcultures," as I argued in the preceding chapter.

Organizational culture is viewed as an organizational-level phenomenon, not an individual- or a group-level one (Robbins and Judge, 2009). Although organizational subcultures could be viewed as a "sub-organizational"-level phenomenon, cultural diversity represents the entire cultural situation of an organization, with some organizations being culturally homogenous, while others are characterized by diverse or heterogeneous subcultures. Therefore, in studying organization-level diversity such as workforce diversity, it would be reasonable to adopt the perspective of multiple cultures as offered in the literature on organizational culture. My theories and hypotheses are thus developed drawing on the work on organizational culture. Figure 7.1 represents the theoretical model to be tested. As voluntary turnover is confirmed to affect net profits by some scholars (e.g., Huselid, 1995), I will not test them in this work.

Cultural diversity as cutting-edge: Its effect on net profits

As I discussed in Chapter 6, one rationale behind the power of cultural diversity to allow an organization to be innovative and adaptive is that the diverse knowledge or perspectives stemming from various subcultures can combine to enrich the knowledge base and create new knowledge (Nonaka, Toyama, and Hirata, 2008). This can ultimately lead to an increase in net profits. In such a way, subcultures are likely to affect organizational adaptability, that is, an organization's abilities to be adaptive or even proactive to its environments. This is the key function of subcultures in affecting organizational performance. It is expected that the greater an organization's cultural diversity, the more likely it is to achieve organizational adaptability.

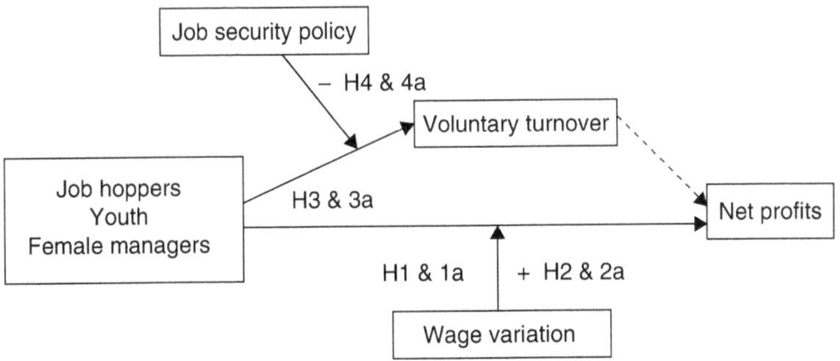

Figure 7.1   The theoretical model[a]
Notes:
[a] The broken line represents the relationship tested in the previous research.

Many scholars (and even the general public) argue that general diversity or heterogeneity is associated with improvements in group or organizational outcomes. However, specifying how diversity contributes to performance rather than providing "blanket statements" that diversity will inevitably lead to better performance is a more realistic message, one that is more likely to be embraced by employees (Jayne and Dipboye, 2004). Pelled (1996) articulated two approaches to analyze diversity's relationship with group outcomes. The first approach is to treat general diversity rather than a particular type of diversity and to make general statements about the impact of diversity on group outcomes. The second approach is to address a specific variable of diversity and examine the distinct impact of such a variable on group outcomes. The second approach assumes that no two types of diversity variable affect a group's or organization's performance in the same manner, and thus, it is imperative to explore the effects of not only general diversity but also specific diversity variables. All organizational subcultures do not have the same effect on organizational performance; subcultures such as countercultures expedite organizational adaptability. Recognizing the significant effects of specific subcultures urges scholars to explore the type of subculture or subcultural group that can enhance the abilities of an organization to be adaptive.

In Japanese companies, where there is traditionally less job mobility than in their Western (especially the US) counterparts, job hoppers, who enter the corporation after quitting a job at another company, can represent a subculture. People in Japanese corporations, characterized by the internal labor market, usually spend their working years at a single company until reaching retirement age (Dore, 1973), which varies across companies, usually around the age of 60. Their working years typically begin after they graduate from technical schools, high schools, colleges, or other schools, and are then hired by a company. Such typical Japanese employees who have a long tenure at a corporation are immersed in its organizational culture and may be considered as embodying the dominant, core values of the corporation. On the other hand, job hoppers are not assimilated into the organizational culture of the corporation, and therefore are likely to think from a perspective different from that of the majority of people at the corporation. They are likely to bring into the company perspectives and styles of leadership different from those of traditional Japanese managers, or even a "market culture" perspective.

Job hoppers are immersed in a market culture that values freedom and competition. They also espouse market principles. Market culture and principles introduced by job hoppers could be implanted in an organization and thus enable it to be adaptive and innovative (Hamel, 2007). Such job hoppers might not be considered as a subculture in the conventional work on diversity because job hopping is not unusual in Western companies. Yet, they could be regarded as a subculture in an organization, especially a typical Japanese organization, if viewed from the multicultural perspective adopted in literature about organizational culture. Therefore, I focus on job hoppers as a subcultural group in this research setting, that is, in the Japanese context.

In addition to job hoppers, female managers and younger generation employees may constitute subcultures in Japanese corporations. According to the famous cross-cultural study conducted by Hofstede (1980), Japanese corporations ranked the highest in "masculinity" index scores among companies worldwide. This suggests that male employees might dominate, particularly managerial positions, and that their values might prevail over female employees. Indeed, the percentage of females occupying managerial positions is especially small in Japanese corporations compared with that of their male counterparts (Okada, 2008). It is expected that the presence of females holding managerial or executive positions is not only symbolically but also practically significant in terms of its impact on organizational performance. Thus, female managers are likely to constitute a subculture in Japanese companies and I also treat female managers as a diversity variable at Japanese workplaces.

Youth culture can be also considered a subculture in Japanese corporations. Older generation employees are traditionally dominant in higher-ranking positions because employees in Japanese companies are promoted to higher levels according to seniority or their tenure. The culture of the older generations at the managerial level could affect the entire organization and become its dominant culture. Thus, youth culture, especially at higher levels in the organization, could represent a subculture in traditional Japanese companies.

In studying group-level diversity, Pelled (1996) used a middle-ground approach by identifying both the common effect, that is, the effect shared by all types of diversity, and the distinct effect of a focal diversity variable. Likewise, this study explores both the common effect of subcultures and the distinct effect of a focal variable of diversity (in this case, job hoppers) on net profits. I provide the formal hypotheses of these effects:

Hypothesis 1: in general, a set of subcultures significantly accounts for an increment in net profits.

Hypothesis 1a: in particular, a constellation of job hoppers is significantly and positively associated with net profits.

Interactive effect of cultural diversity on net profits with wage variation

Some scholars presented interaction or moderation models using growth strategy, personality, or similar elements as a moderator (e.g., Dwyer, Richard, and Chadwick, 2003; Homan et al., 2008), and argued that the associations of diversity with performance are conditional on the second variable. The organizational culture literature states that employment systems can affect organizational culture and subcultures. Thus, it is expected that cultural diversity interacts with employment systems to have an effect on net profits. In the previous chapter, I argued that management practices and employment system can affect the homogenization and heterogenization of organizational culture and become an antecedent to such an organizational phenomenon. It is expected that cultural diversity can be encouraged and sustained when a specific type of employment system, that is, a market-oriented system, is utilized, as I discuss in more detail further. Therefore, in this chapter, I focus on the role of employment system when it can serve as a second variable or a moderator that affects the relationship between cultural diversity and net profits.

Ouchi and Jaeger (1978) addressed how employment systems affect organizational culture. They suggested that Type J organizations, exemplified by Japanese companies, or Type Z organizations, typical of some US companies (e.g., IBM and Hewlett-Packard or HP at the time when their article was written), implement employment practices that facilitate cultural strength, in other words, what Jacoby (2005) called an organization-oriented employment system.

On the other hand, subcultures or cultural diversity are expected to be coexistent with, and encouraged by, what Jacoby (2005) called a market-oriented employment system or what Cappelli (1999) called "the new deal." It is not a shared value or corporate culture, but an explicit contract that unites people in corporations under the market-oriented employment systems. A strong culture is difficult to develop under such an employment system. Subcultures can develop and be common in corporations under the new deal. People who are racially, sexually, or ethnically different from the majority of their colleagues would have more chances to be hired and promoted to higher positions in market-oriented employment systems, as I argued in the previous chapter. They feel a sense of fairness and equity in this environment where they would be treated on the basis not of favoritism or seniority but their efforts or contributions. In particular, job hoppers, the focal diversity variable in this study, would be encouraged by variable or merit-based pay (a crucial part of the new deal), because they would wish to be evaluated not by their tenure or seniority but by their abilities and how much value they have added to the corporation.

To explore the interactive effect of subcultures, I selected wage variation, not variable pay per se, as part of the market-oriented employment system for an empirical reason: I was unable to obtain data on variable wages itself. I assume that the greater the variable wage, the greater the wage variation would be between employees, as is currently apparent in most US companies (O'Toole and Lawler, 2007). I suppose that wage variation can occur as a result of the use of variable wages, such as merit- or performance-based pay. Consistent with the hypotheses on direct effects presented earlier, I hypothesize both the common interactive effect of subcultures, and the distinct interactive effect of a constellation of job hoppers along with wage variation, on net profits:

Hypothesis 2: in general, the set of product terms between subcultures and wage variation significantly accounts for an increment in net profits in such a way that the positive relationships of respective subcultures with net profits are stronger when wage variation is greater compared with those when wage variation is smaller.

Hypothesis 2a: in particular, a constellation of job hoppers interacts with wage variation to have a significantly positive effect on net profits such that the positive relation between a constellation of job hoppers and net profits is stronger when wage variation is greater compared with that when wage variation is smaller.

Cultural diversity as a double-edged sword: Its effect on voluntary turnover

Cultural diversity is not a panacea for achieving organizational goals and targeted profits. It has its downsides as well as upsides. One downside involves organizational instability as a result of lost organizational solidarity. Organizational subcultures may clash not only with each other but also with the dominant culture, which could damage organizational integrity. As some scholars (e.g., Milliken and Martins, 1996) who studied group diversity have pointed out, subcultures or cultural diversity can be a "double-edged sword." In particular, organizational solidarity that is lost by such diversity results in employees voluntarily leaving the organization, or high voluntary turnover (Pelled, 1996). As certain types of diversity have a more positive effect on the organization than other diversity variables, a subculture could also have a more negative or devastating impact on the organization than other subcultures. It is expected that, above all, job hoppers can have a significant effect on voluntary turnover. This is because they are not absorbed into the dominant culture as much as other employees and may be inclined to move between employers. I therefore present the following formal hypotheses on the downside of cultural diversity:

Hypothesis 3: in general, a set of subcultures significantly accounts for an increase in voluntary turnover.

Hypothesis 3a: in particular, a constellation of job hoppers is significantly and positively associated with voluntary turnover.

Interactive effect of cultural diversity on voluntary turnover with a job security policy

Scholars have reported the drawbacks and advantages of diversity, yet they have not answered the key question. That is, given the two opposite sides of diversity, how do people, in particular managerial employees, minimize the drawbacks and reap more benefits? Even if they gained benefits from cultural diversity, the benefits could be offset by the costs they incurred, more specifically voluntary turnover. Consequently, they could gain no profit or even attain net losses. Then, they need to sustain and magnify the benefits of cultural diversity by minimizing the costs as much as possible. Thus, the challenge is to develop the means to mitigate voluntary turnover caused by cultural diversity and gain a higher level of net profits.

One possible method is an extensive screening process in hiring potential employees with diverse cultural backgrounds (O'Reilly and Pfeffer, 2000). Irrespective of differences in race, nationality, age, and the like—which Harrison, Price, and Bell (1998) argued are at the surface level of diversity—organizations could retain their integrity through their hiring practices, even if they embraced the concept of workforce diversity. An extensive screening process allows human resource (HR) staff to screen in only applicants who are considered fit for the organizational culture at the deepest level of the organizational phenomenon, which is equivalent to what Schein (1985) called "basic assumptions," even if the applicants are demographically different from the majority of the company. Alternatively, the HR staff would screen out the applicants whom they find unsuitable for the organizational culture, even if their demographics seem to be similar to those of the majority of the company's employees. Another way to mitigate turnover caused by cultural diversity is the use of a job security policy. Organizations could obtain trust and commitment from members with diverse cultural backgrounds by means of such a policy (O'Reilly and Pfeffer, 2000). Once companies have secured the employees' jobs and gained their commitment and trust, employees would be unlikely to leave. This would compensate for cultural integrity lost by cultural diversity.

The configurational perspective in the strategic human resource management (SHRM) literature assumes that management practices should be congruent with each other if the company would like to maximize benefits from such practices (Delery and Doty, 1996; Dreher and Dougherty, 2002). In light of this perspective, a job security policy is aligned not with merit-based pay but with seniority-based pay. However, Ouchi and Jaeger (1978) proposed a modified Type J organization, that is, a Type Z organization driven by an organization-oriented employment system combined with parts of a market-oriented employment system. Indeed, SHRM researchers found both job security policy and merit-based pay to be parts of a high-performance work system (Huselid, 1995). Because I could not acquire empirical data on the screening process, I focus here on job security policy. I investigate whether the use of a job security policy could mitigate the effects of subcultures or cultural diversity on voluntary turnover, thereby increasing net profits. It has been reported that voluntary turnover reduced in such a manner actually improves profits (Huselid, 1995). Consistent with the hypotheses proposed so far, I hypothesize both the common interactive effect of subcultures, and the distinct interactive effect of a constellation of job hoppers along with a job security policy, on voluntary turnover:

Hypothesis 4: in general, a set of product terms between subcultures and a job security policy significantly accounts for a decrease in voluntary turnover in such a way that the positive relationships between respective subcultures and voluntary turnover are weaker when a job security policy is stronger rather than when it is weaker.

Hypothesis 4a: in particular, a constellation of job hoppers interacts with a job security policy to have a significant negative effect on voluntary turnover in such a way that the negative relationship between a constellation of job hoppers and voluntary turnover is weaker when a job security policy is stronger rather than when it is weaker.

Methods

Data sources

The data for this study involved Japanese companies during the Japanese fiscal year 2006: April 1, 2006 to March 31, 2007. The data sources were disclosed and public. Data were obtained from *Toyokeizai CSR (corporate social responsibility) kigyo soran* (CSR Survey Report for Japanese Companies, published in 2007 by the Toyokeizai Publishing Company), annual reports, and *Toyokeizai yakuin shikiho* (Quarterly Handbook on Japanese Executives, published in 2007 by the same publishing company). The most essential data for this study, including subcultural variables and turnover, were obtained from *Toyokeizai CSR kigyo soran*. The total number of companies whose data were used to conduct statistical analyses was 976. In principle, holding companies were excluded because many of these companies usually specialized in managerial functions and the number of employees hired was considerably small compared to their sales and profits. The companies analyzed in this study operated in a wide range of industries, such as food, construction, electronics, automobile, wholesale, and service. Most were public companies listed on the Tokyo Stock Exchange or other Japanese stock markets.

Variables

Dependent variables

The models included voluntary turnover as well as net profits as dependent variables. I gathered data on voluntary turnovers both for the employees who held college degrees and those who did not, and aggregated the voluntary turnover for these two groups. Voluntary turnover varied across industries. To adjust for industrial heterogeneity, I subtracted from the value of voluntary turnover for each company its industrial average and used the subtracted value as the voluntary turnover. All variables, including dependent, independent, and moderator variables, were measured with different scales, for instance, the Japanese currency of yen and the number of people who left jobs. Hence, the values on voluntary turnover were standardized and the z scores used so that I could readily perceive changes in values on indices with different measurement units (Cohen et al., 2003). Net profits were also standardized to help interpret the results of the statistical analyses.

Independent variables

Independent variables of subcultures consisted of job hoppers, female managers, and youth. As I have discussed earlier, a constellation of job hoppers was the focal independent variable of this study. I used data on the number of job hoppers who were hired by their current company during the fiscal years 2005 and 2006 after they had left their former company. Regardless of whether they held college degrees, I designated job hoppers as those who had left their former employer and were employed by their current employer during the period. Some of them might literally be job hoppers who had changed jobs and employers several times and moved between companies. For some, however, hopping to their current employer might be their first attempt to change employers in working life. Japanese companies traditionally hire new graduates and tend to dislike employing those who have left their former companies and seek new jobs in other companies. Thus, because job hoppers are not a majority in Japanese companies and represent a subculture, I designated job hoppers as those who were hired during these fiscal years, irrespective of the number of times they had changed employers and jobs. Because the number of people designated as job hoppers in such a manner varied across industries, I subtracted from the number of job hoppers at a given company the industrial average and used the subtracted values, as I did for voluntary turnover. The number of job hoppers in Japanese companies is still considerably small compared with that in Western companies. Thus, I did not use the percentage of the entire employees but their absolute number. The variable of job hoppers is the aggregate of the standardized numbers of job hoppers, with and without college degrees, who were hired in the Japanese fiscal year of 2005 or 2006.

Data for female managers were captured on the basis of the percentage of female managers and female executives at the company. The values were standardized and averaged. I was not able to directly obtain data on youth culture or the actual number of younger managers. Thus, I used an estimated number of younger managers, primarily by using the difference between the executives' average age and the average age of all employees of the company. I assumed that the smaller the difference, the more likely it would be that youth were established at the upper organizational levels. I used the reversed and standardized values.

Moderators

As stated earlier, I selected wage variation, not variable wages per se, as the moderator that is expected to affect the effects of cultural diversity on net profits, because I did not gain data directly on wage variables. I assumed that wage variation can take place as a result of the use of variable wages. I captured wage variation primarily by using the standardized difference between the average annual wages for executives in a given company and that for all employees of the company. I assumed that the difference can result from a merit-based pay system, as is seen in US companies. Indeed, Japanese companies that are known for the high salaries paid to their executives compared to general employees, for example, Nissan and Sony, adopt pay-for-performance policies. Nissan's president, Carlos Ghosn, who earned around $12 million in 2010, is believed to be the highest-paid executive in any public Japanese companies that year. (Japanese companies are not obligated to disclose individual-based compensations for CEOs and board members although they have to announce the total amount of salaries of highest-ranking managers in the organization.)

Furthermore, I used job security as a moderator for voluntary turnover models. I defined this as the average tenure for all employees in a given company because I assumed that the longer the tenure per employee, the more eager the company would be to support and implement a job security policy. The values were standardized.

Controls

I used industrial dummies as control variables and categorized the companies by industries following the criteria supplied by the Tokyo Stock Exchange. The baseline industry was the electronics sector, which was coded zero. I also used payroll or the standardized number of employees as a control variable. This is likely to be associated with net profits and voluntary turnover.

Results

To test the hypotheses, I performed hierarchical, moderated (interactive) regression analyses using the ordinary least squares (OLS) method. Table 7.1 shows means, standard deviations, and correlations.

Table 7.2 shows the regression results for testing hypotheses 1, 1a, 2, and 2a. I included the control variables in model 1 (step 1) and added wage variation as a moderator to model 1 in model 2 (step 2). Then, I added the set of independent variables, that is, the set of subcultures, to model 2 in model 3 (step 3) in order to estimate both the common effect of these subcultures and the distinct effect of job hoppers on net profits. Finally, I added the set of product terms between subcultures and wage variation to model 3 in model 4 (step 4) in order to estimate both the common interactive effect of these subcultures, and the distinct interactive effect of job hoppers with wage variation, on net profits.

Table 7.1   Means, standard deviations, and correlations[a]

Variables	Mean	s.d.	1	2	3	4	5	6	7
1. Payroll	0.00	1.00							
2. Job security	0.00	1.00	.26**						
3. Job hoppers	0.05	3.34	.36**	−.08*					
4. Youth	0.00	1.00	.04	.57**	−.09*				
5. Female managers	0.00	1.00	−.02	−.35**	.06	−.15**			
6. Wage variation	0.00	1.00	.09**	.06*	.19**	.02	.06+		
7. Net profits	0.00	1.00	.24**	.07*	.12**	.00	−.01	.09**	
8. Voluntary turnover	0.00	1.00	.43**	−.02	.83**	−.07*	.05	.15**	.23**

Notes:
[a]n = 976. Due to parsimony, correlation results for 24 dummy industries are not reported.
+p < .10
*p < .05
**p < .01

Model 3 indicates that the set of subcultures, including job hoppers, youth, and female managers, did not significantly contribute to the increment in net profits (ΔR^2 = 0.00, n.s.). A constellation of job hoppers was not related to net profits, either (β = 0.00, n.s.). Thus, both hypotheses 1 and 1a were not supported. Model 4 shows that the set of the product terms between subcultures and wage variation significantly accounts for the increment in net profits (ΔR^2 = 0.04, p < 0.01). The product term between youth and wage variation was negative although this effect was marginal (β = −0.23, p < 0.10). The result was mixed and, accordingly, Hypothesis 2 was partially supported. A constellation of job hoppers in particular had a statistically significant and positive interactive effect on net profits along with wage variation (β = 0.18, p < 0.01). I plotted the interactive effect of the constellation of job hoppers on net profits with wage variation in Figure 7.2. The figure shows that a constellation of job hoppers had a positive effect on net profits when the wage variation is greater, as opposed to a negative effect when it is smaller. Thus, Hypothesis 2a was supported. I checked the results by using other outcome variables, for instance, profitability, or the amount of profits per employer, and by rerunning the same statistical analyses. I obtained similar results to those of the analyses I conducted before.

Table 7.3 shows the results for testing hypotheses 3, 3a, 4, and 4a. I entered the control variables in model 1 (step 1) and added job security as a moderator to model 1 in model 2 (step 2). Then, I added the set of independent variables to model 2 in model 3 (step 3) for estimating

Table 7.2   Results of regression analysis for net profits[a]

Predictors	Model 1	Model 2	Model 3	Model 4
Constant	–0.09** (0.03)	–0.09** (0.03)	–0.09* (0.03)	–0.10** (0.03)
Step 1: Controls added				
Payroll	0.47** (0.01)	0.45** (0.01)	0.45** (0.01)	0.40** (0.01)
Step 2: Moderator added				
Wage variation		0.18* (0.08)	0.17* (0.08)	0.10 (0.08)
Step 3: Independent variables added				
Job hoppers			0.00 (0.00)	–0.01* (0.00)
Youth			–0.01 (0.01)	–0.04* (0.01)
Female managers			0.00 (0.02)	0.02 (0.02)
Step 4: Product terms added				
Job hoppers × wage variation				0.18** (0.02)
Youth × wage variation				–0.23+ (0.12)
Female managers × wage variation				0.20 (0.12)
ΔR^2		.01	.00	.04
F for ΔR^2		5.06*	0.31	23.78**
R^2	.60	.61	.61	.65
Overall model F	33.71**	32.85**	29.37**	32.22**

Notes:
[a]n = 569. Values in parentheses are standard errors. Industrial dummies are not reported.
+$p < .10$
*$p < .05$
**$p < .01$

both the common effect of these subcultures and the distinct effect of job hoppers on voluntary turnover. Finally, I added the set of product terms of subcultures with job security to model 3 in model 4 (step 4) for estimating both the common interactive effect of these subcultures and the distinct interactive effect of job hoppers on voluntary turnover.

Model 3 shows that a set of subcultures significantly contributed to the increment in voluntary turnover (ΔR^2 = 0.52, $p < 0.01$). This result was largely due to the effect of job hoppers. That is, a constellation of job hoppers alone was positively associated with it (β = 0.24, $p < 0.01$). Hypotheses 3 and 3a were supported. Model 4 indicates that a set of product terms significantly contributed to a decrement in voluntary

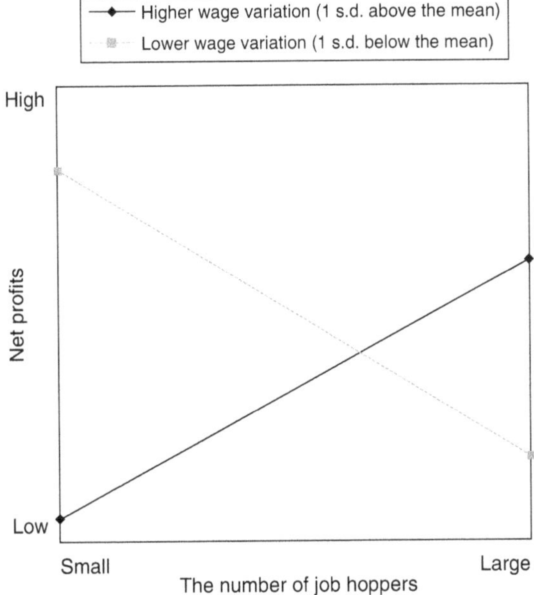

Figure 7.2   The relationship between job hoppers and net profits as a function of wage variation

turnover ($\Delta R^2 = 0.05$, $p < 0.01$) as a product term was significantly and negatively associated with the dependent variable. Thus, Hypothesis 4 was supported. The result was largely due to the negative interaction alone between a constellation of job hoppers and a job security policy ($\beta = -0.09$, $p < 0.01$). Figure 7.3 depicts the interactive effects graphically. The figure shows that job hoppers are less associated with voluntary turnover when they are protected by a job security policy than when they are not (i.e., weaker job security). Thus, Hypothesis 4a was supported.

Discussion

All hypotheses, except hypotheses 1 and 1a, were supported. The results show that the mere presence of general cultural diversity, including job hoppers, cannot affect the bottom line; however, a constellation of job hoppers, among other subcultures, is positively associated with net profits to a greater degree when the wage variation is higher. I discuss the statistical results in more detail further.

Table 7.3   Results of regression analysis for voluntary turnover[a]

Predictors	Model 1		Model 2		Model 3		Model 4	
Constant	−0.08	(0.11)	0.00	(0.11)	0.00	(0.07)	−0.01	(0.06)
Step 1: Controls added								
Payroll	0.56**	(0.05)	0.61**	(0.05)	0.13**	(0.03)	0.35**	(0.03)
Step 2: Moderator added								
Job security			−0.25**	(0.06)	0.00	(0.04)	−0.04	(0.04)
Step 3: Independent variables added								
Job hoppers					0.24**	(0.08)	0.14**	(0.01)
Youth					0.00	(0.04)	0.00	(0.03)
Female managers					0.01	(0.04)	0.08	(0.07)
Step 4: Product terms added								
Job hoppers × job security							−0.09**	(0.00)
Youth × job security							−0.02	(0.02)
Female managers × job security							0.02	(0.04)
ΔR^2			.02		.52		.05	
F for ΔR^2			17.98*		311**		39.70**	
R^2	.17		.19		.71		.76	
Overall model F	4.36**		5.02**		44.76**		53.34**	

Notes:
[a]n = 550. Values in parentheses are standard errors. Industrial dummies are not reported.
+$p < .10$
*$p < .05$
**$p < .01$

Most prior studies on diversity found no support for the hypotheses that predicted the direct impact of diversity on performance, even though they confirmed the effect to be moderated by contingency variables. Likewise, the current study did not yield support for the direct relation hypothesis, but found support for the moderated relation hypothesis. The statistical results indicate that the moderated relation model can predict the impact of workforce diversity within organizations more than can the direct relation model. Importantly, I achieved the same results in the Japanese context as previously reported on the

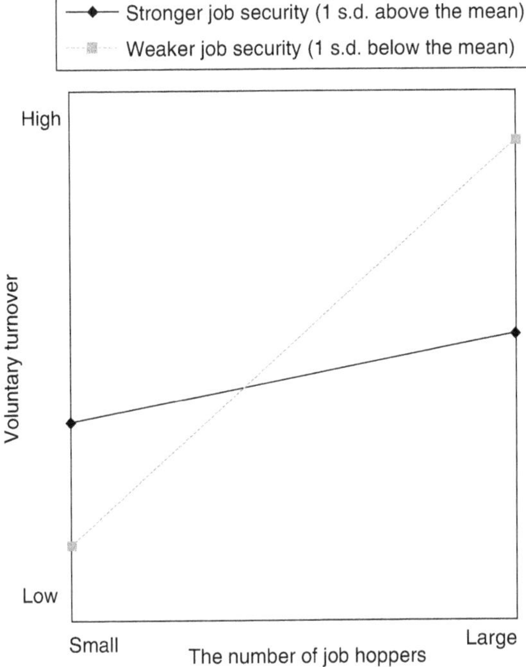

Figure 7.3 The relationship between job hoppers and voluntary turnover as a function of job security

Western context. In addition, interestingly, wage variation as part of the market-oriented employment system moderated the relation between job hoppers and net profits. Note that such wage variation can be a moderator or contingency variable in predicting the impact of diversity variable, here job hoppers, on net profits. The statistical results imply that several variables can be a contingency variable if they are relevant to the research settings.

Theoretical contributions

This research makes theoretical contributions to the studies on the diversity management field. First, it empirically explores the positive consequences of workforce diversity in the Japanese context and demonstrates that Japanese as well as Western firms can enjoy these effects. Research on diversity management usually was conducted in Western countries that have a massive influx of people with different cultural backgrounds into them. My research revealed that job hoppers, representing part of workforce diversity, can play a crucial role in boosting bottom lines, and that workforce diversity matters in Japan as well as in Western countries.

Second, this research found that workforce diversity can also cause negative consequences for Japanese firms, similar to the disadvantages of such diversity in the Western context identified by previous studies. More specifically, it confirms that job hoppers affect voluntary labor turnover as these diversity factors damage cultural cohesiveness and strong culture. Because Japanese firms have been successful owing to their abilities to build strong culture, as Deal and Kennedy (1982) pointed out, the negative consequences caused by diversity might be more serious for Japanese companies than for Western companies. In this manner, this research revealed that workforce diversity has both advantages and disadvantages in the Japanese context and that it can become a double-edged sword to Japanese as well as Western companies.

Third, this research demonstrated that the approaches taken here are effective in addressing issues surrounding organizational-level diversity. It attempted to examine the consequences of workforce diversity by adopting perspectives and theories in the organizational culture literature. Previous and typical work addressed issues concerning group-level diversity by employing theories of social categorization, similarity/attraction, and information/decision making. Meanwhile, assuming that job hoppers, females, and younger people, who have begun to hold managerial positions dominated by males with a long tenure, can constitute subcultures within Japanese firms (although they are not exactly subcultures), I attempted to develop theories and empirically examine the consequences, both positive and negative, of workforce diversity. These approaches would enrich studies on diversity management by allowing scholars in the field to address issues surrounding organizational-level diversity.

Theoretical implications

This research provides theoretical implications. First, all diversity variables or subcultures do not affect bottom lines, and it is important to focus on a specific diversity variable as well as general diversities to enhance an understanding of the nature and impact of workforce diversity.

Second, this research provides an insight into how one can overcome the double-edged sword characteristic of workforce diversity. One of the downsides of workforce diversity is that job hoppers are associated with voluntary turnover. However, in such cases, adopting a job security policy and securing commitment and trust from employees can compensate for lost solidarity and mitigate the negative effect. Then, it would be possible to retain the benefits of cultural diversity while minimizing the negative effect so that one could enjoy the benefits or net profits more than one would without such an effort.

Third, the current research helps guide future work on organizational culture. The perspective of heterogeneous culture and organizational subcultures within companies was proposed in the literature about organizational culture, yet little empirical research or theoretical application has been performed on the grounds of the perspective. This study demonstrates how to theorize workforce and cultural diversity by drawing on the perspective of multiple cultures and how to subsequently empirically test the hypotheses regarding the phenomenon.

Practical implications

This study not only makes theoretical contributions but also provides significant implications for both Japanese and non-Japanese managers. First, this research implies that workforce diversity does matter even in the Japanese context and that Japanese firms and managers can take advantage of it at their traditionally homogenous organizations.

Second, this research shows what actions managers worldwide, irrespective of whether Japanese, should undertake to resolve the double-edged sword of diversity. By adopting a job security policy and securing commitment and trust from employees, managers could diminish the downside of workforce diversity. Then, they could retain the benefits of workforce diversity while minimizing expenses so that they could enjoy the benefits or net profits more than they would without such an effort.

Limitations and future directions

Despite the theoretical contributions provided by this study, it does have certain limitations. First, as I used disclosed and public data, I was unable to capture cultural diversity itself. Thus, I regarded job hoppers, female managers, and younger managers as subcultures and treated this workforce diversity as cultural diversity. Nevertheless, this method might be one way to capture cultural diversity because prior work (Cox, 1993) assumed that workforce diversity can represent cultural diversity.

Second, I did not use a panel data set and test whether net profits could cause workforce diversity. Instead, I tested the same hypotheses set forth in this chapter using the data set for the Japanese fiscal year

2007 and almost the same sample as used in this research, with net profits of 2006 being a control variable. The results were almost the same as revealed in this research.

Third, because I used disclosed and public data, I was unable to capture variable wage itself. Therefore, I could not help but use "wage variation" instead of "variable wage."

Fourth, for the same empirical reason, I was also unable to directly assess the percentage of younger people in managerial positions. Instead, I attempted to estimate the number of younger managers and then used the estimated number of younger managers.

Fifth, I did not examine the mechanism through which cultural diversity affects net profits in greater detail. Such a process is expected to include organizations' abilities to be adaptive and to create knowledge.

My future work will be to develop this study by addressing these remaining issues.

Part III
Transforming Japanese Workplaces Overseas and Conclusion

8
Impact of National Characteristics on HRM Practices

Introduction

In Chapter 5, I theorized and tested the associations between management practices and manufacturing performance on the basis of evidence from Japanese manufacturers. However, I did not consider the impact of different national environments on such associations because I focused only on their Japan-based plants. Considering such a limitation, and to advance my prior work, I began the research discussed in this chapter. Here, I explore the impact of national characteristics on management practices using evidence from not only Japan- but also China-based manufacturers. These China-based manufacturing companies were affiliated with Japanese companies, and thus, my work also provides readers with a glimpse of Japanese companies' overseas workplaces that are in transition.

Facing intense global competition in the mid 1990s, Japanese manufacturers have transferred labor-intensive production work to low labor-cost countries, particularly China. China is, in fact, said to be the "world's factory," and Japanese as well as US, European, and Asian (e.g., Taiwanese and South Korean) manufacturers have concentrated their production function on China over recent years. China, the world's most populous country, has become such a production force by capitalizing on its abundant and cheap labor force. For both Japanese and non-Japanese manufacturers, however, China is not just a production base but also a lucrative market that has rapidly expanded and continued to grow in recent years. In the autumn of 2008, the US, Japan, and European countries were hit hard by the global financial crisis that was triggered by the collapse of the US investment bank, Lehman Brothers. The Chinese economy was also affected by the fallout; however, it recovered swiftly and has since continued to grow, while developed countries' economies have been anemic. Japanese and other nations' companies have, therefore, depended on China's strong economy and growing demands in order to bounce back from the loss of earnings caused by the global economic recession and to reach and exceed their pre-recession earning levels.

Japanese companies have practiced high-variety and small-lot production, typically with manufacturing cells or cell production methods in their Japan-based plants. Meanwhile, they have mass-produced commodity-type products in China. However, their Chinese plants are also reported to have operated with cells in recent years. For example, Canon, a Japanese precision instrument manufacturer, recently saw its Chinese plants becoming more efficient and competitive, armed with cutting edge production technology, including cells (*Nikkei Newspaper*, August 18, 2010).

Against this backdrop of the overseas expansion of Japanese companies' operations and the transformation of their overseas workplaces, I explore the relationships between human resource management (HRM) practices and manufacturing performance. For this purpose, I have studied 206 manufacturing teams working in Japan- and China-based manufacturers. My research will advance knowledge in the field of strategic human resource management (SHRM) studies by identifying the impact of different national characteristics on HRM practices. By answering the call to conduct these studies across nations, my work will also make a theoretical contribution to the development of the burgeoning field of international SHRM. I commence by identifying issues that remain unsolved in the field of SHRM studies.

Unsolved issues in SHRM studies

With its aim of exploring the relationships between HRM and performance, SHRM research is "the whole subject area [HRM]'s Holy Grail" (Boselie, Dietz, and Boon, 2005: 67). In general, previous empirical work has yielded support for the central thesis that HRM generates high performance and that HRM matters. Nevertheless, as Gerhart (2005) suggested, several issues concerning SHRM research still remain unresolved. The first unresolved issue concerns the failure to capture HRM practices as they are actually implemented. Arthur and Boyles (2007) argued that most SHRM research has centered on the more abstract level of policies or programs, as described by HRM managers, rather than on the practices that are actually implemented by real people. SHRM research will stand on firmer ground when it is able to capture and assess actual practices rather than the stated policies (Wright and Boswell, 2002).

The second issue is the lack of a deep understanding of the selected performance indicators. Rather than financial measures such as return on equity (ROE) and Tobin's q, indicators more relevant to HRM practices are needed to increase the understanding of the impact of HRM practices (Guest, 1997). The third issue is the limited support for the efficacy of the contingency perspective in the SHRM literature. SHRM scholars are not only required to take stock of the selected performance measures but also asked to have a deep understanding of contingency variables to verify the contingency hypothesis (Wright and Sherman, 1999; Martin-Alcazar, Romero-Fernandez, and Sanchez-Gardey, 2005). The fourth, and for this chapter's work the most important, issue is a paucity of research on the impact of different national characteristics on the relationship between HRM and performance.

Jackson and Schuler (1995) labeled national characteristics, such as workforce, labor markets, and national cultures, as constituting an organization's external environment. They distinguished this from its internal environment, which is made up of factors such as strategies, structures, and technology. Then, they highlighted the impact of national characteristics on HRM practices. National characteristics are expected to affect the two-way interactions between such practices and the components of the internal environment. In statistical terms, it is presumed that national characteristics can moderate such two-way interactions and hence three-way interactions can be established among HRM practices, the internal environment, and national characteristics. However, little is known about whether and to what extent different national characteristics affect two-way interactions. It is imperative to examine such three-way interactions among HRM practices, the internal environment, and national characteristics to advance knowledge in the field of SHRM research.

Taking into account these unresolved issues, here I examine the relationships between HRM practices and manufacturing performance. I focus particularly on the three-way interactions among HRM practices, manufacturing configuration, and country, drawing on evidence from Japan- and China-based manufacturers. I aim to make several theoretical contributions to the SHRM field. Most importantly, taking into consideration the role of different national characteristics in HRM, I address the question of whether the country in which a manufacturer operates moderates the two-way interactions between HRM practices and the manufacturing configuration. In other words, I explore whether the proposed three-way interactions among HRM practices, manufacturing configuration, and country are established in terms of manufacturing performance. By answering the call from Brewster, Sparrow, and Harris (2005) for conducting SHRM research across nations, this research also aims to make a theoretical contribution to the development of the burgeoning field of international SHRM. Furthermore, this research will make valuable practical contributions, particularly for manufacturers, because I analyze highly significant data collected at the front lines of manufacturing companies facing formidable global competition and provide theory- and evidence-based suggestions for them.

Theoretical background and hypotheses

Direct relationships between HRM practices and manufacturing performance

As stated in Chapter 5, caution must be exercised when examining the relationships between management practices and performance. First, when conducting empirical SHRM research, it is methodologically important to capture and assess those management practices that are actually implemented. I therefore focus on manufacturing lines or cells and collect data on real, solid HRM practices as implemented by rank-and-file workers, unlike those evaluated by HRM personnel at company headquarters. Second, no agreement seems to exist as yet on what, exactly, high-performance work practices (HPWPs) are, and therefore SHRM scholars must select HRM practices relevant to their research frameworks or settings. In response to this, I utilize relevant and effective HRM practices as demonstrated in Chapter 5. According to their inherent functions, these practices are classified in one of the four areas: (1) skill enhancement or multiskilling training (particularly, training aimed at creating multiskilled operators), (2) teamwork practices, (3) motivational practices (with monetary and nonmonetary rewards), and (4) improvement activities. The practices subsumed under each of these areas generally correspond to those proposed by Appelbaum, Bailey, Berg, and Kalleberg (2000) as being effective for manufacturers, namely the opportunity to participate, skills, and incentives. However, my study is more comprehensive than that of Appelbaum and colleagues in that it includes improvement activities that can encourage operators' learning, leading ultimately to high performance for manufacturers (Takeuchi, Wakabayashi, and Chen, 2003). I use the four areas of HRM practices in examining HRM–performance relationships.

Third, SHRM research differs from traditional HRM research as it emphasizes a system of HRM practices as a solution to business problems rather than using individual practices in isolation. I, too, adopt this approach, and in the methods section, I show how I aggregate the scores given to HRM practice questionnaire items developed in terms of the aforementioned four areas.

Fourth, as with HRM practices, relevant outcome variables vary depending on the research setting (Becker and Gerhart, 1996). Because the selected performance measures need to be at the same level as the HRM practices and also meaningful to the research context, I select the following manufacturing performance measures as the focal dependent variables: quality (few incidences of product defects), reduction in work-in-process inventory, productivity (quantity of completed products per worker), and shortening of lead time (the time it takes to make a product, or the throughput time). These are strategically significant for manufacturing companies, being closely connected to and immediately reflected in company-level performance indicators such as profits and profitability (Hyer and Wemmerlöv, 2002).

On the basis of the arguments I have made, I hypothesize the direct relationship between the use of HRM practices (e.g., teamwork practices) and manufacturing performance measures (e.g., quality):

Hypothesis 1: the use of HRM practices is positively associated with manufacturing performance measures; the greater the extent to which those practices are used, the more likely it is that a high level of those performance measures is achieved.

Two-way interactions between HRM practices and manufacturing configuration

The contingency perspective assumes that HRM practices generate high performance when they are in good alignment or fit with environmental factors within an organization, such as its strategies and technology (Dreher and Dougherty, 2002). This proposition has attracted many SHRM scholars, who have attempted to empirically test its efficacy. However, except some studies (such as Batt, 2002: Deepak, Guthrie, and Wright, 2005), such work has failed to support the contingency perspective (Becker and Huselid, 1998; Delery and Doty, 1996; Huselid, 1995).

One problem with theorizing and testing the contingent relationship between HRM and performance is that generic business strategy typologies, such as those proposed by Miles and Snow (1978) and Porter (1980), have been predominantly used to form the contingency variables thought to be complementary to or synergistic with HRM practices (Martin-Alcazar, Romero-Fernandez, and Sanchez-Gardey, 2005; Wright and Sherman, 1999). Such generic typologies apply better to the competitive environment of the 1970s and early 1980s than to that of today. The need for scholars to improve their constructs and measures of contingency is as significant as the requirement for better constructs and measures of HRM practices and performance.

To test the contingency perspective, I treat and conceptualize "manufacturing configuration" as a contingency variable in this research framework, as done in Chapter 5. This is primarily because manufacturing configurations are at the same level (the shop floor) as that of HRM practices and manufacturing performance but also because the success of a specific manufacturing configuration is known to be dependent on the extent to which HRM practices are used (MacDuffie, 1995). As I explained in Chapter 5, the construct of manufacturing configuration is defined as a continuum with a traditional mass production line at one end and a "real" or "genuine" cell at the other (Hyer and Wemmerlöv, 2002). This is because manufacturing cells have emerged as an alternative to the traditional production lines and replaced them. Various forms of a line and a cell, ranging from a typical conventional line, a mixed-flow line, a mixed form of a cell and a line, and a quasi-cell up to a real cell, can be placed along the continuum. Production using manufacturing cells is called cell production by Japanese manufacturers and "cellular manufacturing" by U.S. manufacturers (Hyer and Wemmerlöv, 2002). It has been reported that not only Japanese firms but also some China-based manufacturers currently employ this production method (*Nikkei Newspaper*, August 18, 2010).

The roles of cell operators are different from those of line operators in several regards. For example, cell operators generally handle a wider range of work processes than those handled by their line counterparts. Further, they produce products or parts within a self-sufficient and autonomous production team. Accordingly, cell production has been described as a human-centered production method (Isa and Tsuru, 2002), whose implementation requires greater skills and commitment from operators than those required in conventional mass production. The use of HRM practices is expected to be more conducive to the success of such manufacturing operations and consequently contribute more to performance in cases where the configuration resembles more a cell than a line. Thus, I can construct a hypothesis according to the contingency perspective: I treat manufacturing configuration as a contingency variable in the hypothesis. However, a caveat must be taken into account: there are several types of fits (Venkatraman, 1989). As with much of previous contingency-based work in the SHRM field that Wright and Sherman (1999) reviewed, I adopt a fit-as-moderation approach that views a relationship between a predictor variable (HRM practices) and a criterion variable (manufacturing performance) as being dependent on or moderated by the second and moderator variable (manufacturing configuration). Expanding the direct relationship hypothesis further, I present a formal two-way interaction hypothesis:

Hypothesis 2: the manufacturing configuration moderates the relationships between the use of HRM practices and aspects of manufacturing performance in such a manner that the relationships are positive and stronger at the manufacturing configuration that is more similar to a cell than at that closer to a line.

Three-way interactions among HRM practices, manufacturing configuration, and country

HRM practices interact not only with aspects of an organization's internal environment, such as strategies, technologies, and structures, but also with its external environment or context (Jackson and Schuler, 1995; Chenevert and Tremblay, 2009). Such factors include laws and regulations, cultures, politics, unions, and labor markets. Martin-Alcazar, Romero-Fernandez, and Sanchez-Gardey (2005) proposed that external environmental factors should be treated as not just a contingency variable but a contextual variable (which has been underestimated in previous SHRM work) that conditions or, sometimes, is conditioned by HRM practices. They went on to argue that the use of what they called the "contextual perspective" allows for an understanding of HRM–performance relationships in a macro or global context.

First and foremost, national cultures can affect the implementation of HRM practices and, consequently, play a vital role in supporting or harming them. "Organizations are culture-bound" (Hofstede, 1980: 252), and all HRM practices are not equally applicable to countries with different cultures. A fit between national culture and the HRM practices in use may enhance effectiveness, whereas a mismatch may diminish it. In statistical terms, this situation involves a central question, namely, whether or not there is a statistical interaction between national culture and HRM practices. However, this question has never been empirically explored (Gerhart and Fang, 2005).

I expect national cultures to matter in a global research setting that involves both Japan- and China-based manufacturers. Both countries place strong emphasis on the traditional Asian value of collectivism (House et al., 2004), but some differences exist between their national cultures. A major feature of Chinese culture is respect for age and hierarchy (Lockett, 1988). Chinese managers want a clear distinction between themselves and their subordinates. In effect, Hofstede (1993) estimated that China has a larger power distance as a cultural value than Japan has, suggesting that Japanese society is more egalitarian. This suggests that Chinese groups may be less autonomous or self-managing than their Japanese counterparts. Manufacturing operations typically involve team activities, and social bonds among workers are required to ensure success. A high level of group autonomy and discretion is vital in boosting manufacturing performance (Appelbaum et al., 2000). My case study, noted earlier in this book, also revealed that allowing work groups a certain level of autonomy, if not high, was important for the success of manufacturing activities. It is suggested that strong command-and-control authority structures, deriving from China's cultural attributes, conflict with the world-class manufacturing philosophies (DeFilippo, 1997: Jiang, Baker, and Frazier, 2009). Compared to the Chinese collectivist and authoritarian culture, Japan's collectivist and egalitarian culture is, thus, expected to be much more complementary to teamwork and to enhance teamwork practices necessary for manufacturing teams in general, and manufacturing cells in particular.

The labor market is another factor that affects the implementation and impact of HRM practices. Japanese workers traditionally tend not to leave their companies and move to others because the labor market is well established inside Japanese organizations. However, this situation does not exist outside Japanese organizations (Jacoby, 2005). Furthermore, Japanese companies have suffered prolonged economic stagnation since the burst of the asset-inflated bubble economy in the early 1990s, which has made Japanese workers in general more reluctant to quit a job. By contrast, China's economy has been growing at an average annual rate of around 10 percent over the past decade. Within this continuously growing economy, Chinese workers tend to migrate between companies, seeking more generous wages and better working conditions than those provided by their current employers. A high turnover rate of Chinese workers is detrimental to manufacturing operations for several reasons: no other workers are available owing to the overall labor shortage; employers cannot recoup their investment in training them (Jiang, Baker, and Frazier, 2009); and organizations cannot accumulate experience, skills, or knowledge held by operators (Nonaka, Toyama, and Hirata, 2008).

Thus, a combination of national culture, labor markets, and other national characteristics can influence the implementation of HRM practices and their impact on manufacturing performance. Therefore, the country in which a manufacturer operates is expected to influence the two-way interactions between HRM practices and the manufacturing configuration, as proposed in Hypothesis 2. Cell production relies more on operator skill and commitment than does mass production. Therefore, it is more sensitive to the effect of the HRM practices enhanced or diminished by different national characteristics. Japan-based manufacturers are more likely to find their nation's cultural characteristics enhancing the impact of their HRM practices on performance when using a cell rather than a line. Conversely, for China-based manufacturers, using a cell in the context of their national environment is more likely to diminish the effect of HRM on performance than using a line arrangement. Enriching the two-way interaction hypothesis, the previous arguments lead to the following three-way interaction hypothesis:

Hypothesis 3: the country in which a manufacturer operates moderates the two-way interactions between the use of HRM practices and the manufacturing configuration on manufacturing performance indices. More specifically, operating in a Japanese production site enhances the effect of HRM on performance more within a manufacturing configuration that tends toward a cell rather than a line. In contrast, using this configuration in a Chinese production site diminishes such an effect.

Methods

Research design and sampling

To test the earlier hypotheses, I collected data by conducting questionnaire surveys. To advance research on Japanese manufacturers discussed in Chapter 5, I combined the data from the Japan- and China-based manufacturer surveys. On the basis of the questionnaire items used for the Japanese survey, I developed items for the Chinese survey. Questionnaire items are presented in the Appendix. Although the questionnaire items used for the two studies were presented in two different languages, Japanese and Chinese, their contents were almost identical. However, some questions were added to the questionnaire developed for the Japanese survey. The survey method used in Japan is already explained in Chapter 5. Here, I discuss the method used for the Chinese survey.

I created two types of questionnaire sheets: one for managers and another for team or group leaders responsible for a cell or line. The managers' questionnaire focused on manufacturing performance, configurations, and control variables. By contrast, the team leaders' survey centered on HRM practices because they were, what Huselid and Becker (2000) called, "key informants." This means that they are supposedly more knowledgeable about practices that are actually implemented than anyone else, even the operators who often quit jobs voluntarily and have less experience with current jobs than their team leaders. It should be noted that the unit of analysis is a manufacturing team or, to be more precise, a cell or line.

In principle, dyads of managers and leaders were instructed to complete their respective questionnaire sheets. However, there were exceptions, such as a Chinese manager who was also a team leader and completed both questionnaire sheets. Furthermore, a Chinese manager was in charge of eight teams at a participating China-based manufacturer and was asked to fill out the same number of questionnaire sheets. However, as this posed a burden on the manager, the leaders completed the questionnaires on his behalf, and he then reviewed the completed surveys. I also checked the completed questionnaire sheets when I revisited the participating China-based manufacturers for follow-up research. Thus, during these visits, I reviewed and checked the questionnaire sheets that had been completed and submitted, while I asked the respondents or the people who had supervised the survey (e.g., plants' managerial staff or production engineers) for their explanations and reasons for their responses. I corrected the responses that I found wrong according to respondents' or survey supervisors' accounts. I undertook this measure to increase the reliability of the survey.

First, during the autumn of 2006 through the beginning of 2007, I collected data from Japan-based manufacturing companies. These companies were located across Japan. I developed Japanese versions of the questionnaires and conducted the Japanese survey as explained in Chapter 5. The Japanese versions were later translated into Chinese by Chinese graduate students majoring in economics at my home institution. While management-related words tend to have somewhat different connotations between China and Japan, manufacturing terms are also technical. It was, therefore, very difficult and time-consuming for these students to translate the original Japanese version into Chinese and back-translate this version into Japanese. Hence, while the graduate students worked on the translation, I explained and discussed the content with them on many occasions to convey what I meant, both explicitly and implicitly, in the Japanese version.

Using the completed Chinese version of the questionnaires, I gathered data from China-based manufacturing companies in the first quarter of 2010 and again in the summer of the same year. China is a huge country and collecting data from across the country is both difficult and costly. I therefore focused on a specific region and collected data from the manufacturing companies located in the city of Dalian, Liaoning province. Dalian is home to many Japanese corporations and hence the participating companies were owned by or affiliated with Japanese companies.

I combined data from the Japan- and China-based manufacturers. As noted previously, there was a three-year gap between the times of data collection in Japan and China. However, both survey periods were relatively favorable, in business terms, to the manufacturers, which means that the participating companies were operating under relatively good economic conditions when I conducted the surveys. Although the Japanese economy is still reeling from the aftermath of the 2008 global economic crisis and the 2011 natural disasters, the environment at the time when I conducted my survey was relatively favorable to Japan-based manufacturers, compared to the current situation. Similarly, although the Chinese economy was also affected by the economic crisis, it recovered rapidly and has since expanded, and the period in which I undertook the Chinese survey was fairly comfortable for China-based manufacturers.

As mentioned in Chapter 5, 20 Japan-based manufacturing companies participated in my survey. To conduct my survey in China, I directly visited the same number (namely, 20) of manufacturers located in Dalian. I first explained to the companies I visited the survey's purpose and method and asked managing directors or managerial employees at these companies to participate. Of these, 16 companies agreed to participate. However, the four companies that declined allowed me to observe their plants or interview their managerial employees. This method of data collection may lead to response bias (Ichniowski et al., 1996). However, participation in the survey—given that this involved dyads of managers and leaders completing two different types of questionnaires containing numerous items—was painstaking for both the individuals and their companies in the face of severe global competition. This approach was, therefore, necessary to ensure that participating companies had an understanding of and involvement with the research.

Table 8.1 provides information about the Chinese survey participants. A total of 129 production teams from 16 manufacturing companies participated. All can be categorized in general as either electronics manufacturers or metal-making companies, except one chemical producer. At this chemical company, the mechanical department in charge of the metal-making process participated in the survey. Thus, all participating manufacturing teams from China were engaged in assembly or metal-making work, as were the teams from Japan. Most of the participating China-based companies had been designated as crucial foreign manufacturing sites by their Japanese headquarters because they shipped completed products to the Japanese, Chinese, and international (such as US) markets. In that sense, these manufacturers constituted an important sample to conduct such a survey. To conduct statistical analyses, I combined data from all China-based manufacturers and the 77 teams from 20 Japan-based manufacturers (see information on

Table 8.1   Chinese survey participant information

Manufacturer Codes	Manufacturing teams	Managers	Leaders
Manufacturer 1	13	3	13
Manufacturer 2	19	11	19
Manufacturer 3	8	1[a]	8
Manufacturer 4	10	10	10
Manufacturer 5	8	3	8
Manufacturer 6	8	3	8
Manufacturer 7	4	4	4
Manufacturer 8	2	1	2
Manufacturer 9	1	1	1
Manufacturer 10	8	8	0[b]
Manufacturer 11	10	5	10
Manufacturer 12	1	1	1
Manufacturer 13	3	3	1[c]
Manufacturer 14	4	1	4
Manufacturer 15	15	7	15
Manufacturer 16	15	9	15
Total Number	129	71	119

Notes:

[a] In manufacturer 3, in practice, leaders also responded to questionnaire items for managers because one manager had to fill out the eight questionnaire sheets and this work was a heavy burden on the manager. But, along with me, the manager reviewed all the questionnaire sheets returned from leaders.

[b] Manufacturer 10 was a small company, and people in managerial positions were also responsible for operations. Thus, these managerial employees responded to questionnaire items both for managers and leaders.

[c] I did not receive completed questionnaire forms from two leaders at manufacturer 13. I revisited the plant and observed no major differences in operations between lines. The plant manager also acknowledged the fact. Thus, I used responses from leaders at other lines to cope with missing data problems.

participants in the Japanese survey in Chapter 5). Thus, a total of 206 production teams were observed or used as cases for my analyses.

Variables

Criterion variables

As discussed in Chapter 5, I adopted a five-point Likert scale and measured components of manufacturing performance. Managers evaluated the current performance of a specific cell or line of which they were in charge. The evaluations were made by making comparisons such as (1) with other cells or lines at the same plant, (2) with the level of the same performance indicator for a typical team of production workers that had made the same type of product at the same plant about five years earlier, and (3) with the average level of the corresponding performance indicator in the same industry. The Chinese survey included additional questionnaire items in which Chinese managers compared aspects of manufacturing performance (e.g., productivity and quality) for their line or cell with those of affiliated plants (i.e., Japanese plants). Because of the additional items, the Japanese sample had missing data, and hence I imputed the dataset and performed a confirmatory factor analysis (CFA) of the four-factor model, using the Statistical Analysis System (SAS) MI (to perform multiple imputation of missing data), Covariance Analysis of Linear Structural Equations (CALIS), and MIANALYZE (to combine the results of the analyses of imputations and generate valid statistical inferences) procedures. The results demonstrated convergent validity, with all factor loadings being significant. The SAS MIANALYZE procedure does not produce overall fit indexes, and I demonstrate only convergent validity. Scores on a set of several question items were then aggregated and averaged according to the different areas of manufacturing performance (such as productivity). The average values were manufacturing performance indices used for subsequent statistical analyses. Internal consistency reliabilities (Cronbach's α) for all performance indexes were high (.70 for productivity, .61 for reduction in work-in-process inventory, .69 for shortening of lead time, and .73 for quality) and, hence, these indexes were used as criterion variables.

Predictor variables

I developed 24 items covering all areas of skill enhancement training (6 items), teamwork practices (5 items), improvement activities (7 items), and motivational practices (6 items). Leaders assessed HRM practice items using a five-point Likert scale ranging from 1 (strongly disagree) to 5 (strongly agree). I performed CFA using the SAS CALIS procedure with maximum likelihood (ML) estimation to test the four-factor model and demonstrate convergent or discriminant validity. Overall fit statistics for the four-factor model were relatively, if not strongly, favorable (χ^2 = 553, df = 246, p < .01; GFI = .81, RMSEA = .07, CFI = .83), because the sample size was not large enough to perform a factor analysis, in comparison to the number of indicator variables used (Brown, 2006). Internal consistency reliabilities (Cronbach's α) were .75 for skill enhancement training, .74 for teamwork practices, .83 for improvement activities, and .65 for motivational practices. I aggregated and averaged values on the questionnaire items by each of the four HRM practice areas, following the work of others (e.g., Takeuchi, Wakabayashi, and Chen, 2003; Takeuchi, 2009). This method is different from that used in the Japanese survey research, in which I aggregated all the variables and regarded the average value as a system of the (human resource) HR system. By unbundling the system, I examine the effects of a set of HRM practices within the respective HR areas in more detail. I used an additive rather than a multiplicative approach for the reason mentioned in Chapter 5.

Moderators

Manufacturing configuration is used as the second and moderating variable in this research framework to explore the interactive effects of HRM practices. Managerial employees assessed technological aspects of a cell or line under their supervision in terms of not only form but also the strategic intent behind the technical designs, that is, lot size, product variety, and frequency of change both in production volume and models. This assessment was made using five questionnaire items on a five-point Likert scale. I then performed CFA with ML estimation. The overall fit statistics for the one-factor model were favorable (χ^2 = 26, df = 5, p < .01; GFI = .95, RMSEA = .14, CFI = .80). The internal consistency reliability coefficient was .43, indicating that the value is generally considered low (Nunnally and Bernstein, 1994). This might have been because it was the first attempt to assess manufacturing configurations. Despite the low value, I adopted averaged values of the five questionnaire items as the index with which to capture manufacturing configurations. A manufacturing configuration with a greater value can be represented as being more similar to a manufacturing cell, while a lower value signifies something closer to a line. To analyze the interactive effect between HRM practices and manufacturing configurations, I used the product terms between those two variables.

Country where the manufacturer operates is the other moderator and a third variable. This is nominal and treated as a dummy variable. If the production site of a manufacturing company was in Japan, it was coded 1, and if it was in China, it was coded 0. Product terms among HRM practices, manufacturing configuration, and country were then used to examine three-way interactive effects on manufacturing performance.

Control variables

I have already discussed control variables in detail in Chapter 5, and hence I only briefly explain them here. These are also assessed using a five-point Likert scale. *Mizusumashi* (Japanese for "whirligig beetles") replenishment workers were used as a control variable to test the work-in-process inventory and lead time models. *Pokayoke* (Japanese for "mistake-proof") tools or equipment was selected as the control variable for the quality models. Production volume was used as the control variable to test the productivity models.

Results

To test the hypotheses, I performed hierarchical moderated regression analyses using the ordinary least squares (OLS) method. I used an increment in the criteria (manufacturing performance indices) accounted for when a set of variables (such the four areas of HRM practices in a set) is added to another set or a variable already entered in the previous stage—that is, an increase in the multiple squared correlation coefficient (ΔR^2)—as the test statistic to assess whether the hypotheses were true. I also considered the coefficients on individual variables in verifying the hypotheses. When conducting the analyses, I followed the advice of Cohen et al. (2003) and mean-centered predictors (HRM practices) and a moderator (manufacturing configuration), but not controls, country, and the criteria. Thus, I subtracted from these variables their mean values to avoid multicollinearity among the predictors, moderator, and product terms between them. Table 8.2 presents the descriptive statistics including means, standard deviations, correlations, and reliabilities. Given that the sample size was not large, I considered regression coefficients at a probability level of less than .1 to be significant.

Table 8.3 presents results of the hierarchical moderated regression analyses. As step 2 shows, the inclusion of the four categories of HRM practices in a set led to improvements across all manufacturing performance models. Regarding the productivity model, this inclusion caused a significant increase in the criterion of productivity ($\Delta R^2 = 0.05$, $p <$ .05). Among the four categories of HRM practices, improvement activities, in particular, had a statistically significant and positive association

Table 8.2 Means, standard deviations, correlations, and reliabilities[a]

Variables	Mean	S.D.	1	2	3	4	5	6	7	8	9	10	11	12	13
1 Production volume	3.85	1.13													
2 *Mizusumashi*	3.08	0.71	.24**												
3 *Pokayoke*	3.31	0.70	.22**	.33**											
4 Manufacturing configuration	3.21	0.57	−.21**	−.18**	−.11+	(.43)									
5 Country	0.37	0.48	−.61**	−.31**	−.43**	.12+									
6 Productivity	3.54	0.60	.26**	.17*	.34**	−.13*	−.24**	(.70)							
7 Reduction in work-in-process inventory	3.39	0.72	.08	−.11+	.03	.22**	−.17**	.22**	(.61)						
8 Shortening of lead time	3.57	0.57	.20**	.10	.21**	−.05	−.18**	.56**	.34**	(.69)					
9 Quality	3.58	0.66	.26**	.24**	.36**	−.01	−.28**	.42**	.25**	.56**	(.73)				
10 Skill enhancement training	3.47	0.66	.39**	.22**	.16*	.07	−.55**	.11+	.18**	.10	.13+	(.75)			
11 Teamwork practices	3.82	0.61	.41**	.29**	.16*	.00	−.47**	.13*	.06	.09	.11	.67**	(.74)		
12 Improvement activities	3.45	0.65	.45**	.22**	.19*	.02	−.51**	.29**	.16*	.18**	.19**	.68**	.65**	(.83)	
13 Motivational practices	3.37	0.53	.32**	.19**	.21**	.14*	−.51**	.17*	.21**	.32**	.25**	.68**	.54**	.62**	(.65)

Notes:

[a]$n = 206$. Internal consistency reliability coefficients (Cronbach's α) appear on the diagonal.

+$p < .10$

*$p < .05$

**$p < .01$

Table 8.3 Results of hierarchical moderated regression analyses[a]

Predictors	Model 1: Productivity		Model 2: Reduction in work-in-process inventory		Model 3: Shortening of lead time		Model 4: Quality	
	Entry b	Final b	Entry b	Final b	Entry b	Final b	Entry b	Final b
Step 1: Control variable								
Production volume	0.14**	0.07+						
Mizusumashi			−0.12+	−0.17*	0.08	0.02		
Pokayoke							0.34**	0.24**
F	15.42**		2.92+		2.25		30.38**	
r^2	0.07		0.01		0.01		0.12	
Step 2: HRM practices								
Skill enhancement training	−0.16+	−0.10	0.11	−0.01	−0.20*	−0.08	−0.10	−0.06
Teamwork practices	−0.07	−0.20	−0.13	0.00	−0.07	−0.24+	−0.06	−0.35*
Improvement activities	0.30**	0.40**	0.10	0.00	0.09	0.26*	0.11	0.26+
Motivational practices	0.09	−0.07	0.23+	0.19	0.47**	0.41**	0.27*	0.12
ΔR^2	0.05		0.07		0.12		0.02	
F for ΔR^2	3.30*		3.95**		7.44**		2.60*	
R^2	0.12		0.08		0.13		0.17	
Step 3: HRM practices × manufacturing configuration								
Manufacturing configuration	−0.13+	0.10	0.21*	0.11	−0.09	0.12	0.01	0.17
Skill enhancement training × manufacturing configuration	−0.21	0.18	−0.60**	−0.40	−0.12	−0.08	−0.25	0.13
Teamwork practices × manufacturing configuration	0.19	−0.39	0.27	0.29	0.17	−0.28	0.33+	−0.21
Improvement activities × manufacturing configuration	−0.10	0.47	−0.15	0.02	0.14	0.53*	0.03	0.22

(continued)

Table 8.3 Continued

Predictors	Model 1 : Productivity		Model 2: Reduction in work-in-process inventory		Model 3: Shortening of lead time		Model 4: Quality	
	Entry *b*	Final *b*	Entry *b*	Final *b*	Entry *b*	Final *b*	Entry *b*	Final *b*
Motivational practices × manufacturing configuration	0.06	−0.26	0.38+	0.19	−0.08	−0.21	0.05	0.02
ΔR^2	0.03		0.07		0.03		0.02	
F for ΔR^2	1.07		3.38**		1.12		0.90	
R^2	0.15		0.15		0.16		0.19	
Step 4: HRM practices × country								
Country	−0.08	−0.05	−0.23+	−0.25+	−0.03	−0.05	−0.11	−0.10
Skill enhancement training × country	−0.18	−0.03	−0.12	0.08	−0.20	−0.11	−0.16	−0.11
Teamwork practices × country	0.05	0.18	−0.24	−0.23	0.13	0.23	0.41*	0.53*
Improvement activities × country	−0.10	−0.30	0.17	0.16	−0.22	−0.37*	−0.25	−0.38+
Motivational practices × country	0.31	0.36	−0.04	−0.05	0.08	0.09	0.28	0.28
ΔR^2	0.01		0.02		0.02		0.03	
F for ΔR^2	0.54		0.89		0.88		1.44	
R^2	0.16		0.17		0.18		0.22	
Step 5: Manufacturing configuration × country	−0.60**	−0.67**	0.18	0.17	−0.42*	−0.52**	−0.32+	−0.39+
ΔR^2	0.05		0.01		0.02		0.01	
F for ΔR^2	11.58**		0.79		6.63*		3.00+	
R^2	0.21		0.18		0.20		0.23	

Step 6: HRM practices × manufacturing configuration × country				
Skill enhancement training × manufacturing configuration × country	−0.33	0.05	0.15	−0.35
Teamwork practices × manufacturing configuration × country	0.76*	0.02	0.60[+]	0.69[+]
Improvement activities × manufacturing configuration × country	−1.08**	−0.39	−0.88*	−0.46
Motivational practices × manufacturing configuration × country	−0.04	0.00	−0.17	−0.26
ΔR^2	0.06	0.00	0.05	0.02
F for ΔR^2	3.66**	0.25	2.53*	1.58
R^2	0.27	0.18	0.25	0.25

Notes:
[a]$n = 206$
[+]$p < .10$
*$p < .05$
**$p < .01$

with productivity (β = 0.30, p < .01). Meanwhile, skill enhancement training was negatively related to productivity (β = –0.16, p < .1). The inclusion of the four categories of HRM practices in a set also reduced work-in-process inventory (ΔR^2 = 0.07, p < .01). Motivational practices had a marginal relationship with this indicator (β = 0.23, p < .1). A set of those HRM practices shortened lead time (ΔR^2 = 0.12, p < .01), among which, motivational practices had a positive relationship with lead time (β = 0.47, p < .01). Further, skill enhancement training was negatively related to the criterion (β = –0.20, p < .05). An added set of HRM practices accounted for the significant variance in the criterion of quality beyond that accounted for the control variable (ΔR^2 = 0.02, p < .05), and motivational practices were also positively related to quality (β = 0.27, p < .05).

Final bs in Table 8.3 indicate the final regression coefficients on individual (each of the four areas of) HRM practices after all relevant variables have been entered into the equations in the sixth and final step. Regarding moderated regressions, the final coefficients represent the regressions of the criterion on predictors at the value of zero on all other individual variables (moderators) with which the predictors interact (Cohen et al., 2003: Jaccard and Turrisi, 2003). If both predictors and moderator are mean-centered, as they are here, the predictors' final coefficients indicate slopes at an average on the moderator with which the predictors interact. The third and moderator variable, country, is a nominal and dummy variable and is not mean-centered. Its zero value means that the production site is located in China. Thus, the final coefficients of the predictors, namely HRM practices, represent regressions of the manufacturing performance indexes on the predictors at the value of zero (in this case, average) on manufacturing configuration and on country (in this case, China). Accordingly, the second step's results need to be checked. On the basis of the results, it can be said that Hypothesis 1 is partially supported.

As the results of step 3 indicate, the inclusion of a set of four product terms between the four categories of HRM practices and manufacturing configuration caused no significant increase in the criteria across all models except the work-in-process inventory model. However, the coefficient on the product term between skill enhancement training and manufacturing configuration was significant but negative on the model (β = –0.60, p < .01). Thus, the results did not support Hypothesis 2.

Hypothesis 3 predicted three-way interactive effects among the four categories of HRM practices, manufacturing configuration, and country. The inclusion of a set of three-way interaction terms in the sixth and final step caused significant increments in productivity ($\Delta R^2 = 0.06$, $p < .01$) and shortening of lead time ($\Delta R^2 = 0.05$, $p < .05$). However, the test statistics were not significant in the other two models. To facilitate an understanding of these three-way interactions, I plotted the two-way interactions between HRM practices and manufacturing configuration separately for Japan and China. I defined the manufacturing configurations that were closer to a cell/line as one standard deviation above/below the mean according to the procedure proposed by Cohen and colleagues (2003). Figure 8.1a reveals a two-way interaction, with teamwork practices being positively associated with productivity at the combination of a cell and Japan and negatively associated at that of a line and Japan. In contrast, Figure 8.1b shows that teamwork practices have a negative relationship with productivity at the combination of a cell and China while the slope is barely flat at the combination of a line and China. This pattern corresponds with Hypothesis 3.

However, effects of the three-way interaction among improvement activities, manufacturing configuration, and country on productivity, as depicted in Figures 8.2a and 8.2b, indicate that the two-way

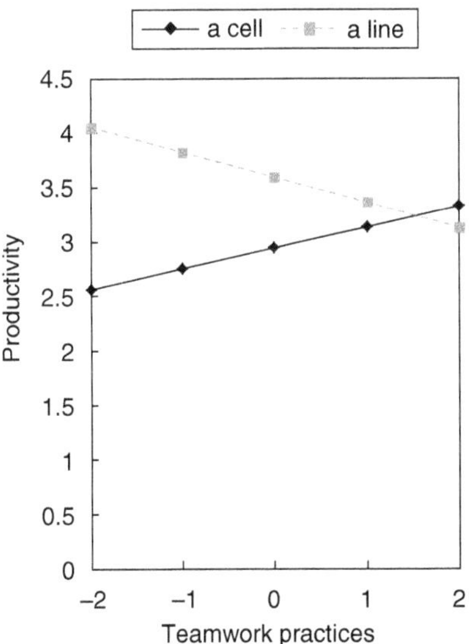

Figure 8.1a   The relationship between teamwork practices and productivity as a function of manufacturing configuration for Japan

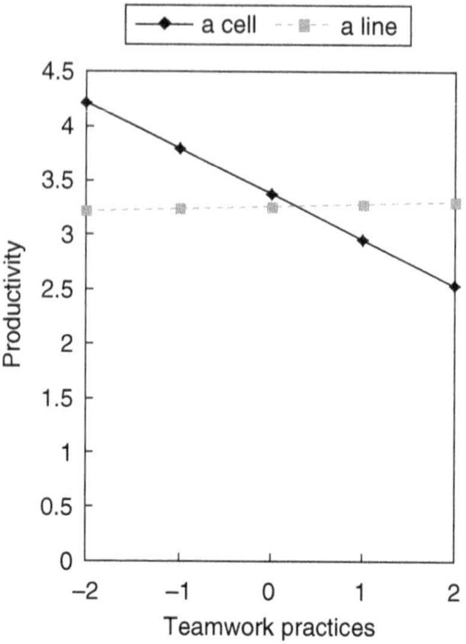

Figure 8.1b   The relationship between teamwork practices and productivity as a function of manufacturing configuration for China

interactive relationships for both Japan and China contrast with those expected by Hypothesis 3. The relationship between improvement activities and productivity is positive and stronger at the combination of a cell and China than of a line and China. By contrast, the association is negative for the combination of a cell and Japan and positive for a line and Japan. I tested the significance of the simple slope for the regression of productivity on improvement activities at the combination of a cell and China, using the procedure presented by Aiken and West (1991), and found it significant ($t = 2.60$, $p < .01$). I conducted a similar test for the combination of a line and China, but it was not significant. The pattern of the effects of the three-way interaction among teamwork practices, manufacturing configuration, and country on shortening of lead time was as predicted by Hypothesis 3, similar to that seen in Figures 8.1a and 8.1b. The effect of the three-way interaction among improvement activities, manufacturing configuration, and country on the shortening of lead time was in a pattern similar to that depicted in Figures 8.2a and 8.2b, which was contrary to the prediction of Hypothesis 3. It may be concluded, thus, that Hypothesis 3 is partially supported.

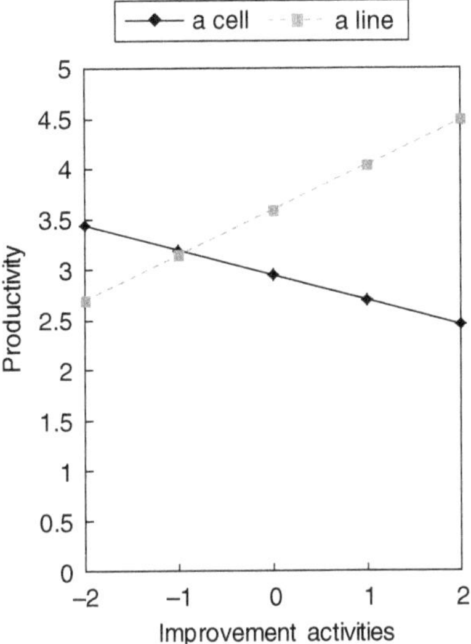

Figure 8.2a The relationship between improvement activities and productivity as a function of manufacturing configuration for Japan

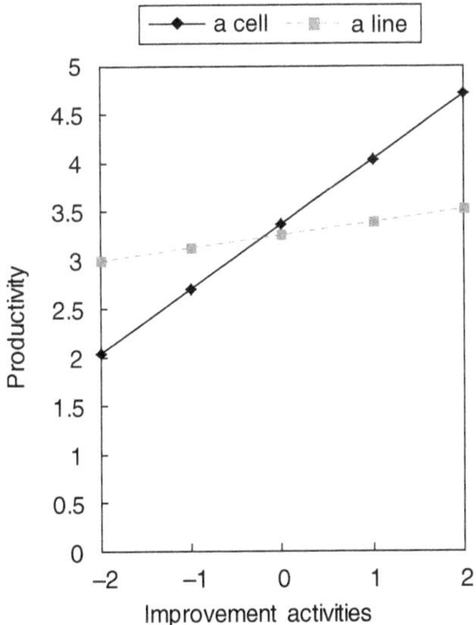

Figure 8.2b The relationship between improvement activities and productivity as a function of manufacturing configuration for China

Discussion

Follow-up research and interpretation of the results

To increase my understanding of these results, I conducted follow-up research for the Chinese survey in August 2010 and March 2011. I revisited China-based participating companies and exchanged opinions and insights with survey respondents as well as individuals who had supervised the survey, such as plant managers, HR managers, and production managers. On the basis of both the previous work conducted on SHRM and this follow-up research, here, I interpret and discuss these results in more detail.

In general, and in line with previous empirical work on SHRM, these results indicate that HRM does matter. However, HRM practices do not necessarily have positive relationships with manufacturing performance. Surprisingly, skill enhancement training was negatively related to productivity and shortening of lead time. Such training as studied in this survey primarily aims at developing multiskilled operators. Training programs and tasks requiring the multiskilling ability may make operators feel stressed. Production activities to drive Lean Production System have sometimes been dubbed "management by stress" (MacDuffie, 1995). Firms that require their employees to engage in these activities are criticized for making operators work harder to meet targets and achieve higher performance goals. Work stress stemming from executing multiskilling work practice might sometimes hinder rather than improve manufacturing performance.

Consistent with previous SHRM research, the two-way interaction hypothesis, built on the contingency perspective, was not supported here. The relationships between HRM practices and manufacturing performance were not contingent on or moderated by the second and moderator variable of manufacturing configuration. However, when considering the country of operation, moderated relationships emerged. The pattern of such interactions was different between the two nations, supporting the hypothesis that country moderates such two-way interactions. These results suggest that three-way interaction models are better than two-way models at predicting the manufacturing performance.

The results for the three-way interactions among improvement activities, manufacturing configuration, and country contradicted my hypothesis. The relationship between improvement activities and productivity was negative for the combination of a cell and Japan but positive for a line and Japan. The relationship was positive at both a cell and a line for China, with the slope steeper at the cell. One explanation for this apparently contradictory pattern is that the China-based participants of the study were affiliated with Japanese companies. Therefore, they might be more aware about the importance of improvement activities in boosting efficiency, and hence be more engaged in these activities than were the Japan-based manufacturers. Managers and leaders at certain China-based manufacturers accepted this explanation when I revisited them for my follow-up research.

Three-way interactions were not confirmed to either the work-in-process inventory or quality models. I chose several measures of manufacturing performance because these indicators are considered relevant to this research setting, that is, the manufacturing sector, apart from other reasons. Despite my effort to carefully choose my measures, the statistical results were not consistent across the three-way interaction models. This might indicate that the relationships between HRM practices and manufacturing performance are not straightforward despite their proximity, and in fact their links may be more complex than they appear to be, as I argued in Chapter 5.

Theoretical implications

This research makes a theoretical contribution to the field of SHRM primarily by identifying the impact of national characteristics or, more generally, the external context on HRM practices. It identifies the importance of national characteristics, including national cultures and job markets, in explaining the impact of HRM practices on manufacturing performance. The results demonstrate that the countries where manufacturers operate, or are even bound and embedded, can plausibly explain why the relationships between HRM practices and performance are not always moderated by contingency variables such as strategies, technologies, structures, and other environmental factors within an organization.

This research makes another theoretical contribution to the body of literature on SHRM in that it tests the contingency perspective-based hypothesis by employing the manufacturing configuration as a contingency variable. It shows that three-way interaction models that take into account the country of operation are better than two-way models at predicting manufacturing performance.

Furthermore, by answering the call from some scholars (e.g., Brewster, Sparrow, and Harris, 2005) to conduct SHRM research in the global context, this research also contributes to the development of the burgeoning field of international SHRM. In recent years, empirical studies have been conducted in both Western and Asian countries (Takeuchi,

Wakabayashi, and Chen, 2003; Chow, Huang, and Liu, 2008; Takeuchi, 2009). Nevertheless, more recently, there have also been calls for SHRM research to be conducted in a global context or across multiple countries, and some scholars have done so (e.g., Ahmad and Schroeder, 2003; Lawler et al., 2011). In this study, I attempted to explain two-way interactions that are not supported by the existing SHRM literature, taking into consideration the importance of different national characteristics and designating country as the third and moderator variable. These attempts will encourage the building of more advanced theories and the invention of more sophisticated methodologies in the burgeoning field of international SHRM research.

Practical implications

This research also makes practical contributions, particularly for manufacturers. First, it underscores the need for creating awareness about the nuanced but significant effect that a mix of cultural attributes, labor markets, and other characteristics specific to a given nation can have on the implementation of HRM practices. For managers planning to transfer their production facilities abroad, such awareness will result in the success of a specific manufacturing method and, eventually, outstanding manufacturing performance. Otherwise, they will encounter the method's failure and, then, mediocre outcomes.

Second, this research suggests actions or measures for China-based manufacturers in transition toward new manufacturing methods. Attracted by the country as a rich source of workforce, manufacturers from around the world have made direct investment here. China has served, quite literally, as the world's factory. Previously, it has been considered difficult to run sophisticated operations driven by the principles of Lean Production System, such as cellular manufacturing, in Chinese factories (Lockett, 1988; DeFilippo, 1997). However, the results of this study suggest that Chinese production sites should not be viewed as places where implementing new types of manufacturing is unsuitable and unthinkable. Chinese manufacturers are expected to benefit from these manufacturing innovations as long as they carry out appropriate HRM practices, such as improvement activities, to ensure the success of the new production methods.

Third, the statistical results imply that Chinese workers in China-based Japanese companies may be engaged in advanced production work as opposed to the monotonous and standardized work typical in conventional Chinese workplaces, and hence, they may be achieving a high standard of manufacturing performance. China-based manufacturers that participated in my survey were affiliated with Japanese companies. A typical image of Chinese factories—whether or not they have any connections with Japanese companies—seems to be that they are places where, deployed on long production lines, a large number of unskilled operators engage in simple and monotonous work and mass produce commodity-type or low-end products. However, the results of the three-way interactions revealed unpredicted patterns: improvement activities can boost manufacturing performance at a cell in China to a greater extent than in Japan. The results might prove that Chinese workers in China-based Japanese companies engage in advanced production, their skills and knowledge are harnessed and developed by means of sophisticated management practices, and their Chinese workplaces are thus transforming into new ones. In such a manner, my work offers a glimpse inside Japanese overseas workplaces that are undergoing transformations.

Limitations and future directions

Despite the theoretical and practical contributions outlined previously, this research has some limitations. First, I did not directly assess national characteristics. Instead, I coded the countries where manufacturers operate and used this scheme to evaluate each country's impact. However, such a method might be considered imprecise. In my future work, I will need to develop new questionnaire items that directly assess national characteristics, and more precisely explore the extent to which national characteristics affect the impact of HRM practices. Second, the China-based manufacturers that participated in my survey were owned by or affiliated with Japanese companies. Firms owned by companies from other countries such as the US, Taiwan, or South Korea—some of which hire tens of thousands of Chinese workers—as well as Chinese state- or privately run enterprises, were not included. Had I done so, the results might have been different. Third, I focused my research activities on the northern city of Dalian because it was difficult and costly to collect data from across the country. China is a large country that has significantly varied culture and workforce. Had I collected data in cities other than Dalian, the results might also have been different. My next project will focus on collecting data from several parts of China and conducting large-scale comparative studies between China and Japan.

9
Conclusion

Introduction

So far I have examined the landscape of Japanese workplaces undergoing transformation since the turn of the twenty-first century. Furthermore, I have attempted to conceptualize the new approaches (regarding management practices and organizational culture) that Japanese companies took and to empirically test their effectiveness. In this chapter, I summarize those transformations and identify lessons that companies outside Japan can learn, including those transformations that Japanese companies have undergone over the past decade or more. Finally, I mention future Japanese workplaces and conclude this book.

Summary of transformations at Japanese workplaces

I summarize the transformations occurring at Japanese workplaces in Table 9.1 and discuss these transformations in more detail in this section. The transformations are those that have occurred over more than a decade since the turn of the century.

Transformations at the shop-floor level

Over the past decade, major Japanese companies have abandoned parts of their traditional and organization-oriented management and employment systems and adopted those based on market principles, such as merit-based pay and personnel outsourcing, following their Western, particularly, US counterparts (Jacoby, 2005). These changes in the management system are concerned with management or human resource management (HRM) policies that are formulated by higher-ranking managerial or human resource (HR) staff. Rather than paying attention

Table 9.1 Summary of the transformations at Japanese workplaces since the dawn of the new millennium

---

At the shop-floor level (in the manufacturing sector)
Management practices:
The use of team-based practices
→ The use of a system of high performance work practices

Triggers to the transformation:
The collapse of the nation's bubble economy and threats from overseas competitors, and the ensuing introduction of cell production

Expected consequences of the transformation:
A higher standard of manufacturing performance

At the company level
Organizational culture in terms of the homogeneous and heterogeneous nature:
Homogeneous and strong culture
→ Heterogeneous culture, multiple subcultures, and culture's greater diversity

Triggers to the transformation:
Adoption of parts of a market-oriented employment system in addition to changes in macro environments, for instance, demographics

Expected consequences of the transformation:
Adaptability, innovation, and lost cultural integration

---

to these policies at the abstract level, I focused on management practices at the operational level, which are actually being implemented by front-line or rank-and-file employees. These management practices are also workplace practices in the sense that they are unique to and performed at workplaces. For my investigation, I chose the manufacturing sector, particularly the electronics industry, because the Japanese economy has been bolstered largely by the electronics and automotive industries since World War II. Moreover, Japanese electronics manufacturers represent the Japanese companies that are struggling to compete with their overseas rivals and regain their lost competitiveness.

Japanese companies were believed to espouse and utilize high commitment and high-performance work practices (HPWPs) and other advanced management practices. Indeed, my case study of Toyota Motor Corp. (TMC) revealed that the Japanese automobile manufacturer implemented these practices in its operation. For instance, Toyota Motor Kyushu Inc. (TMK), a manufacturing company wholly owned by TMC, espoused teamwork. The ability of TMK's operators to handle multiple tasks allowed for effective team activities. Those operators were trained to perform multiskilling tasks. Production teams comprising these operators were autonomous or self-sufficient in that they assumed responsibility for accomplishing a spectrum of work processes assigned on a mini production line.

As my studies of Japanese electronics companies illustrated, however, utilizing HPWPs as a set was uncommon among Japanese manufacturers. Instead, Japanese electronics manufacturers utilized HPWPs in isolation, even if these practices were put in place at their workplaces. Even though the manufacturers used team-based management practices as part of a high-performance work system, they did not utilize them in line with other HPWPs that can bolster these team-based practices, such as multiskilling training and several means to motivate employees. In conclusion, teamwork, quality control (QC) circles, and other team-based practices would have been common among Japanese manufacturers although a set of HPWPs or high-performance work system was not widely used among them, except by automotive manufacturers, before the turn of the century. Thus, the effects of those team-based practices could have been limited.

However, Japanese electronics manufacturers and other manufacturers started utilizing a set of HPWPs after the turn of the century, while introducing cell production. By doing so, they attempted to be more efficient and competitive and to survive in the face of the economy's decade-long stagnation and challenges from overseas competitors. As they have made efforts to turn themselves around, their traditional workplaces have been transformed. Japanese manufacturers are still in transition in terms of the use of high-performance work systems. To assess the effectiveness of the newly introduced management practices, I theorized the associations between the management practices and manufacturing performance. Then, I tested the direct and interactive effects with the manufacturing configuration (a cell or line), by collecting data from Japanese manufacturers. I confirmed the effects but not fully.

Moreover, I attempted to duplicate the effects by collecting data from China-based manufacturers as well. In addition, I assessed the impacts of different national characteristics on these effects by combining the two data sets. China-based manufacturers that were surveyed were affiliated with Japanese companies. Their teamwork activities had negative effects on autonomous team activities required for effective manufacturing, which was supposedly caused by the nation's authoritarian culture. Meanwhile, these China-based manufacturers utilized improvement activities sufficiently well to ensure the success of their manufacturing activities and to obtain a high standard of manufacturing performance. Thus, their workplaces seem to be transforming. Although

I only presented the results of the Chinese survey, I could conclude that Japanese workplaces overseas are also in transition.

It is apparent that Japanese workplaces are transforming in terms of the management practices considered in this book. However, it is also important to know the outcomes of those transformations from the perspective of managers and scholars interested in the effects of management practices, such as strategic human resource management (SHRM) scholars. Japanese manufacturers expect to become more competitive and ensure a higher standard of manufacturing performance than they previously achieved by employing HPWPs or a system of those practices. As the results of my empirical studies demonstrated, particularly when using combined data from the Japanese and Chinese surveys, these new practices were indeed associated with a high standard of manufacturing performance. However, it should be noted that the effects were not fully verified.

In sum, shop floors at home and abroad in Japanese manufacturing companies seem to have transformed or still be transforming into workplaces where people implement high- performance work systems. They do so because it enables them to ensure the success of cell- or team-based production and achieve a higher standard of manufacturing performance than they did in the days of traditional mass production.

Transformations at the company level

In this book, I have investigated transformations in Japanese workplaces not only at the shop-floor level but also at the company level by taking both micro and macro approaches. I examined the organizational culture of Japanese companies, which is an aspect of the organization-level phenomenon, by paying attention to the organizations' upper echelon. I attempted to explore the changing nature of Japanese companies' organizational culture in terms of cultural homogeneity or diversity as an approach in the literature about organizational culture. Japanese companies have been known for their homogeneous workforce, which has allowed them to develop a homogeneous and strong organizational culture. Such culture has been considered a source of their competitive advantages because a strong culture can allow an organization's members to become well integrated and directed toward achievement of the organization's goals. The organization can benefit from its strong culture in the form of a high standard of efficiency and productivity. Japanese companies, particularly their upper echelon or managerial staff, are still dominated by older, male Japanese employees. These employees typically have a long tenure with their current employers, having landed a job at the company immediately after having graduated from college. The situation in which the upper echelon was dominated by such similar people has helped to homogenize the organizational culture of Japanese companies at all levels, from the upper echelon to the front lines. The organizational culture reflects these people's values, such as masculinity, and other traditional values of Japanese society, including collectivism and egalitarianism.

On the whole, Japanese companies' organizational culture remains homogeneous, but there is a slow, but growing trend toward workforce diversity. Recently, these companies seem to have become culturally more diverse than they were before, at least in the 1980s, when their strong culture attracted attention from scholars and even the general public from around the world. Those who can constitute subcultures in Japanese companies, such as job hoppers, female managers, and younger generation employees, have started to hold managerial and other key organizational positions. As a result, the organizational culture of Japanese companies has not been as strong as it was and, instead, has become heterogeneous. In other words, cultural diversity or the extent to which an organization is heterogeneous due to the presence of subcultures has become salient and greater in Japanese companies over recent years. Thus, workplaces have transformed or are transforming into culturally diverse organizations. However, it should be noted that this phenomenon is still in its nascent stage.

The heterogenization of Japanese companies' culture was triggered by several environmental factors such as changes in demographics, labor markets, and the central government's policies. In addition to these macro-level changes, organizational and managerial factors have generated the new organizational phenomenon, and they are more significant from the perspective of management theories and practices. Adoption of parts of a market-oriented employment system was a key driver in transforming the culturally homogeneous workplaces of Japanese companies into culturally heterogeneous ones. The strong culture of these companies was developed and sustained by their traditional employment system, parts of which include job security, seniority-based evaluation and pay, internal promotion, and other organization-oriented practices. Meanwhile, parts of the market-oriented employment system, such as variable pay, external recruitment, personnel outsourcing, and short-term employment, can weaken this cultural strength but encourage cultural diversity by bringing new perspectives and knowledge to the organizations. The introduction of these elements seems to have served to transform traditional Japanese workplaces into culturally new ones.

Such cultural transformations appear to damage the cultural strength and integrity built up by Japanese companies over a long period of time, which is a source of their competitive advantages. However, cultural diversity can allow organizations to be adaptive and innovative. Indeed, my empirical work demonstrated that even those Japanese companies that traditionally had a homogenous culture can benefit from workforce and cultural diversity and improve their bottom lines by means of such diversity. It also revealed that Japanese companies might lose their cultural integrity owing to the cultural diversity, causing employees to leave the companies. My statistical results suggested that companies, irrespective of being Japanese or non-Japanese, are required to embrace cultural diversity by taking certain measures such as securing employees' jobs and enhancing their commitment, thereby compensating for any solidarity lost due to cultural diversity. In sum, as some Japanese companies have become more diverse in terms of their workforce, workplaces have transformed or are transforming into culturally diverse organizations.

Lessons to learn from Japanese companies

Management practitioners and scholars outside Japan may believe that their companies can learn nothing from Japanese companies, a majority of which are still struggling to survive the two decade-long economic stagnation and increasingly fierce global competition. Even the Japanese may think so and wish to learn from highly acclaimed foreign companies such as Apple Inc., Google Inc., Amazon.com Inc., General Electric Co., South Korea's Samsung Electronics Co., Ltd., the social network giant Facebook, and other celebrity companies, instead of indigenous Japanese companies. However, Japanese companies have experienced events that foreign companies have not yet faced but might encounter in the future. Hence, there are several lessons that foreign companies can learn from Japanese companies, including failures and successes of their strategies and corporate governance practices. Among countless lessons to be drawn from Japanese companies, I focus on those that accord with the subjects in this book: lessons in management practices and organizational culture.

First, companies outside Japan, particularly those in emerging economies, can learn the measures that they should take in the face of serious threats from competitors and the end of their nation's economic growth. Many Japanese companies have struggled and continue to struggle to regain their competitive edge and re-emerge in the global business scene. Toward this aim, they have made several attempts to be competitive with foreign rivals and have strived to be more efficient and profitable over the past two decades in which they have been bogged down by a declining economy. One of the means adopted by Japanese manufacturers to address these difficulties was to become lean by employing Toyota Production System (TPS). Specifically, they replaced traditional mass production with cell production, as Japanese electronics manufacturers had done. The replacement entailed not just technical but also organizational and HR transformations. Operators were required to gain multiple skills and perform multiskilling tasks. Their multiskilling abilities allowed for effective team activities that were required for new team-based production methods. Companies in emerging economies are currently enjoying an economic boom. However, economic growth will not last forever, and they, too, will face competitors who are fiercer than their current ones. At that time, these companies will have to take measures or even turn themselves around to deal with these new challenges. They will also have to become more efficient and competitive than they are at present. Companies outside Japan can learn a lot from the experiences and efforts that Japanese companies have made over the past decades, including their organizational and HR as well as production transformations.

Second, companies in the rest of the world can learn how Japanese companies continued their manufacturing operations in Japan despite transferring large parts of production functions overseas. The production facilities have been transferred to cheap-labor countries such as China and South Asian countries so that the companies can become more cost-competitive and tap into the cost advantages inherent in those countries. However, they did not transfer all production functions overseas and continued to operate in Japan with manufacturing cells. They decided to mass produce abroad while producing high-end products in a small-lot size with manufacturing cells in Japan. Companies outside Japan, particularly in the US, have closed their factories in their home countries and shifted their entire manufacturing operations offshore. Even Asian companies, including those from South Korea, Taiwan, and Singapore, have transferred production facilities to more cost-competitive sites overseas in recent years. Closures of production facilities lead to job cuts and even the loss of skills and knowledge so far accumulated by workers. The events affect manufacturing capabilities built up over years, as US electronics manufacturers have learned. Japanese manufacturers have countered such threats by continuing to operate in the home nation with manufacturing cells, looking at cell production as a means to maintain manufacturing in Japan. However, this advanced manufacturing method alone would not necessarily guarantee that manufacturing companies in Japan and the rest of the world can become more competitive than they are now and maintain manufacturing in their home countries. To be competitive with these team-based or cell production methods, manufacturers need to capitalize on human capital and elicit worker skills and capabilities by utilizing relevant management practices, as shown in this book.

Third, foreign companies can learn how to educate and motivate people through management practices so as to develop flexible work organizations and improve performance. This question concerns the important theme of SHRM studies. Educating people to handle several work tasks and become multiskilled was one means whereby Japanese manufacturing companies successfully implemented cell production and improved manufacturing performance. Developing multiskilled workers was a key factor in driving effective work teams and in implementing cell- or team-based production. Prior SHRM work suggested the importance of education to performance improvement, but did not mention in detail how people should be educated. Japanese companies used several means to develop multiskilling abilities, including on-the-job training (OJT), extensive training, and job rotation, as well as in-house qualification systems and multiskilled worker maps to encourage and motivate people to become multiskilled. Japanese companies used education programs and other management practices such as improvement activities and teamwork practices to implement cell production and be more efficient and profitable. Foreign companies can learn much from Japanese companies about how to actually exercise HPWPs and then improve performance.

Fourth, companies in the rest of the world can learn how to operate in different national environments, in which it seems difficult to operate using advanced manufacturing methods. In recent years, Japanese companies have started operating in China and other parts of Asia such as Malaysia with advanced manufacturing methods, including cell production. These advanced manufacturing methods do not seem to function well in a nation that is culturally different from and unfamiliar with them. For example, China, a nation known for high power distance and accustomed to traditional mass production, might not be a good place to implement cell and other advanced production techniques. However, my work revealed that China-based manufacturers affiliated with Japanese companies operated with those new methods by taking advantage of the abilities of younger Chinese workers to learn faster and be more adaptive than their older counterparts working at Japan-based plants. Consequently, China-based manufacturers improved their manufacturing performance. American, European, and Asian companies operating in China and other Asian countries can learn how to operate with advanced manufacturing methods through effective management practices and improve performance in different national environments from Japanese manufacturing companies.

Fifth, foreign companies can learn about the advantages and disadvantages of workforce and cultural diversity. My work revealed that even traditionally homogenous Japanese companies benefit from diversity while being vulnerable to the loss of cultural integrity and coherence among employees. Asian companies, such as those in China, Taiwan, and South Korea, are homogeneous, although their countries and regions, particularly China, are multicultural societies in which ethnically diverse groups live. Managerial positions at these companies are held by people with similar cultural backgrounds. These homogeneous companies can learn from Japanese companies how to benefit from diversity at work. By contrast, culturally diverse Western companies can also learn that putting too much emphasis on diversity can damage cultural integrity and coherence and result in their facing a cultural backlash.

Future Japanese workplaces

While I have been writing this book, Japanese companies have been facing new challenges, one after another, such as a high surge in the Japanese yen against the US dollar, the disruption of supply chains caused by the massive March 11 earthquake and tsunami, and the shortage of electricity in the aftermath of the nuclear crisis following those natural disasters. In the case of Toyota, which exports roughly half its cars produced in Japan, a mere one yen rise against the US dollar generated a loss of 30 billion yen, or approximately US$355 million, in operating profits (Ingrassia, 2011). The earthquake and tsunami caused explosions of the nuclear reactors at the Fukushima nuclear power plant and the ensuing radioactive leakage, events that precipitated a thorough inspection of the nation's operating nuclear power reactors by the Japanese government. This means that utilities companies have to stop running their reactors for a long time, some of which might never be restarted. Then, Japanese residents and companies will have to make ends meet with less electricity provided by the nation's energy companies. In addition to the yen's high appreciation against the US dollar and other foreign currencies such as the euro, the power shortage, high corporate taxation, excessive regulation of carbon dioxide emissions, and other economic and social factors, including a shortage of younger workforce and weak domestic demand owing to the low birthrate and increasing elderly population, may accelerate the transfer of production functions by Japanese companies to overseas sites. Non-manufacturing Japanese companies have followed suit. For instance, Japanese retailers such as Fast Retailing Co., Ltd. and Aeon Co., Ltd.—Japan's major super-market operator—are expanding their overseas operations and sales while reducing the number of their outlets and chain stores in Japan. It is uncertain whether those Japanese companies will continue to oper-ate in Japan, but they would be unlikely to expand operations in Japan for at least a little while. The current situation might promote a hol-lowing-out of the domestic industries, even as the Japanese economy is recovering from the March 11 triple disasters. The shifting environ-ments surrounding Japanese companies might cause further changes in Japanese workplaces. For manufacturing companies, all production functions might be transferred to overseas sites. Additionally, research and development, as well as other non-manufacturing functions such as logistics, might be conducted overseas. Indeed, some Japanese manufacturers are already doing so (*The Japan Times*, February 4, 2012; February 17, 2012). Offices located in Japan might only serve as com-pany headquarters, employing only a small number of managerial and staff employees in administrative positions.

There are adversities and uncertainties surrounding Japanese com-panies, but the current landscape of Japanese workplaces is unlikely to change radically in the near future. Japanese companies will strengthen their competitiveness that was built on advanced manufacturing meth-ods or technology. They will do so on the basis of their flexible and resilient approach to the organization of work that can also be bolstered by an array of management practices, such as team-based practice and other elements of high-performance work systems. Japanese workplaces will continue to be characterized by their teamwork and resilience, among several other positive qualities. Even at overseas workplaces, Japanese companies will retain an atmosphere characterized by team-work and associated management practices. The upper echelons of Japanese organizations are likely to be more diverse than they are now. The trend for which I argued in this book will grow further. More peo-ple with different careers and cultural backgrounds will work together with the typical, homogenous type of Japanese managerial employee in the future. Thus, different cultural values are likely to develop within

Japanese companies in the future, and, consequently, Japanese companies will be more culturally diverse organizations from their upper echelon through their front lines. Then, Japanese companies will take advantage of the dynamism stemming from the new phenomenon to a greater extent than they are doing now, even if they might encounter backlashes, including conflicts between subcultures and the dominant culture and the loss of cultural integrity owing to the presence of numerous subcultures within the company.

Japanese companies and their workplaces have transformed several times since the nation opened the door to foreigners and started modernizing and westernizing itself around 150 years ago. Some current leading Japanese companies were established immediately after the 1868 Meiji restoration that marked the end of centuries of the nation's feudalism and the founding of modern Japan. Those Japanese firms modernized themselves and built their competitiveness in the early days of modern Japan by introducing state-of-the-art technology and institutions from Western societies. Japanese companies again transformed after World War II. Then, they developed their cutting-edge technology while building the foundation for so-called Japanese management styles such as lifetime employment, seniority system, and enterprise unionism. These efforts to transform led to the prosperity of Japanese companies in the 1980s. In the wake of the collapse of the bubble economy in the early 1990s and as a result of competitive threats from foreign rivals during the same period, Japanese companies have transformed themselves to address the difficulties accompanying the changes in their environments. They are transforming further now, a time when, facing the March 11 triple disasters and increasingly harsh business environments, they have reached the most significant turning point since World War II. It might be slow, but Japanese companies and workplaces are surely transforming.

Appendix

Questionnaire items, all on the five-point Likert scale, are presented next.

Questionnaire items for managers

Manufacturing configuration (five items)

1. Please circle one of the following line layouts that best describes your assembly line.
   (1: "Genuine" mass production line, that is, one on which a small variety of products are manufactured at large-lot sizes. 2: "Quasi" mass production line, that is, one that can be rearranged to adapt to changes in product models. 3: "Hybrid" or mixed production line, that is, one on which small quantities of various products are manufactured. 4: "Quasi" cell or team-based line, that is, one operated with a large number of operators, compared to that of other cells that produce comparable products at the plant. 5: "Genuine" cell or team-based line, that is, one that is operated with a small number of operators, compared to other cells that produce comparable products at the plant.)
2. On your assembly line, at what lot size are products manufactured, compared to that of other lines that produce comparable products at the plant? (1: very large and 5: very small)
3. On your assembly line, how many items of products are manufactured, compared to those of other lines that produce comparable products at the plant? (1: very small and 5: very large)
4. On your assembly line, how frequently are changes in production volume made, compared to those of other lines that produce comparable products at the plant? (1: rarely and 5: very frequently)
5. On your assembly line, how frequently are changes in product models made, compared to those of other lines that produce comparable products at the plant? (1: rarely and 5: very frequently)

Capacity utilization (one item)

1. What percentage of the maximum or potential production capacity of your line is currently utilized? (1: 0–20 percent, 2: 20–40 percent, 3: 50–60 percent, 4: 60–80 percent, 5: 80–100 percent)

Roles of *Mizusumashi* replenishment workers (one item)

1. To what extent are you satisfied, overall, with outcomes, such as timeliness and accuracy, achieved by procurement workers (sometimes called *Mizusumashi* replenishment workers in Japanese plants) who replenish your assembly line with part components? (1: not at all satisfied and 5: very satisfied)

Pokayoke or error-proof tools (one item)

1. To what extent are you satisfied with *pokayoke* or error-proof tools on your assembly line, through which minor mistakes can be prevented and manufacturing quality can be improved? (1: not at all satisfied and 5: very satisfied)

Productivity (five items)

1. On your assembly line, how large is the number of products assembled per worker or labor productivity, compared to that of other lines that produce comparable products at the plant? (1: very small and 5: very large)
2. On your assembly line, how large is the number of products assembled per worker, compared to the level achieved by the assembly lines that produced comparable products at the plant approximately three years ago? (1: very small and 5: very large)
3. On your assembly line, how large is the number of products assembled per worker, compared to that of other lines that produce comparable products at the affiliated plants? (1: very small and 5: very large. This item was not used in the Japanese survey.)
4. On your assembly line, how large is the number of products assembled per worker, compared to the "average level" of the industry? (1: very small and 5: very large)
5. On your assembly line, how strongly is the number of products produced per worker associated with the ability of your plant to compete against rival plants? (1: very weakly and 5: very strongly)

Reduction in work-in-process inventory (five items)

1. On your assembly line, how large is the work-in-process inventory, compared to that of other assembly lines that produce comparable products at the plant? (1: very large and 5: very small)
2. On your assembly line, how large is the work-in-process inventory, compared to the level achieved by the assembly lines that produced comparable products at the plant approximately three years ago? (1: very large and 5: very small)
3. On your assembly line, how large is the work-in-process inventory, compared to that of other assembly lines that produce comparable products at affiliated plants? (1: very large and 5: very small. This item was not used in the Japanese survey.)
4. On your assembly line, how large is the work-in-process inventory, compared to the "average level" of the industry? (1: very large and 5: very small)
5. On your assembly line, how strongly is the level of work-in-process inventory associated with the ability of your plant to compete against rival plants? (1: very weakly and 5: very strongly)

Shortening of lead time (five items)

1. On your assembly line, how long is the lead time or throughput time (i.e., the time taken to complete all assembly work on the line), compared to that of other lines that produce comparable products at the plant? (1: very long and 5: very short)

2. On your assembly line, how long is the lead time, compared to the level achieved by the assembly lines that produced comparable products at the plant approximately three years ago? (1: very long and 5: very short)
3. On your assembly line, how long is the lead time, compared to that of other lines that produce comparable products at affiliated plants? (1: very long and 5: very short. This item was not used in the Japanese survey.)
4. On your assembly line, how long is the lead time, compared to the "average level" of the industry? (1: very long and 5: very short)
5. On your assembly line, how strongly is the lead time associated with the ability of your plant to compete against rival plants? (1: very weakly and 5: very strongly)

Quality (five items)

1. On your assembly line, how high is the percentage of defective products in all products assembled, compared to that of other lines that produce comparable products at the plant? (1: very high and 5: very low)
2. On your assembly line, how high is the percentage of defective products in all products assembled, compared to the level achieved by the assembly lines that produced comparable products at the plant approximately three years ago? (1: very high and 5: very low)
3. On your assembly line, how high is the percentage of defective products in all products assembled, compared to that of other lines that produce comparable products at the affiliated plants? (1: very high and 5: very low. This item was not used in the Japanese survey.)
4. On your assembly line, how high is the percentage of defective products in all products assembled, compared to the "average level" of the industry? (1: very high and 5: very low)
5. On your assembly line, how strongly is the percentage of defective products in all products associated with the ability of your plant to compete against rival plants? (1: very weakly and 5: very strongly)

Questionnaire items for leaders, all assessed on the five-point scale: strongly disagree (1) and strongly agree (5)

Multiskilling or skill enhancement training (six items)

1. Workers deal with multiple work processes.
2. Most of the workers are experienced employees who have long careers in manufacturing work.
3. Workers acquire new skills and broaden the range of their skills while doing their jobs on the line.
4. Workers get more skillful supervisors or colleagues to instruct them in new tasks whenever they need to do so.
5. Through off-the-line job training (OffJT), workers learn and upgrade skills required of a multiskilled worker who can handle multiple work processes.
6. Workers upgrade their skill level while they achieve within-plant-certifications.

Teamwork practices (five items)

1. Workers not only focus on their own work but also maintain a balance with the pace of co-workers' work so that they do not disturb it.
2. Workers help adjacent co-workers on the line who have trouble with their work.
3. Workers bear shared responsibility for the results of the line, such as quantity, cost, and quality.
4. Workers gain an understanding of each other's tasks while working on the line.
5. The team of production workers competes against other production teams at the plant on performance measurements such as quality and lead time (all the time taken to make products).

Improvement activities (seven items)

1. Workers attempt to improve the work environment through suggestion systems.
2. Solutions that workers present through suggestion systems are useful in making the manufacturing line more efficient.
3. Workers regularly (e.g., once a week) hold and participate in a QC circle or other off-the-line improvement activities.
4. Every worker, whether regular or nonregular (e.g., dispatched or part-time), participates in off-the-line improvement activities.
5. Solutions that workers find through improvement activities are adopted as standardized procedures to prevent the same major or minor trouble with the line from occurring again.
6. Workers on the line exchange know-how and solutions with people on other lines.
7. Workers are allowed to suggest ideas for improving products and work processes directly to technical staff members (such as manufacturing engineers).

Motivational practices (six items)

1. Promotion of workers to a higher position is closely linked to their skill levels.
2. As a line's leader, you make a point of recognizing any efforts and attempts made by workers on your production team to improve work, even if they failed.
3. Within-plant qualifications are useful in getting workers to upgrade the level of skills involved with their jobs.
4. Workers describe their own manufacturing job as challenging or creative.
5. Workers feel a sense of achievement by performing their manufacturing jobs.
6. Workers have chances to meet corporate executives who are on a plant tour.

Workers' job attitudes (five items)

1. Assembly workers are willing to deal with changes and contingencies they face in working on the line, such as changes in product models and production volume.

2. Assembly workers are willing to participate in various improvement activities.
3. Assembly workers try to implement important work improvement ideas that they have come up with.
4. Assembly workers are willing to work beyond the range of tasks specified by their job descriptions.
5. When operating on the line, assembly workers value harmony or cooperation among co-workers.

References

Adler, P. S. 1993. "The 'learning bureaucracy': New United Motor Manufacturing, Inc." In L. L. Cummings and B. M. Staw (eds), *Research in organizational behavior: An annual series of analytical essays and critical reviews*, vol. 15: 111–194. Greenwich, CT: JAI Press.

Ahmad, S. and Schroeder, R. G. 2003. "The impact of human resource management practices on operational performance: Recognizing country and industry difference." *Journal of Operations Management*, 21: 19–43.

Aiken, L. S. and West, S. G. 1991. *Multiple regression: Testing and interpreting interactions*. Thousand Oaks, CA: Sage Publications.

Aoki, M. 1990. "Toward an economic model of the Japanese firm." *Journal of Economic Literature*, 28: 1–27.

Appelbaum, E., Bailey, T., Berg, P., and Kalleberg, A. L. 2000. *Manufacturing advantage: Why high-performance work systems pay off*. Ithaca, NY: Cornell University Press.

Argyris, C. and Schön, D. A. 1978. *Organizational learning: A theory of action perspective*. Reading, MA: Addison-Wesley.

Arthur, B. J. and Boyles, T. 2007. "Validating the human resource system structure: A levels-based strategic HRM approach." *Human Resource Management Review*, 17: 77–92.

Arthur, J. B. 1994. "Effects of human resource systems on manufacturing performance and turnover." *Academy of Management Journal*, 37: 670–687.

Baldwin, C. Y. and Clark, K. B. 1997. "Managing in an age of modularity." *Harvard Business Review*, 75(5): 84–93.

Barnard, C. I. 1938. *The functions of the executive*. Cambridge, MA: Harvard University Press.

Baron, R. M. and Kenny, D. A. 1986. "The moderator-mediator variable distinction in social psychological research: Conceptual, strategic, and statistical consideration." *Journal of Personality and Social Psychology*, 5: 1173–1182.

Baron, J. M. and Kreps, D. M. 1999. *Strategic human resources: Framework for general managers*. New York, NY: John Wiley & Sons.

Batt, R. 2002. "Managing customer services: Human resource practices, quit rates, and sales growth." *Academy of Management Journal*, 45: 587–597.

Becker, B. E. and Gerhart, B. 1996. "The impact of human resource management on organizational performance: Progress and prospects." *Academy of Management Journal*, 39: 779–801.

Becker, B. E. and Huselid, M. A. 1998. "High performance work systems and firm performance: A synthesis of research and managerial implications." In G. R. Ferris (ed.), *Research in personnel and human resources management*, vol. 16: 53–101. Greenwich, CT: JAI Press.

Becker, B. E. and Huselid, M. A. 2006. "Strategic human resource management: Where do we go from here?" *Journal of Management*, 32: 898–925.

Berggren, C. 1992. *The Volvo experience: Alternatives to lean production in the Swedish auto industry.* Ithaca, NY: Cornell University Press.

Bloor, G. and Dawson, P. 1994. "Understanding professional culture in organizational context." *Organization Studies*, 15: 275–295.

Bohlander, G., Snell, S., and Sherman, A. 2001. *Managing human resources* (12th edition). Mason, OH: South-Western College Publishing.

Boselie, P., Dietz, G., and Boon, C. 2005. "Commonalities and contradictions in HRM and performance research." *Human Resource Management Journal*, 15: 67–94.

Bowen, D. E. and Ostroff, C. 2004. "Understanding HRM-firm performance linkages: The role of the 'strength' of the HRM system." *Academy of Management Review*, 29: 203–221.

Brewster, C., Sparrow, P., and Harris, H. 2005. "Towards a new model of globalizing HRM." *International Journal of Human Resource Management*, 16: 949–970.

Brown, T. A. 2006. *Confirmatory factor analysis for applied research.* New York, NY: The Guilford Press.

Cannella, Jr., A. A., Park, J., and Lee, H. 2008. "Top management team functional background diversity and firm performance: Examining the roles of team member collocation and environmental uncertainty." *Academy of Management Journal*, 51: 768–784.

Cappelli, P. 1999. *The new deal at work: Managing the market-driven workforce.* Boston, MA: Harvard Business School Press.

Cappelli, P. and Neumark, D. 2001. "Do 'high-performance' work practices improve establishment-level outcomes?" *Industrial and Labor Relations Review*, 54: 737–775.

Chenevert, D. and Tremblay, M. 2009. "Fits in strategic human resource management and methodological challenge: Empirical evidence of influence of empowerment and compensation practices on human resource performance in Canadian firms." *International Journal of Human Resource Management*, 20: 738–770.

Chow, I. H., Huang, J. C., and Liu, S. 2008. "Strategic HRM in China: Configurations and competitive advantage." *Human Resource Management*, 47: 687–706.

Cohen, J., Cohen, P., West, S. G., and Aiken, L. S. 2003. *Applied multiple regression/correlation analysis for the behavioral sciences* (Third edition). Mahwah, NJ: Lawrence Erlbaum Associates.

Colbert, B. A. 2004. "The complex resource-based view: Implications for theory and practice in strategic human resource management." *Academy of Management Review*, 29: 341–358.

Cox, T. H. 1993. *Cultural diversity in organizations.* San Francisco, CA: Berrett-Koehler Publishers.

Cutcher-Gershenfeld, J. C. 1991. "The impact on economic performance of transformation in workplace relations." *Industrial and Labor Relations Review*, 44: 241–260.

Deal, T. E. and Kennedy, A. A. 1982. *Corporate culture: The rites and rituals of corporate life.* Reading, MA: Addison-Wesley.

Deepak, K. D., Guthrie, J. P., and Wright, P. M. 2005. "Human resource management and labor productivity: Does industry matter?" *Academy of Management Journal*, 48: 135–145.

DeFilippo, J. S. 1997. "World-class manufacturing in Chengdu: A case study on China's first aviation joint venture." *International Journal of Technology Management*, 13: 681–694.

Delery, J. E. and Doty, D. H. 1996. "Modes of theorizing in strategic human resource management: Tests of universalistic, contingency, and configurational performance predictions." *Academy of Management Journal*, 39: 802–835.

Delong, T. and Darwall, C. 2003a. *Xilinx, Inc. (A)*. Harvard Business School Case.

Delong, T. and Darwall, C. 2003b. *Xilinx, Inc. (B)*. Harvard Business School Case.

Dore, R. 1973. *British factory–Japanese factory: The origin of national diversity in industrial relation*. Berkeley, CA: University of California Press.

Dreher, F. G. and Dougherty, T. W. 2002. *Human resource strategy: A behavioral perspective for the general manager*. New York, NY: McGraw-Hill/Irwin.

Dwyer, S., Richard, O. C., and Chadwick, K. 2003. "Gender diversity in management and firm performance: The influence of growth orientation and organizational culture." *Journal of Business Research*, 56: 1009–1019.

Eisenhardt, K. M. 1989. "Building theories from case study research." *Academy of Management Review*, 14: 532–550.

Ely, R. J. and Thomas, D. A. 2001. "Cultural diversity at work: The effects of diversity perspectives on work group processes and outcomes." *Administrative Science Quarterly*, 46: 229–273.

Emery, F. E. and Trist, E. L. 1960. "Socio-technical systems." In C. W. Churchman and M. Verhulst (eds), *Management sciences: Models and techniques*, vol. 2: 83–97. New York, NY: Pergamon Press.

Erickson, C. L. and Jacoby, S. M. 2003. "The effect of employer networks on workplace innovation and training." *Industrial and Labor Relations Review*, 56: 203–223.

Fishman, C. 2000. "Moving toward a balanced work life." *Workforce*, March: 38–42.

Frost, J. P., Moore, L. F., Louis, M. R., Lundberg, C. C., and Martin, J. (eds). 1985. *Organizational culture*. Beverly Hills, CA: Sage Publications.

Fu, H. 2012. *An emerging non-regular labor force in Japan: The dignity of dispatched workers*. London: Routledge.

Fujimoto, T. 1999. *The evolution of a manufacturing system at Toyota*. New York, NY: Oxford University Press.

Galbraith, J. 1973. *Designing complex organizations*. Reading, MA: Addison-Wesley.

Gerhart, B. 2005. "Human resources and business performance: Findings, unanswered questions, and an alternative approach." *Management Revue*, 16: 174–185.

Gerhart, B. and Fang, M. 2005. "National culture and human resource management: Assumptions and evidence." *International Journal of Human Resource Management*, 16: 971–986.

Guest, D. E. 1997. "Human resource management and performance: A review and research agenda." *International Journal of Human Resource Management*, 8: 265–276.

Guest, D. E., Michie, J., Conway, N., and Sheehan, M. 2003. "Human resource management and corporate performance in the UK." *British Journal of Industrial Relations*, 41: 291–314.

Hackman, J. R. 2002. *Leading teams: Setting the stage for great performances*. Boston, MA: Harvard Business School Press.

Haghirian, P. (ed.). 2010. *Innovation and change in Japanese management*. Basingstoke: Palgrave Macmillan.

Hamel, G. 2007. *The future of management*. Boston, MA: Harvard Business School Press.

Hamel, G. and Prahalad, C. K. 1994. *Competing for the future*. Boston, MA: Harvard Business School Press.

Harrell-Cook, G. 2001. Book reviews (*Manufacturing Advantage: Why High-Performance Work Systems Pay Off*). *Academy of Management Review*, 26: 459–462.

Harrison, D. A., Price, K. H., and Bell, M. P. 1998. "Beyond relational demography: Time and the effects of surface- and deep-level diversity on work group cohesion." *Academy of Management Journal*, 41: 96–107.

Hofstede, G. 1980. *Culture's consequences: International differences in work-related values* (Abridged edition). Newbury Park, CA: Sage Publications.

Hofstede, G. 1993. "Cultural constraints in management theories." *Academy of Management Executive*, 7: 81–94.

Homan, A. C., Hollenbeck, J. R., Humphrey, S. E., van Knippenberg, D., Ilgen, D. R., and van Kleef, G. A. 2008. "Facing differences with an open mind: Openness to experience, salience of intragroup differences, and performance of diverse work groups." *Academy of Management Journal*, 51: 1204–1222.

House, R. J., Hanges, P. J., Javidan, M., Dorfman, P. W., and Gupta, V. 2004. *Culture, leadership, and organizations: The GLOBE study of 62 societies*. Thousand Oaks, CA: Sage Publications.

Huang, X., Rode, J. C., and Schroeder, R. 2011. "Organizational structure and continuous improvement and learning: Moderating effects of cultural endorsement of participative leadership." *Journal of International Business Studies*, 42: 1103–1120.

Huber, V. L. and Brown, K. A. 1991. "Human resource issues in cellular manufacturing: A sociotechnical analysis." *Journal of Operations Management*, 10: 138–159.

Huselid, M. A. 1995. "The impact of human resource management practices on turnover, productivity, and corporate financial performance." *Academy of Management Journal*, 38: 635–672.

Huselid, M. A. and Becker, B. E. 2000. "Comment on 'Measurement error in research on human resources and firm performance: How much error is there and how does it influence effect size estimates?' by Gerhart, Wright, McMahan, and Snell." *Personnel Psychology*, 53: 835–854.

Hyer, N. L. and Brown, K. A. 1999. "The discipline of real cells." *Journal of Operations Management*, 17: 557–574.

Hyer, N. and Wemmerlöv, U. 2002. *Reorganizing the factory: Competing through cellular manufacturing*. Portland, OR: Productivity Press.

Ichniowski, C., Kochan, T. A., Levine, D., Olson, C., and Strauss, G. 1996. "What works at work: Overview and assessment." *Industrial Relations*, 35: 299–333.

Ingrassia, P. J. 2011. "The road ahead for Japan's car industry." In McKinsey and Company (ed.), *Reimagining Japan: The quest for a future that works*: 242–246. San Francisco, CA: VIZ Media, LLC.

Isa, K. and Tsuru, T. 2002. "Cell production and workplace innovation in Japan: Toward a new model for Japanese manufacturing." *Industrial Relations*, 41: 548–578.

Iwamuro, H. 2004. *Handbook for cell production*. Tokyo, Japan: Nikkan Kogyou Press (in Japanese).

Jaccard, J. and Turrisi, R. 2003. *Interaction effects in multiple regression* (Second edition). Thousand Oaks, CA: Sage Publications.

Jackson, E. S. and Schuler, R. S. 1995. "Understanding human resource management in the context of organizations and their environment." *Annual Review of Psychology*, 46: 237–264.

Jacoby, S. M. 2005. *The embedded corporation: Corporate governance and employee relations in Japan and the United States*. Princeton, NJ: Princeton University Press.

Jayne, M. E. A. and Dipboye, R. L. 2004. "Leveraging diversity to improve business performance: Research findings and recommendations for organizations." *Human Resource Management*, 43: 409–424.

Jiang, B., Baker, R. C., and Frazier, G. V. 2009. "An analysis of job dissatisfaction and turnover to reduce global supply chain risk: Evidence from China." *Journal of Operations Management*, 27: 169–184.

Johnson, D. J. 2005. "Converting assembly lines to assembly cells at sheet metal products: Insights on performance improvements." *International Journal of Production Research*, 43: 1483–1509.

Kanji, G. K. and Wong, A. 1999. "Business excellence model for supply chain management." *Total Quality Management*, 10: 1147–1168.

Kast, F. E. and Rosenzweig, J. E. 1985. *Organization and management: A system and contingency approach* (Fourth edition). New York, NY: McGraw-Hill Book Company.

Kerr, J. and Slocum, Jr., J. W. 1987. "Managing corporate culture through reward systems." *Academy of Management Executive*, 1: 99–108.

Kitazume, T. 2010. "Japan Inc. urged to rethink Asia view: New ideas, human resources, local knowledge needed to take part in region's growth." *The Japan Times*. December 29. www.japantimes.co.jp/text/nb20101229d1.html. Last accessed July 10, 2012.

Koike, K. 1994. "Learning and incentive systems in Japanese industry." In M. Aoki and R. Dore (eds), *The Japanese firms: The source of competitive strength*: 41–65. Oxford, NY: Oxford University Press.

Kotter, J. P. and Heskett, J. L. 1992. *Corporate culture and performance*. New York, NY: The Free Press.

Koufteros, X. A. 1999. "Testing a model of pull production: A paradigm for manufacturing research using structural equation modeling." *Journal of Operations Research*, 17: 467–488.

Kumazawa, M. 2004. "A study of comparison among the method for handling multiple work processes, cell production, and the assembly line system with conveyor-belts." *Journal of Yokkaichi University*, 16(2): 57–73 (in Japanese).

Lafley, A. G. 2007. *Ongoing transformation: Leading change to sustain growth and leadership*. http://meeting.aomonline.org/2007/downloads/podcasts/Distinguished_Executive_AG_Lafley_Speech.pdf. Last accessed July 10, 2012.

Lawler, J. J., Chen, S., Wu, P., Bae, J., and Bai, B. 2011. "High-performance work systems in foreign subsidiaries of American multinationals: An institutional mode." *Journal of International Business Studies*, 42: 202–220.

Liker, J. K. and Hoseus, M. 2008. *Toyota culture: The heart and soul of the Toyota way*. New York, NY: McGraw-Hill.

Lockett, M. 1988. "Culture and the problems of Chinese management." *Organization Studies*, 9: 475–496.

Lorsch, J. W. 1986. "Managing culture: The invisible barrier to strategic change." *California Management Review*, 28: 95–109.

MacDuffie, J. P. 1991. *Beyond mass production: Flexible production systems and manufacturing performance in the world auto industry.* Unpublished doctoral dissertation, Sloan School of Management, M.I.T.

MacDuffie, J. P. 1995. "Human resource bundles and manufacturing performance: Organizational logic and flexible production systems in the world auto industry." *Industrial and Labor Relations Review*, 48: 197–221.

Makino, S. and Roehl, T. 2010. "Learning from Japan: A commentary." *Academy of Management Perspective*, 24(4): 38–45.

March, J. G. and Simon, H. A. 1958. *Organizations.* New York, NY: John Wiley & Sons.

Martin, J. 1992. *Cultures in organizations.* New York, NY: Oxford University Press.

Martin, J. 2002. *Organizational culture: Mapping the terrain.* Thousand Oaks, CA: Sage Publications.

Martin-Alcazar, F., Romero-Fernandez, P. M., and Sanchez-Gardey, G. 2005. "Strategic human resource management: Integrating the universalistic, contingent, configurational, and contextual perspectives." *International Journal of Human Resource Management*, 16: 633–659.

Miles, R. and Snow, C. 1978. *Organizational structure, strategy and process.* New York, NY: McGraw-Hill.

Milliken, F. J. and Martins, L. L. 1996. "Searching for common threads: Understanding the multiple effects of diversity in organizational groups." *Academy of Management Review*, 21: 402–433.

Miltenburg, J. 2001. "U-shaped production lines: A review of theory and practice." *International Journal of Production Economics*, 70: 201–214.

Miyoshi, H. and Nakata, Y. (eds). 2011. *Have Japanese firms changed? The lost decade.* Basingstoke: Palgrave Macmillan.

Mossholder, K. W., Richardson, H. A., and Settoon, R. P. 2011. "Human resource systems and helping in organizations: A relational perspective." *Academy of Management Review*, 36: 33–52.

Nicholas, J. M. 1998. *Competitive manufacturing management: Continuous improvement, lean production, and customer-focused quality.* Boston, MA: Irwin/McGraw-Hill.

Nikkei Newspaper. 2010. "Canon to take Japanese production methods global." August 18: 9 (English and electronic version). http://t21.nikkei.co.jp/. Last accessed July 10, 2012.

Nikkei Newspaper. 2011. "Renewing Japan." November 4: 15 (in Japanese).

Noguchi, H. 2003. *Japan's production revolution.* Tokyo, Japan: Nikkan Kogyou Press (in Japanese).

Nonaka, I. and Takeuchi, H. 1995. *The knowledge-creating company.* New York, NY: Oxford University Press.

Nonaka, I., Toyama, R., and Hirata, T. 2008. *Managing flow: A process theory of the knowledge-based firm.* Basingstoke: Palgrave Macmillan.

Numagami, T., Kawabe, M., and Kato, T. 2010. "Organizational deadweight: Learning from Japan." *Academy of Management Perspective*, 24(4): 25–45.

Nunnally, J. C. and Bernstein, I. H. 1994. *Psychometric Theory* (Third edition). New York, NY: McGraw-Hill.

Okada, K. 2008. "Diversity key to corporate growth." *The Japan Times*. October 29. http://www.japantimes.co.jp/text/nn20081029f2.html. Last accessed July 10, 2012.

Okamoto, Y. (ed.). 2002. *Competitive advantage of Japanese manufactures: Rebuilding and transferring it worldwide.* Unpublished Grant-in-Aid for Scientific Research (*Kakenhi*) report submitted to The Japan Ministry of Education, Culture, Sports, Science and Technology (in Japanese).

O'Reilly, C. A., and Pfeffer, J. 2000. *Hidden value: How great companies achieve extraordinary results with ordinary people.* Boston, MA: Harvard Business School Press.

Osterman, P. 1994. "How common is workplace transformation and who adopts it?" *Industrial and Labor Relations Review*, 47: 173–188.

Osterman, P. 2000. "Work reorganization in an era of restructuring: Trends in diffusion and effects on employee welfare." *Industrial and Labor Relations Review*, 53: 179–196.

O'Toole, J. and Lawler, E. E. 2007. *The new American workplace.* Basingstoke: Palgrave Macmillan.

Ouchi, W. G. 1981. *Theory Z.* Reading, MA: Addison-Wesley.

Ouchi, W. G. and Jaeger, A. M. 1978. "Type Z organization: Stability in the midst of mobility." *Academy of Management Review*, 3: 305–314.

Pascale, R. T. 1990. *Managing on the edge: How the smartest companies use conflict to stay ahead.* New York, NY: Simon & Schuster.

Pelled, L. H. 1996. "Demographic diversity, conflict, and work group outcomes: An intervening process theory." *Organization Science*, 7: 615–631.

Peters, T. J. and Waterman, Jr., R. H. 1982. *In search of excellence: Lesson from America's best-run companies.* New York, NY: Harper & Row.

Pfeffer, J. 1994. *Competitive advantage through people.* Boston, MA: Harvard Business School Press.

Pfeffer, J. 1998. "Seven practices of successful organizations." *California Management Review*, 40(2): 96–124.

Porter, M. E. 1980. *Competitive strategy: Techniques for analyzing industries and competitors.* New York, NY: Free Press.

Robbins, S. P. and Judge, T. A. 2009. *Organizational behavior* (13th edition). Upper Saddle River, NJ: Pearson Education.

Sackman, S. A. (ed.) 1997. *Cultural complexity in organizations: Inherent contrasts and contradictions.* Thousand Oaks, CA: Sage Publications.

Sakatsume, Y. 2002. "Continuous improvement of cell production lines." *IE Review*, 43(1): 69–75 (in Japanese).

Sakatsume, Y. 2004. "Effects of continuous improvement activities after introducing cell production." *IE Review*, 45(2): 6–13 (in Japanese).

Sakikawa, T. 2010. *The new Japanese workplace.* Unsold book, Graduate School of Modern Society and Culture at Niigata University.

Schein, E. D. 1985. *Organizational culture and leadership: A dynamic View.* San Francisco, CA: Jossey-Bass Publishers.

Scott, W. R. 1995. *Institutions and organizations.* Thousand Oaks, CA: Sage.

Shinobu, C. 2003. *Post-lean production systems: Toward an adaptable enterprise in the age of uncertainty.* Tokyo, Japan: Bunshin-Do (in Japanese).

Shinobu, C. and Mori, K. 2003. "A design framework for cell production systems: From the viewpoint of autonomy and decentralization." *Journal of JIMA (Japan Industrial Management Association)*, 53(6): 491–495 (in Japanese).

Shirai, K. 2001. "Cell production and managing human resources." In T. Tsuru (ed.), *Innovation and evolution of production systems: Diffusion of cell production among Japanese firms*: 87–121. Tokyo, Japan: Nihon Hyoron Sya (in Japanese).

Staw, B. M. 1986. "Organizational psychology and the pursuit of the happy/productive worker." *California Management Review*, 28(4): 40–53.

Svyantek, D. J. and Bott, J. 2004. "Received wisdom and the relationship between diversity and organizational performance." *Organizational Analysis*, 12: 295–317.

Takeuchi, N. 2009. "How Japanese manufacturing firms align their human resource policies with business strategies: Testing a contingency performance prediction in a Japanese context." *International Journal of Human Resource Management*, 20: 34–56.

Takeuchi, N., Wakabayashi, M., and Chen, Z. 2003. "The strategic HRM configuration for competitive advantage: Evidence from Japanese firms in China and Taiwan." *Asian Pacific Journal of Management*, 20: 447–480.

Tamaki, K. 1996. *Strategic production system*. Tokyo, Japan: Hakuto Syobo (in Japanese).

Tani, T. and Mitsuya, Y. 1998. "Management accounting for micro profit centers: A case of NEC Saitama." *Journal of Economics and Business Administration (Kobe University)*, 177(3): 17–34 (in Japanese).

The Japan Times. 2012. "Panasonic expects to book record ¥780 billion net loss." February 4: 1.

The Japan Times. 2012. "Industrial revival claims ring hollow as makers flee Japan." February 17: 3. http://www.japantimes.co.jp/text/nn20120217f1.html. Last accessed July 10, 2012.

The Japan Times. 2012. "Nonregulars at record 35.2% of workforce." February 22: 7. http://www.japantimes.co.jp/text/nb20120222a3.html. Last accessed July 10, 2012.

Trist, E. L. and Bamfortrh, K. W. 1951. "Some social and psychological consequences of the longwall method of coal-getting." *Human Relations*, 4: 3–38.

US Department of Labor. 1993. *High performance work practices and firm performance*. Washington, DC: US Government Printing Office.

Van der Vegt, G. S., Emans, B. J., and Van de Vliert, E. 2001. "Patterns of interdependence in work teams: A two-level investigation of the relations with job and team satisfaction." *Personnel Psychology*, 54: 51–69.

Vedantam, S. 2007. "In boardrooms and in courtrooms, diversity makes a difference." *The Washington Post*. January 15: A02. http://www.washingtonpost.com/wp-dyn/content/article/2007/01/14/AR2007011400720.html. Last accessed July 10, 2012.

Venkatraman, N. 1989. "The concept of fit in strategy research: Toward verbal and statistical correspondence." *Academy of Management Review*, 14: 423–444.

Vogel, E. F. 1979. *Japan as number one: Lessons for American*. Tokyo, Japan: Charles E. Tuttle Company.

Wageman, R. 1995. "Interdependence and group effectiveness." *Administrative Science Quarterly*, 40: 145–180.

Weick, K. E. 1996. *Sensemaking in organizations*. Thousand Oaks, CA: Sage Publications.

Williams, K. Y. and O'Reilly, C. A. 1998. "Demography and diversity in organizations: A review of 40 years of research." In B. M. Staw and L. L. Cummings (eds), *Research in organizational behavior*, vol. 20: 77–140. Greenwich, CT: JAI Press.

Womack, J. P., Jones, D. T., and Roos, D. 1990. *The machine that changed the world*. New York, NY: Rawson Associates.

Wright, M. P. and Boswell, W. R. 2002. "Desegregating HRM: A review and synthesis of micro and macro human resource management research." *Journal of Management*, 28: 247–276.

Wright, P. M., Dunford, B. B., and Snell, S. A. 2001. "Human resources and the resource based view of the firm." *Journal of Management*, 27: 701–721.

Wright, P. M. and Sherman, W. S. 1999. "Failing to find fit in strategic human resource management: Theoretical and empirical problems." In G. F. Ferris (ed.), *Research in personnel and human resources management* (Supplement 4): 53–74. Greenwich, CT: JAI Press.

Yanai, T. 2011. "Dare to err." In McKinsey and Company (ed.), *Reimagining Japan: The quest for a future that works*: 59–61. San Francisco, CA: VIZ Media, LLC.

Yin, R. K. 2003. *Case study research: Design and methods* (Third edition). Thousand Oaks, CA: Sage Publications.

Youndt, M. A., Snell, S. A., Dean, Jr., J. W., and Lepak, D. P. 1996. "Human resource management, manufacturing strategy, and firm performance." *Academy of Management Journal*, 39: 836–866.

Index

Printed in the USA
CPSIA information can be obtained
at www.ICGtesting.com
LVHW011020011023
759814LV00008B/988